Sympathy for the Devil

www.**transworldbooks**.co.uk

Sympathy for the Devil

The Birth of the Rolling Stones and the Death of Brian Jones

Paul Trynka

BANTAM PRESS

LONDON · TORONTO · SYDNEY · AUCKLAND · JOHANNESBURG

TRANSWORLD PUBLISHERS
61–63 Uxbridge Road, London W5 5SA
A Random House Group Company
www.transworldbooks.co.uk

First published in Great Britain
in 2014 by Bantam Press
an imprint of Transworld Publishers

This book is a work of non-fiction. In some limited cases names of people have been
changed solely to protect the privacy of others. The author has stated to the publishers that,
except in such minor respects not affecting the substantial accuracy of the work, the contents
of this book are true.

A CIP catalogue record for this book
is available from the British Library.

ISBNs 9780593071229 (cased)
9780593071236 (tpb)

Addresses for Random House Group Ltd companies outside the UK
can be found at: www.randomhouse.co.uk
The Random House Group Ltd Reg. No. 954009

The Random House Group Limited supports the Forest Stewardship Council® (FSC®), the
leading international forest-certification organisation. Our books carrying the FSC label are
printed on FSC®-certified paper. FSC is the only forest-certification scheme supported by
the leading environmental organisations, including Greenpeace. Our paper procurement
policy can be found at www.randomhouse.co.uk/environment

Typeset in 11.25/16pt Minion by Falcon Oast Graphic Art Ltd.
Printed and bound in Great Britain by
Clays Ltd, Bungay, Suffolk

2 4 6 8 10 9 7 5 3 1

To Hubert Sumlin, Pops Staples and
all their fellow, forever-young pioneers.

Contents

Prologue

IT WAS ONLY a raggle-taggle bunch of musicians, kids really, and the way history normally unfolds, there should have been no way any witnesses would have spotted that something world-changing was happening. Yet, the leader of the band did have something special about him – the way he sneered at the audience, getting in their faces, coaxing out shimmering glissandos from his guitar in a style no one had ever seen before, or switching over to an amplified blues harp, still a radically new instrument for most of the teenagers who watched him and his companions intently. Elmo Lewis, as he called himself, introduced several of the numbers and ministered to the rest of his band lovingly, like a mother hen, checking that the singer Mick had got the beat, and keeping a close eye on his fellow guitarist's fretboard. Occasionally, when the riffs cohered into something stirring and electrifying, he and the piano player – the other more obviously experienced musician – would look at each other and smile in satisfaction.

Truth is, though, that some people in that decent-sized crowd watching the Rolling Stones, crammed on to the Marquee stage, in July 1962 – and some among those at other little clubs around London over the next few weeks – did spot that something unique was happening. One girl felt the ground beneath her shifting as the band ripped through twenty songs, picked out and overseen by the blond guitarist. At her London grammar school, Cleo Sylvestre had been taught that the role of black people in culture was as 'heathens and savages'. Now, as the band hot-wired this obscure music from deep within the black ghettos of the Chicago Southside and the Mississippi Delta, a new world opened up – a world in which black people like her would have a voice, a role.

Some musicians spotted it, too. Ginger Baker, an aggressive young drummer who had cut his teeth in the trad jazz clubs and was being persuaded into the blues scene by the silver-tongued club owner Alexis Korner, was dismissive of the Stones' upstart singer. Yet still he reckoned that the band's exuberant, snotty, teenage take on this deep, resonant music was something radical and new.

Businessmen got it. Harold Pendleton, manager of the Marquee and a mainstay of the jazz scene, was likewise unimpressed by the band's music yet still noted something powerful about their attitude – a challenging of authority, a disregard for convention that emanated principally from Brian Jones, the twenty-one-year-old who styled himself Elmo Lewis. Jones was a visionary, Pendleton reckoned, although there was something he didn't like about him. He used the term 'evil genius'.

As for Brian himself, the momentary satisfaction he felt as the band he'd masterminded took to the stage was itself world-changing. The music was the one thing that gave meaning to a life that was fractured, restless and unhappy. Now, over fifty years on, that situation endures. Brian Jones got many things wrong in his life, but the most important thing he got right, for his music was world-changing.

History is written by the victors, and in recent years we've seen the proprietors of the modern Rolling Stones describe their genesis, their discovery of the blues, without even mentioning their founder. We've seen Brian Jones described as a 'kind of rotting attachment'. This phrase in itself gives an idea of the magnitude of this story. The dark power of the Stones' music derives from their internal battles, a sequence of betrayals, back-biting, sexual oneupmanship, violence, madness and mania.

The aim of this book is not to gloss over the many flaws of Brian Jones, for if ever a man was driven by his flaws, it was he. His contrariness, his vulnerability and his unhappiness prompted his estrangement from the establishment, and ultimately would underpin the values of the band, which challenged that establishment so provocatively. There was a darkness in his heart that inspired his exploration of the Devil's music, of the story of Robert Johnson, the man who traded the secrets of guitar playing for his immortal soul. Brian sought out those secrets, and was the first man to communicate them to a new generation. It was he who opened the doors to that new world, unlocking its secrets both for his bandmates and for us.

In the course of writing this book I've travelled far, and plumbed deep. It's a sad story – of messy lives, unwanted children, ruthlessness and misogyny, of feuds both petty and profound. But great art can come from messy situations. As we shall see, right from the start there was something of the Devil in Brian Jones. And as we know, the Devil has the best tunes.

1

Secrets and Lies

NEW WORLDS ARE often dreamed up in the most mundane locations. Few people would have imagined the genteel, manicured spa town of Cheltenham as a cradle for a radical new musical manifesto. But the place turns out to be funny that way, countless secrets having been harboured behind those deceptively staid facades. Brian Jones was in fact a typical Cheltonian. By the time he left the place he'd discovered more musical secrets than were ever supposed to exist, as well as amassing more secret children, and heartbreak, than can ever have been imagined.

The word 'genteel' seems to get applied to Cheltenham with monotonous regularity. And yes, perhaps it is an appropriate adjective, as long as you bundle in alongside it the following words: secretive, exotic, futuristic, sordid, elegant, decadent and artistic. Nearly all of those terms capture the early life of Lewis Brian Hopkins Jones, a boy whose destiny seemed more than any other dictated by his surroundings and upbringing. He was the son of an ambitious man who worked at the cutting edge of a world-changing technology. Lewis Blount Jones was, like the son who carried his name, a genius; yet his life was defined by secrets, repression and the traditional British stiff upper lip. This legacy would also define the life of Lewis Jones Jr, for better and for worse.

Any visitor who's new to the town would be instantly struck by the serene beauty of its gleaming white Regency buildings. A long, wide promenade runs south from the high street (location of Brian's grammar school) down to a group of buildings around Lansdown Crescent and Montpellier Walk, all airy shops and coffee bars, framed by caryatids – pillars in the shape of serene women, like those of the Acropolis. Over the road lie the fine green lawns of Imperial Gardens, with the Queens Hotel just in front; a little further down is the Pump Room, another jewel of Georgian architecture, based on the Pantheon; Regency terraces stretch in every direction, the very model of taste and discretion. But as Barry Miles, founder of counter-culture journal *International Times* and the Indica Gallery, who fled Cheltenham in 1962, points out, 'it's all a facade'. The elegant stone frontages of many buildings are in fact cheap painted stucco; the interiors are rickety and damp, thrown up quickly by speculative builders. With its exclusive Ladies' College, arts and music festivals, and well-heeled populace, many of them ex-colonials, post-war Cheltenham was indeed a centre of decorum and conservatism. But behind that lay a hotbed of intrigue and vice.

This secretive character became more formal, more acknow-ledged, from the early fifties, when Cheltenham became the capital for the nation's spooks after GCHQ, the centre of the British eaves-dropping and intelligence community, moved from Bletchley to two government-owned sites in the town. Modern apartment buildings started to spring up and then to fill with mysterious people, many of them European and multilingual; sometimes, if you spotted them drinking at the town's exclusive wine bars, you'd glimpse a security pass.

The James Bond vibe was intensified by the Gloster Aircraft Company, builders of Britain's first operational jet fighter, the Meteor: its top-secret prototypes were assembled at a building on Cheltenham High Street. By the mid fifties Gloster were producing the Javelin, a glossily futuristic delta-wing interceptor. Gloster and Rotol, a part-owned subsidiary of Rolls-Royce launched as a joint venture with the Bristol Aeroplane Company, were the town's leading employers, drawing scientists and engineers like Brian Jones's father from around the country.

Alongside the world's modern secretive industries, Cheltenham was a centre of the world's oldest secretive industry. The town hosted several US Air Force bases, and the presence of US and British military personnel encouraged a bounteous supply of prostitutes: according to one count, those elegant Regency facades hid a total of forty-seven brothels. Right up to the 1960s, Bayshill Road, two blocks down from the Promenade, was a haunt for street-walkers, who'd cheekily ask any passing men if they were 'looking for business'. The Queens Hotel dominated the town's main drag and became a regular haunt for the teenage Brian Jones, all shirt and tie, formal and correct. Yet during the Cheltenham Festival horse-racing week the old colonial types were cleared out to make way for hard-core gamblers and intimidating Irish gangster types who'd play cards until dawn surrounded by high-class call girls who regarded the festival as a cornerstone of the year's working calendar. Even the political establishment had its louche side: the town's most popular mayor, Charles Irving, who became a favourite of Tory icon Margaret Thatcher, drove around town in a white Ford Thunderbird alongside a chauffeur who was dressed in mauve – a spectacle 'so gay it was unbelievable', say witnesses.

Perhaps the best evidence of Cheltenham's Jekyll and Hyde character can be found in the pages of the refined, stately daily newspaper the *Gloucestershire Echo*. The *Echo* majored on issues military and religious, its attitude proudly High Church of England. Its readers were often subject to shocked homilies berating the town's lax morality. In 1956, the Reverend Ward bemoaned 'some innate tendency, a particular evil, that is more marked in Cheltenham than in most places in this country', namely the town's rate of illegitimate births – the highest in the country outside London's inner city. Concerned burghers commissioned further research to establish whether Americans or Irish were responsible for this appalling statistic; the figures revealed it was the English. In later years, Brian's fellow Stones wondered how someone so sexually voracious could have come from a town like Cheltenham. Little did they realize that he was Cheltonian through and through.

Lewis Blount Jones, a talented graduate in engineering from Leeds University, scored a prestigious job at Rotol in 1939, and soon after that married Louisa Simmonds. The couple set up home on Eldorado Road, in a somewhat gloomy red-brick house near the town centre. This was where the young Lewis Brian Hopkins Jones, born in Cheltenham's Park Nursing Home on 28 February 1942, grew up. Brian was soon joined by a sister, Pamela, who was born on 3 October 1943. Just over two years later, on 14 October 1945, the family was touched by tragedy when Pamela died of leukaemia. Lewis and Louisa never spoke about their child's death – it became another of Cheltenham's secrets. The following summer, on 22 August, another sister for Brian was born – Barbara, who would always resemble him.

Around 1950, the family moved to Hatherley Road, in what we'd describe today as quintessential suburbia. In the austerity of the immediate post-war years a new home in a leafy location, complete with garage and modern kitchen, was a badge of high status. 'It was a prestigious place,' remembers next-door neighbour Roger Jessop. 'Those houses were built as special one-offs, much sought after, and the people in our area were eminently middle class. And of all of them, Lewis Jones was about as middle class as you could get.'

Lewis Jones would become a symbol of the Generation Gap – the fault line that opened up when boys like Brian Jones reached adolescence. Brian's life was lived in flagrant opposition to the values of his father, who was repressed and domineering, and who never, ever used the word 'love'. Yet Lewis was anything but an old fogey. Just as Brian became the embodiment of a cultural revolution, Lewis was the embodiment of a technological revolution: his duties at Rotol included work on the most advanced propellors and turbines of the day. Not only did he own a desirable suburban residence, Lewis also owned a car and a phone, both of them rare possessions in the early fifties, and was typical of the new wave of modern British engineers who'd led the world in the development of radar, the jet engine and military electronics. 'He was far-sighted, concerned about the future of British engineering, and would write well-argued letters to the newspapers suggesting it should be given higher priority,' says Roger Jessop.

The young Keith Richards witnessed Hurricanes and Spitfires chasing lone Dorniers out of Kent – there's a good chance their propellors were made by Rotol, as were vital engine parts for Britain's pioneering jets. Like GCHQ and the Dowty company (with which Rotol later merged), Rotol was a prestigious Cheltonian workplace. Lewis commanded huge respect and eventually became head of the crucial airworthiness department. 'He was a learned gentleman,' says colleague Robert Almond, 'formal, as people were in those days.' Linda Partridge, another

Dowty Rotol worker, calls him 'delightful; a very nice, gentle sort of man'. Linda's brothers knew Brian well, and thought Lewis and his son were pretty similar, in looks and size – small feet, delicate musician's hands, modest height – and a certain shyness.

Louisa Simmonds had met Lewis in South Wales and shared with her husband a Welsh 'chapel' background: both were brought up in the traditions of the Welsh Methodist Church. Most surviving accounts of her come from Brian's teenage girlfriends, like Pat Andrews, who remember Louisa's household as 'a morgue', gloomy and oppressive – but by this time, of course, Brian's wilful behaviour was already causing crippling tension in the Jones family.

Back in the 1950s, though, Louisa – a slim, neatly dressed woman with practical mid-length hair – was well known in Cheltenham middle-class circles. She and her husband were social in that earnest, self-improving, almost Victorian way. The couple were proud of their Welsh roots and were key members of the local Cymmrodorion group, which organized talks on Welsh literature and history. The Welsh Church, says family friend Graham Keen, had a strong presence in Cheltenham: 'there was a lot of Welsh economic migration from 1917, after the coal bust'. Graham's parents, Marian and Arthur, knew the Joneses well from Welsh and musical circles, and shared the same ethos of self-improvement, with one crucial difference. 'The chapel beliefs were that you didn't drink, you didn't smoke,' Graham explains. 'But there was a certain flexibility – it was mixed with common sense.' Graham's dad Arthur enjoyed a drink without believing it would condemn him to Hell, but the Keens reckoned the Joneses' attitude was 'fairly fundamental'.

Louisa boasted one undeniably positive character trait: her enthusiasm for music. Although a busy housewife, she gave piano lessons and got involved with the local arts scene. By the late 1940s she was a member of the Cheltenham Townswomen's Guild, an urban, artier version of the Women's Institute. She was also a mainstay of the Guild Choir, conducted by Marian Keen. They'd work on Elgar, Vaughan Williams and choral pieces by other modern composers at the Keens' house on Old Bath Road, or at the Congregational Church on Priory Terrace. The little group became a regular attraction at Guild events and local arts competitions. When Louisa's choir won a cup at the Cheltenham Festival of Performing Arts, judged by a professional panel, the triumph was a source of pride for months.

Music was at the heart of one of Louisa's closest friendships, with next-door neighbour Muriel Jessop, Roger's mother: both families owned pianos, so Muriel and Louisa spent many hours at each other's houses practising light classical music and vocal duets (Debussy, Gilbert and Sullivan) with which they'd enter competitions at the Cheltenham Music Festival and other events. 'They would be outperformed by the professionals, but they would always put up a very creditable, educated, middle-class ladies' performance,' says Roger. Louisa owned a gramophone – again, like the modern semi, the car and the telephone, fairly unusual in early fifties Britain – and there was always music around the house.

So, for all the generation divide, the young Brian – softly spoken, with an impeccably middle-class accent, fascinated by music from an early age – was recognizably his parents' son.

The Joneses were, say their neighbours, quiet and punctilious; they kept their drive swept, and were the first to take action if there was a problem with noise or minor vandalism in the area. 'You couldn't have a more conventional English middle-class family than that,' says Roger Jessop. 'I don't mean that in a snide way.' The

Jessops were close with the Joneses and found them 'reserved but friendly'. They didn't socialize in the way we would today – no dinner parties or trips to the pub – but Roger's dad Frederick, a geography teacher at the boys' grammar school, helped the ten-year-old Brian out with homework, while Lewis assisted Roger with maths and engineering-related problems. Lewis was a patient, logical teacher – he'd work through a problem methodically, enjoying the elegance of the correct mathematical solution.

The young Brian Jones certainly looked like the son of a science geek. He was well spoken and confident but looked gawky, with his horn-rimmed specs and gap-toothed smile, and was a serious, earnest boy, 'almost priggish' according to one of his teachers. 'He *was* quite nerdy,' says Roger, who remembers Brian disappearing for long trainspotting sessions at a vantage point close to the nearby private school Dean Close, which Brian attended.

Yet a couple of people noticed the sensitivity that set him apart from his dutiful, conventional parents. Trudy Baldwin's family attended church with the Joneses, at St Philip's and St James, where Brian, wearing crisp white robes, sang in the choir from around the age of ten. The two families grew fairly close, and Trudy, a few years older than Brian, became a regular babysitter for the Jones children. She remembers the young Brian well, in particular his revelation about a sister who was completely unknown to the Baldwins: 'Brian told me there was another child in the family – a sister who died. He showed me photos of her. He seemed to need to let me know, as if it was something not talked about – my parents were quite close friends, but I don't think they ever knew. It must have been awful, to hide something like that away.'

Trudy Baldwin, like many Cheltonians, looks back on her upbringing and marvels at how strict, how grim it was, bound by deference and repression of emotion. Happiness and approval came from pleasing your elders. These were also the rules for the young Brian Jones, at home and at Dean Close, all tall gothic buildings in sprawling grounds, where he was easily one of the brightest kids in his year, exceptionally adept at English and French, but good at maths, too.

Brian's conventional, slightly nerdy look was complemented by the many interests he shared with his dad, particularly a fascination with engineering. Around the age of ten his parents bought him an expensive, finely engineered green mini steam engine, which he'd tinker with in a state of rapt attention, fuelling it with methylated spirits. His interest in machinery survived well into his teens: he could often be seen examining the shelves of toy trains in the model shop on the high street, or cycling off for an afternoon of trainspotting with his friend Tom Wheeler; while in his later teens he shared an interest in Derbyshire's tram system with friends John Appleby and Tony Pickering, spending hours sanding tram body-work or shovelling cinders for the track.

This dutiful schoolboy was also good at the traditional sports practised at Dean Close, especially cricket. Lewis often moved his dark-coloured Wolseley out of the drive so Brian and Roger could practise batting and bowling against the garage door. Brian spent a fair amount of time at the Jessops', too, especially around the time when he was preparing for the eleven-plus, the traditional and, for some, intimidating exam that decided a child's eligibility for Cheltenham's ancient grammar school – which, with distinguished alumni like Handley Page, founder of the famous aircraft company, was arguably a more prestigious educational establishment than Dean Close. Active and intelligent, Brian seemed the epitome of the grammar school boy who was likely to achieve. But Roger saw the first problems behind the middle-class facade: 'He was a good spin bowler. We'd play cricket down the drive. But then he'd start to wheeze and splutter: he was asthmatic, extremely asthmatic. He was good enough to play in the school team – for two overs he'd be good, but he didn't have the stamina to play in a match. And always, I think, he resented that.'

It was probably Brian's asthma that inspired his parents to pick out a clarinet for him: playing a wind instrument was standard therapy in the fifties for British kids suffering from this condition. Otherwise, treatment was rudimentary, and relied on blowing a pingpong ball around, or inhaling water vapour from a pan of boiling water – more or less placebos. The clarinet-playing was the one positive aspect of an illness that was at that time rare, sometimes terrifying, and above all isolating.

Brian sailed through his eleven-plus, and on 8 September 1953 enrolled at Cheltenham Grammar School, an intimidating edifice whose Victorian spires and crenellations dominated the high street. It took kids from Cheltenham and the suburbs, and there was a strict pecking order: older pupils were more important than younger pupils, and top streams – once the boys were tested for academic ability at the end of the first term – were more important than lower streams. It was repeatedly drummed into new arrivals how the school's origins harked back to Elizabethan times; a couple of days after starting, the nervous new first years would be 'ducked' under a tap in the central courtyard in an ancient bonding ritual.

The eleven-year-old Brian was one of a small group of boys who seemed unfazed by such things. He was well turned out and at ease in this sort of company, one of just two boys in his form who'd arrived from Dean Close. Indeed he stood out: blond-haired, relaxed, academically ahead of most of his peers and looking 'like a cherub' says one friend from Year 7, Philip 'Pip' Price, who sat at an adjoining desk. 'That was my first impression, with his blond hair and smiley face.' Many kids struggled with new subjects, but for Brian it seemed 'like plain sailing'. He actually seemed to enjoy lessons, and although Dr Arthur Bell, who joined the same year, later described Brian as 'essentially a sensitive and vulnerable boy', Pip and others thought the opposite. 'I couldn't describe him as a shy person. Not the way he was around town, and with the people he knew.' Compared to most of the Cheltenham kids he was confident, put his hand up often, and 'helped other kids'.

In those post-war years, grammar schools took boys from a wide range of backgrounds, hence Brian and his classmates embodied a new social mobility. But before they came to define, or subvert, the system, they had to conform to it. Grammar school boys from working-class Cheltenham families frequently ended up as doctors or professors, and there was heavy emphasis on how many boys achieved scholarships to Oxford or Cambridge. There was a large contingent whose fathers worked at Dowty, or GCHQ – an elite crowd who seemed destined for success, bright boys of whom the teachers approved.

In those first years, L. B. Jones, too, made a powerful impression on his teachers. '*Very* able,' one of his internal report cards notes, 'with signs of brilliance.' In a school that relied on rigorous county-wide selection, this was a significant accolade. 'He was a clever bloke,' confirms Colin Dellar, who became friends with Brian around the beginning of 1954, 'and confident too, there's no doubt about that.' Roger Jessop, whose father was by now Deputy Head at the school, regarded Brian as one of the group who studied in 'an intellectual, rigorous way. He was the top of an A stream in which there were some very bright people, who later got starred entry to Oxbridge. You could see he had the ambition, too.' Frederick Jessop approved of the boy who lived next door, thought he had the kind of 'striving ambition' which the school aimed to foster. In those first couple of years at the grammar school, says Roger, 'my father was very pleased with him'.

It wasn't to last.

Many years later, Lewis Jones would speak to the BBC about Brian. There was much puzzlement in his account, for Lewis seemed to know little of the internal life of his son. The pair, alike in some key ways, were separated by a generation gap that in their case was a yawning chasm. It opened up in 1956. The cause was jazz – or, more accurately, jazz and sex.

The broadcaster Alistair Cooke once recalled the day his mother first heard him listening to a Louis Armstrong record: she burst into tears, mortified to hear what her contemporaries regarded as 'degraded, negro depravity'. For boys like Brian and his friends Graham and John Keen, this music was 'a revelation'. But even the Keen brothers, with their comparatively enlightened parents, 'just had to keep quiet about it, for the time being. It was considered a bad influence.'

Brian didn't keep quiet about it. Jazz, and the other black music forms that exploded into British teenagers' consciousness that year, would become the major focus of his life from that moment on. Ultimately, the way his parents dealt with this dreaded new phenomenon would come to define his life.

Plenty of British youngsters discovered jazz, or rock'n'roll, in 1956, the Year Zero for teenagers, symbolized by the cinematic release of *Rebel Without a Cause*, the James Dean movie which defined the iconography of youthful rebellion. That year, according to Brian's future bandmates, there were also seismic changes in Dartford, Kent: 'it was the start of teenage culture, and from that time on our class was divided into musical sects,' says Dick Taylor, a future Stone. Dick's A-stream classmate Michael Jagger was already a Yankophile, famously obsessed with baseball, and seized on to this music, as did friends like Bob Beckwith. But Dick and Mick's parents were indulgent of this new obsession, happy to see their sons' friends turn up with a guitar and make a noise in their living room. The same turned out to be true of Keith Richards, whom Dick met at Sidcup Art College three years later. But for Brian and his parents, the advent of 'degraded' music opened up a rift that would within three years become un-bridgeable. Plenty of people have heard second-hand reports of Brian's affection-free upbringing as a child; by the time we reach his teens, they become first-hand reports. If they did have affection for Brian, it was conditional on his adhering to their rules. 'It's difficult to pinpoint this with psychological accuracy,' John Keen comments, 'but my mother knew his mother quite well – and I don't think his parents treated him with the love most kids get.'

Cheltenham Grammar tracked the progress of its pupils year by year, and there is something poignant about their judgements on Brian, how the brilliant, confident child who's singing in the church choir at the age of eleven, keeps a rabbit, is a keen scout and a member of the Gloucester Youth Club (Railway Section) becomes estranged. His form teacher, Jim Dodge, noticed a change in Brian's behaviour as early as the summer of 1955, commenting that Brian 'suffers from a dominating father, and has to show off to com-pensate'. Mr Dodge was, his pupils remember, a shrewd, worldly man, and he'd hit on a key element of the young Brian's psyche. 'It was a tension-ridden family,' Roger Jessop recalls. 'I would have hated to have Lewis as my father. Whatever [Brian] did wasn't right for him.' Compared to the anodyne lines in other boys' reports, Mr Dodge's venture into psychology in Brian Jones's case is hugely significant; it's followed, year on year, by reports that Brian is clever but 'needs careful handling'. Ultimately, his teachers would never learn to handle him.

There was another factor to add to the music and the rush of teenage hormones: Brian's asthma. It was this that became the final nail in the coffin of his future as a grammar school high-achiever. For the first year or two he'd held his own at sports. Then, says Roger Jessop, who cycled to school with him most mornings, he simply dropped out of the sporty set. 'Often he wasn't fit enough for proper games. And I think he resented himself – gave himself a complex. He didn't have the physical well-being to overcome what were nature's blockages.' Brian's teachers remarked on his health problems: there were fifteen days of absence from school in the summer of 1956, and comments that he was sleeping poorly.

At Cheltenham Grammar School, boys who got ahead played rugby or cricket – they were the only ones worthy of mention in the annual school magazine. So Brian's health alone marked him as a boy apart. Roger Jessop was one of many grammar school boys who stayed in touch with each other and went on to make their mark in respectable professions. But after the first couple of years cycling to school with Brian, he and Brian began to take different routes – in their lives, too. 'He was popular in the early years,' says Roger, 'in the way that young boys who were good at classes and could help with homework would be. But very quickly he lost street cred with the mainstream. So he wasn't popular, I would say, when he left.'

If Brian's parents ever read the rush of British newspaper headlines from the mid 1950s on that fulminated against the corrupting influence of rock'n'roll, jazz or the 'Beatnik horror', as the *Sunday People* put it, they would have felt they were living through a case study. Their inflexibility was, it seems, the downfall of the Jones family. Louisa occasionally confided in her choir friend, Marian

Keen, telling her that Brian was out of control. Marian, once she was told her sons were obsessed with Louis Armstrong, bent with the wind, letting them listen to jazz. 'My parents were adaptable,' says John Keen. 'I got the feeling Brian's parents were rigid, quick to reject anything outside what they were comfortable with.' The result of this was that Brian Jones turned into a wild child, in Cheltenham terms, within twelve months. When his schoolmates talk about that period, they start to use the same words and phrases, many of them ones that recur through his life: 'chip on his shoulder', 'rebellious'. From that point on, too, everyone starts to talk of him as a musician, almost exclusively, always seen with a clarinet or a guitar. One person uses another term that also crops up later: 'the devil'.

When the music first hit Brian, it all came at once. It's likely that Bill Haley, whose Rock Around The Clock streaked to the top of the UK charts in November 1955, was the first harbinger of a new way of life. Immediately, Brian started to work out where this music had come from: he investigated all the rawer country records that had fed into rock'n'roll, including Johnny Cash and, as we shall see, Tennessee Ernie Ford. Along with a younger music fan, Phil Crowther, he got into skiffle in 1956 when Lonnie Donegan enjoyed a string of hits and inspired thousands of British kids – including, of course, John Lennon and Paul McCartney – to try their hands at this defiantly DIY genre. Via Donegan, Brian learned about Leadbelly, whose music was also being spread around the Cheltenham coffee bars; this was probably one of the factors that inspired him to acquire a guitar, around the winter of 1956. In the coffee bars, from the new set that he started to hang out with, he learned more, about trad jazz and more modern jazz from Count Basie and Duke Ellington through to Charlie Parker and, by the late fifties, Cannonball Adderley. He devoured all this music, obsessively, as if it were a code to a new way of existence. Which of course it was.

Music was a means of escape, as well as a form of therapy. For there's another word that describes Brian from that period on: lonely. Pat, Brian's girlfriend of 1960, remembers his loneliness. But that sense of isolation, the claustrophobia he felt at home, was a spur to get the young Brian out of the house. Mick Jagger, Dick Taylor and others played their music in the living room; Brian would strap his guitar to his back and get on his bike. The gulf between Lewis Jones and his son meant that over the next few years Brian would amass playing experience far beyond his fellow Stones, and possibly any aspiring blues guitarist in England.

Cheltenham, boring, staid Cheltenham, was now a hotbed of musical experimentation. A little jazz coterie had begun to coalesce at a celebrated building, 38 Priory Street, where an indulgent mum, Mrs N. E. Filby, had allowed her daughters Jane and Ann to open a basement coffee club. 'It started with four grammar school boys, a band led by John Picton,' says Jane. 'All my sister's friends, basically. They'd do their homework upstairs first. Then it was friends of friends – it was never open to the public.' Within a year or so, visiting musicians like Lonnie Donegan and bandleader and trombonist Chris Barber were dropping by when they came to play the Town Hall; by late 1956, the little club had become a second home for Bill Nile, whose Delta Jazzmen were the town's hottest ticket. Brian was a regular at the club by the age of fifteen. 'I saw him at Filby's by early 1957,' says Graham Keen, who was going out with Ann Filby. 'He'd brought a guitar with him, although I can't remember much about his playing. But I do remember he was really worried about getting home on time, cos his mum and dad wanted him in around ten o'clock.'

Brian's interest in being the top kid in class may by 1957 have completely evaporated – 'an awkward attitude', his teachers noted – but he'd turned that formidable focus on to music. At home, he'd spend hours playing records on the family gramophone, obsessively working out riffs and chords and sounds with a devotion that would soon make him stand out. At the grammar school, a small bunch of boys had started to arrange lunchtime music sessions under the supervision of teacher Bill Neve. Neve brooked no nonsense – he'd cuff Brian around the ear if he talked back – but was open-minded musically, and allowed the boys to form a jazz band, led by clarinettist Colin Partridge. The band-leader got on reasonably well with Brian, who turned up with a guitar for the sessions, and it was immediately obvious to Partridge that he'd been practising: 'He'd clearly been playing a while and had been listening to the right music, although I felt there was more to his vision than strictly jazz.' Or at least Partridge's version of jazz, a purist New Orleans revival style in the vein of Bunk Johnson. 'It was rigid, not Brian's style at all,' says the band's singer Dave Jones, who would continue to play with his near namesake. 'My impression,' Partridge states, 'was that he was a loner.'

That is indeed what he was as far as the establishment kids went. As he built new relationships through music, Brian's old friends fell away – or rather he pushed them away, keen to shock those he considered bores or jobsworths. One friend turned enemy was Colin Dellar, who'd sat next to him in the A stream. 'We were friends for two years. And then we were not friends. In the end it was like two gangs, the Jones Gang and the Dellar Gang. And I used to say that the Dellar Gang used to represent good, and the Jones Gang represented evil.' The pair started to fall out, says Dellar, when he visited the Joneses' semi-detached home. It was neat and prim inside but Brian used to delight in leaving a mess for his mum to clean up. 'He'd say, "That'll give her something to do!"' Some of

29

Brian's other friends put this down to a typical schoolboy showing off, aiming to shock. If so, it worked: it was Dellar who thought there was something of 'the devil' about Brian Jones.

Their feud didn't quite descend into violence but there was constant sniping. One time Dellar pulled off a particularly satisfying coup when groups of kids were marking each other's history essays. His group managed to get hold of Brian's to assess. 'It was a very good piece of work because he was a highly intelligent boy. But we managed to get the history teacher, Mr Campbell, to give him a low mark. That was fun.'

Brian's counter-attack was devious, and effective. At some point during their fourth year, Deputy Head Frederick Jessop was walking along the school hallway when suddenly he heard a string of obscenities being shouted at him. He hurried up the stairwell in search of the offender, but whoever it was had disappeared. Mr Jessop was certain he'd recognized Dellar's voice, and questioned the pupil. 'He was really annoyed with me, but it wasn't me who'd shouted at him – it was Brian Jones.' The Deputy Head didn't believe Dellar. A full year later, Dellar was shocked to find that having joined the sixth form he wasn't appointed a prefect. Later still he learned that the Head, Dr Bell, 'had heard all these stories from the Deputy Head about me, that I'd been saying all these things. Which was Brian Jones getting his own back. In the end they realized it was Brian imitating my voice and I did become a prefect – a year later than all my friends. And Brian did that to me.'

Dellar was exceptional in his detestation of Brian Jones, but plenty of other boys noticed his total lack of respect for, even hatred of, authority. 'He'd lampoon the establishment,' says classmate Ian Standing. 'There was always this aura of slight aggression, or obstinacy. It would all have been a big front, but it was very noticeable. He resented authority, no question.' One or two others in the year also challenged the teachers, but as classmate Robin Pike points out, 'there would be misbehaviour but not being directly rude to a teacher. Because this was the fifties there was still corporal punishment, hence that certain amount of fear.'

Brian Jones courted punishment openly, most conspicuously in February 1957, when Bill Haley, the chubby kiss-curled rock'n'roller who'd been adopted (for the want of anyone better) as an icon of youthful rebellion, announced extra dates for his UK tour, including a show in Cheltenham. On the 22nd, teenagers queued for tickets, causing a stir in the town: the civic authorities were paranoid about troublemaking youngsters, in particular Teddy Boys, who had generated many outraged headlines in the local paper and were banned from the Town Hall. Police kept a close eye on the crowd, and the *Gloucestershire Echo* printed a photo of the rock'n'roll fans lined up outside the Gaumont. Soon, the talk of the grammar school was the boy a few dozen places back. 'He was in a grammar school uniform, and it was Brian Jones,' says Robin Pike. 'The magnitude of the occasion is difficult to explain. I'd been strictly forbidden to go, and of course this was in school hours. It was outrageous, really. This was a pivotal moment.'

Brian got his ticket and ventured to the concert on his own. The show, however, turned out to be a disappointment, with no riots and oddly formulaic stage announcements by Haley, whose band featured, of all things, an accordion.

He was only just turning fifteen, but Brian was becoming completely self-sufficient. He was affable enough: he'd got off his bike to chat with Robin Pike when they shared a post round that Christmas. But the fact he'd done so felt unusual to Pike: 'he was particularly friendly – and that in itself was striking'. Where there were shared interests, he'd put the effort in – he continued his visits to Phil Crowther's house to work on songs together – but in other respects his take on life had diverged noticeably from the mainstream.

There was another distinctive aspect of Brian's life that struck a few people – local girls such as Carole Woodcroft and June Biggar, who cycled a similar route on their way to the girls' grammar school, Pate's Grammar, to the west of the town. Both of them noticed Brian stopping at Albert Road and meeting a Pate's girl with fairish hair in a long ponytail. Hope (not her real name) and Brian were 'all over each other', says June, 'which was unusual. You might meet a grammar school boy at the Gaumont – where it was dark. Because people talk, and you wouldn't want your parents to find out.'

Brian, the geeky ugly duckling, had grown into a muscular, clear-skinned youth. He wasn't too tall but had a fey, puckish charm all of his own which meant that most of the Pate's girls knew of him. The romance with Hope lasted a few weeks or months, remembers Carole. She liked Hope, who was intelligent, pretty and rang the school bell each morning. 'Then Brian moved on, I think, to another girl.'

For all his defiance and the teachers' comments about his declining academic performance, Brian's results in the O levels he sat that summer were respectable: he got seven, including English, Maths, French, German and two sciences – enough to get him into the sixth form, where for his A levels he took on General Studies plus Biology, Physics and Chemistry. These were notoriously difficult subjects, but the best ones to help him to a career as a vet or pharmacist – two strait-laced professions which Lewis, his neighbours reckon, had picked out for him. When Brian joined the sixth form in September 1957, his teachers pronounced his attitude 'good', although once again there were signs of the inescapable presence of Lewis, who reported an 'awkward attitude at home' to the teachers.

Amid the negativity, the crushing sense of being constantly under supervision, the one meaningful avenue of escape in Brian's life continued to open up. That summer he'd started depping regularly on guitar for Bill Nile's Delta Jazzmen, playing a string of shows at their HQ in a backroom of the grand Victorian swimming baths in Alstone. 'He was a good guitarist, probably better than many on the London scene,' says Nile's singer Dave Jones. 'He wasn't a regular, but he played a lot of times, maybe a dozen.' Then the pair branched off to form Brian's first band, the Barn Owls, with drummer (and twitcher) Steve Keegan. Already Brian was venturing beyond the conventional trad jazz repertoire, exploring the work of guitarists James and Lonnie Johnson and, soon, John Lee Hooker, the most stripped-down and primal of the new electric bluesmen. The little band's set was eclectic – Ain't Misbehavin', CC Rider, Careless Love and a couple of Lonnie Donegan numbers – which they'd strum out at local pubs like the Montpellier Arms, Duke of Sussex and Reservoir Inn. Dave and Brian became fairly close friends, meeting at each other's houses or rehearsing at a garage near Hatherley Road. Dave liked Brian. 'He was easy to work with musically, always turned up for gigs and rehearsals, which was the main thing. He was a worker.'

Dave knew that Brian was trying out other musicians outside their trio, always experimenting and learning; and in the spring of 1958, Brian joined up with two jazzer friends, Mac White and Martin Fry, to open a little club at the Wheatsheaf Inn on the Old Bath Road. Mac's band played there most Wednesdays, while Brian checked tickets on the door.

Brian continued to seek out new songs, in the random ways of kids in the pre-internet age: asking friends for recommendations, using the listening booths in the Curry's electrical shop, poring over the pages of *Jazz News*. He suggested to one school friend, Tim (not his real name), that they start up a record club together. The idea was that Brian would supply the record player, and Tim the records. It was probably early in 1958 when they put their plan into action, catching the bus together out to Gloucester, checking through the record racks at Bon Marche, a big department store, and returning to Brian's house with a copy of 16 Tons by Tennessee Ernie Ford. There was no sign of Brian's parents or sister as they settled down in the neatly tended living room, put the 78 on the little record player, and listened to it again and again. 'It's gritty, real life,' they remarked to each other. 'The guy's speaking from experience.' It fitted with Brian's diverse tastes. He was absorbing new music, whatever it was, savouring the deep, doleful tones of Ernie Ford and Johnny Cash just as much as he loved the brash energy of Little Richard.

Now, as a sixteen-year-old, Brian attracted more interest around the city. Perhaps it was his recent transformation from an ugly duckling which inspired his oft-noticed narcissism, but with his blond hair cropped short, high cheekbones and fine features, he seemed well aware of his physical appeal. He turned the eye of many a Pate's girl. 'He was very attractive,' says June Biggar, 'with lovely ivory skin and blue eyes'; perhaps adding to the allure, as another Pate's girl, Penny Farmer, points out, he was already known as 'a wild one'. He was one of those people who might come down the street in a mood and walk right past you without saying hello. 'He wouldn't share things,' say other grammar school boys who were mainly still interested in sports, academia and 'normal' pursuits.

Tim, also sixteen, was a fairly shy schoolboy and his friendship with Brian, not to mention their record club, didn't endure. As he describes their relationship, Tim – a pleasant, friendly man who still lives in Cheltenham – pauses for a while before remarking, 'There was something about his personality I didn't feel comfortable with.' The awkwardness was caused, Tim eventually explains, by an incident one afternoon at Brian's house. 'It was one occasion when he and I were together . . . and he suggested we mutually masturbate. It totally threw me. And I never told anybody else about it, not even my wife.'

Now, in 1950s Britain a little mutual masturbation wasn't especially deviant – John Lennon once famously recalled his own youthful circle jerk, while in some private schools it was positively de rigueur. None the less, 'It was a precocious thing to do,' says Brian's friend John Keen. 'That kind of thing happened in public schools, but here it would have been beyond the pale.' That was certainly Tim's reaction: 'He did have this dark air about him, from a sexual point of view. I call *that* dark. I think that was why we didn't continue that friendship.'

It was early in 1958 that Brian's sexual explorations had their first lasting consequence, when news spread that the sixteen-year-old Hope had disappeared from Pate's and had given birth to Brian's first child. The matter was hushed up – only Hope's immediate classmates were aware – and the baby was given up for adoption (the normal procedure in what was becoming a common event at the girls' grammar school: Hope's classmates remember at least two other secret births that year). It seems Hope did go on to a fulfilling life, later moving overseas. It appears unlikely that the child ever managed to discover the identity of his father, especially as news of the pregnancy and birth were banished to the arena of rumour and speculation.

Some of those privy to the secret disliked Brian from that moment, such as Carole Woodcroft, who went on to the art college, and took a couple of coach trips to West End clubs with Brian in 1959. 'He was a rogue. But not in a glamorous way, not one of the flirty smiley guys. He seemed very cold, as if he was very focused on what he wanted.' John Keen, later a psychologist, liked and respected Brian, but agrees on the point about coldness. 'It's hard to categorize psychologically, but Brian did have a streak in him which was lacking in conscience. He didn't suffer or act as if anything had happened.' In rebelling against his parents' values, against society's conventions, he gave himself licence to be selfish. Barry Miles, a student at the art college who'd meet Brian often over the following years and who also 'had issues' with Cheltenham, remembers Brian as 'a difficult character to be around, but that's because he didn't belong there – he belonged in London'.

With news of the business with Hope carefully suppressed – the boys' grammar school staff were unaware – Brian remained a popular boy around the area, despite the suspicions of the town's parents. His skills and growing reputation as a musician lent him a certain glamour and – says Penny Farmer, who went out on a date to Filby's with him in 1959 – 'he had a naughtiness about him that made him quite interesting'. The pair's date was a fun, sparky evening that started out at Filby's; then they took a long, meandering walk up to All Saints, another jazz club on the high street. He was sexy – 'a naughty face, a twinkly face, he had personality' – and a lot of the talk was about music. An acquaintance of Brian's was playing in the band they were going to see; Brian joked about him, did a little mime to poke gentle fun at him. He kept the conversation going, energetically, talking about other friends on the scene, doing little imitations of them. 'He was all about music. Music was him. It was in everything he did.'

The band, it turned out, was forgettable, but many people in

Filby's and All Saints saw the pair together and soon word got back to Penny's mum. That's how Cheltenham was. 'She went ballistic. She must have heard things my brother David was saying about [Brian], and told me, "Keep clear of that one!" But he really was one of those kids you didn't want to touch for long, or you'd get burnt.'

In the claustrophobic Cheltenham scene, plenty of girls knew about Brian. He was a regular at the sixth form dancing lessons above the Gaumont Cinema, where Brian had seen Bill Haley (Pate's headmistress Miss Lambrick had banned the joint grammar school dances for a short time in an attempt to curb her school's humiliatingly high pregnancy rate, but relented after a few months). Robin Pike remembers Brian disappearing outside with the odd girl, and making out with some French students who were on an exchange around 1959. Yet most of Brian's school friends remember rather more romantic evenings, when Brian danced with a girl he'd met at dancing sessions, or the Friday afternoon sixth form club held jointly with Pate's.

Valerie Corbett lived nearby in Hatherley and was a pupil at Pate's Grammar; she and Brian became a fixture on the scene, chatting at Filby's or on the driveway out of Pate's where Brian would wait, leaning against his bike. 'I remember them particularly from the dance classes,' says Brian's classmate Roger Limb. 'There'd be waltzes, quicksteps, the cha-cha-cha, and I remember Val and Brian being there, with Val just gazing at Brian. She had no eyes for anybody else.'

Anna Livia was in Val's class at Pate's, and like most of her schoolmates she found Val 'really sweet and kind, and when she was happy she had a really sweet smile'. Four months younger than Brian, Valerie was a quiet girl with a pretty face and high cheekbones, mid-length brown hair and well-developed breasts; she and Brian, in his slim suit and with his Gerry Mulligan-style cropped blond hair, made an attractive couple. They were omnipresent at Filby's and other trendy haunts like the Waikiki wine bar and the Patio restaurant throughout the spring of 1959, Brian's final year at school. Colin Partridge, Brian's grammar school contemporary, was one of many who thought the pair looked 'blissfully happy. Although I'm sure they had disagreements from time to time, they seemed joyful.'

Back at the grammar school, though, life was anything but joyful. There were many minor incidents during Brian's final year – benzene ignited in the chemistry lab, throwing of mortar boards around the school grounds – that saw him carpeted or questioned. His absences increased, and in the spring of 1959 this 'unreliable development and conduct' prompted his form master to write to Brian's father. Other teachers tried a more personal approach: the head of biology, Ron Bennett, had high hopes for Brian, as did his bluff deputy Fred Dempsey, who took him aside for a man-to-man talk. 'You've had it all cushy, Brian,' he remonstrated with him. 'You haven't seen the world yet, you don't know how difficult it is to make a living!'

'I really appreciate you telling me this,' the seventeen-year-old replied, with fake sincerity, 'I really will make an effort.'

Instead, his behaviour deteriorated further, into open confrontation.

In the almost textbook list of causes for the teenage rebellion of Brian Jones, the grammar school's bias towards conformist rugby-playing types seems especially to blame. The most potent symbol of this favouritism was David Protherough, prefect and Captain of the Rugby XV, a classic 'jock' esteemed by the teachers and recommended for admission to Cambridge despite the fact he'd not even made the A stream, like Brian. Protherough was popular with the rugby crowd, regarded as 'a bit of a bully' by others, and detested by

Brian. This one-man embodiment of the establishment inspired particular contempt, reckon a couple of classmates, because his girlfriend, Glitch, seemed immune to Brian's advances.

The feud – what teachers would later term 'The Protherough Affair' – came to a head during Brian's final term. 'It was a staged affair during the lunch hour,' remembers Roger Jessop. Brian and a friend had arranged a showdown with the rugby captain which 'ended up in a confrontation, a hell of a scrap, with Brian acting as a ringleader'. Teachers broke up the fight and Brian was once again carpeted, but there was insufficient evidence to penalize him without jeopardizing Protherough's prospects too. Despite talk of expulsion, Brian survived his first act of open rebellion. Protherough duly went up to Cambridge, and in his one-man campaign against jobsworths and authority figures Brian Jones dug his trench a little deeper.

2

Crossroads

SECOND WEEK AT Alexis Korner's club in Ealing and you'd think they would have sorted the teething problems, but no. Condensation dripped steadily on to the stage, the place smelt funky, and the beers were warm. Yet while Keith Scott rippled through the piano parts, Alexis Korner laid down a simple rhythm guitar, and a young drummer called Charlie skipped lightly along a funky path, all led by the grizzled, ornery harmonica of the grizzled, ornery Cyril Davies, no one minded. It was the glorious spring of 1962 and British rock was being hotwired, jump-started, Frankensteined into life, so who cared about being electrocuted?

Mick Jagger was the one who'd sorted the trip, as usual persuading his Yankophile dad to lend him the family motor for the forty-five-minute drive from Dartford. He looked carefully around the room, his usual bounce and cheeky confidence just a little dampened. For the past year he, Keith Richards and Dick Taylor had pretended they were grizzled blues buffs, but really they'd only ever played in a living room. Yet when Mick sidled over to talk to

Korner, with his little band's tape in hand, he got a warm Greek welcome. Korner liked the boyish sincerity, and spoke to the skinny would-be bluesman like an exotic moustachioed uncle. Sure, he'd listen to the Blue Boys' tape, he assured him, and there'd probably be a slot free soon.

Someone else had snaffled the guest slot for this week. There was a hurried conversation on the rickety eight-inch-high stage before Korner announced, in a rich, gravelly voice, his special guest for the evening: 'Ladies and gentlemen, I present, on guitar Elmo Lewis, on vocals P. P. Pond!'

As the swooping, glassy, erotic sound of the slide guitar filled the basement, Dick and Keith craned their necks, trying to work out how the hell he achieved it. Korner, one of the first electric blues guitarists they'd seen, was pretty good; Elmo was far better, the way he kept up that loping, clipped rhythm as Pond sang out the vocals, then swooped up the strings with a glass bottleneck for his lead licks. The guitarist, short hair, serious expression, white shirt and houndstooth trousers, looked impossibly cool. What the hell tuning was that? How the hell did he get that sound? Who the hell was he?

Dick and Keith, the two Blue Boys guitarists, didn't bother trying to hide their shock. 'He's not just good,' Dick told his art college mate, 'he's really, really good.'

It was a hell of an evening, as you'd expect of the time when the future Rolling Stones met each other, when the focused, driven Brian Jones so impressed Mick Jagger, Keith Richards and Dick Taylor who in that spring of 1962 were merely schoolboy fans of the music Brian had already mastered. Ideas and thoughts ran through the Dartford trio's minds, and one question above all: How the hell did he get to be so good?

*

The contrast between the musical development of Brian Jones and his future fellow Stones was obvious within minutes of their first encounter. What wasn't obvious was the tortuous, gruelling nature of the journey Brian had undertaken into the heart of the blues. For the first time we can document that Elmo Lewis, aka Brian Jones, had notched up a hundred or more gigs before he walked on to that stage in Ealing, every one of which separated him just a little bit more from his exasperated parents.

As the 1950s, that grim British decade of repression and conformity, dwindled away, Brian still seemed locked in its clutches. He was treated like a child, forced to comply with his parents' wishes. His three A levels – Physics, Chemistry and General Studies (he failed Biology) – while hardly stunning, were respectable for those days, enough to get him into a red-brick university or polytechnic, so Louisa and Lewis decided this merited a special holiday. But not a family holiday. Lewis couldn't take time off from Rotol that summer of 1959, so Brian was sent to stay with friends in Germany for six weeks. In his future retellings, Brian embellished the trip into a hobo adventure, one boy and his guitar hitch-hiking around Europe. In fact his hosts were elderly, like his parents, and the whole experience was like 'being in an open prison', as he'd tell friends later. The pressure to conform increased on his return, and Brian acceded to his father's wish that he map out a respectable professional career as an optician by enrolling on a course in Applied Optics in London, reportedly at the Northampton Institute (later City University), to start in September.

From what we can tell, Brian missed Val – but not as much as Val missed Brian. 'Her life at that time really centred around Brian,' says Carole Goodsell, a friend of Val's. 'She was quite outgoing, happy and friendly – but he really *was* her entire life.' In the time

Carole spent with Brian and Val she found the aspiring musician 'arrogant and self-centred – but Valerie loved him, which is all that mattered'.

Then, some time in the autumn of 1959, Valerie discovered she was pregnant. As so often happens, the news spread rapidly, but randomly. Initially, says Val's school friend Anna Livia, Val seemed overjoyed. 'She was all excited. I remember her saying, "Oh, I'm going to live in London with Brian." And then there was some incident . . . she broke down in tears and ran out of the room. I suppose that must have been when it had all fallen through.'

The story shared around the coffee bars and basement clubs in Cheltenham was pretty straightforward: Brian had done a runner. Everyone around the tiny scene knew the couple well and shared much the same opinion as Jane Filby, who declares, 'Brian was a big shit. Or, as my husband says, he was actually a little shit. After all, he wasn't that tall.' But none of them really knew the full story. In the 1950s, the outcome of a teenager's pregnancy was decided not by the teenagers but by their parents. Only years later would Graham Ride, one of Brian's friends, who later married Val, discover what had happened: 'Brian made an offer to marry Val, but it all went wrong. It surprised me, when I found out, but that's what happened.'

In the early weeks of her pregnancy, Val, her mother and Brian exchanged letters; for just a few weeks, Val was happy, indulging fantasies of family life with Brian in London. But her parents, seemingly in collusion with Lewis and Louisa, soon put paid to that notion. They were horrified by the thought of their daughter heading for the bright lights to live with Brian and refused to give the necessary permission for him to marry her. This, it seems, was what caused Val's tears, rather than Brian's cold-hearted refusal.

In the spring of 1960, the messy situation turned tragic. Val's father, whom everyone remembers as idolizing his daughter, died of a heart attack. Ken Corbett had worked with Lewis Jones at Rotol; Brian's father, says Graham Ride, blamed his errant son for the tragedy – another outrage to compound the pregnancies of Hope and Val. It was in the traumatic aftermath of Mr Corbett's death that the decision was made to have Val's baby adopted.

Years later, Graham saw the paperwork on the adoption, including various correspondence which showed that Brian renewed his offer to marry Val. Some time around June 1960, Brian arrived from London to visit Val and his son, Barry David, who was recuperating following surgery on his stomach after his birth on 29 May. Yet at some point in the weeks that followed, Val received a letter from Brian that persuaded her to have nothing more to do with him. No one knows its contents, but the most likely explanation is probably the simplest one, which is that while Brian had offered to marry Val, he said he'd felt pressured to do so, and that he wasn't in love with her.

Val was forced into a commonplace, heartbreaking routine, and gave Barry David up for adoption. She would, it turned out, see Brian again; but her Cheltenham friends, like Roger Limb, mostly share a similar impression when they encountered her over the following year: 'She seemed a rather defeated sort of person. Certainly not the bright smiling young thing I had known before.' Brian's younger sister Barbara suffered, too: Miss Lambrick, the Head at Pate's, resented her lothario brother and reportedly would only supply a terse, ungenerous college reference which hampered Barbara's ambitions to become a teacher.

Graham Ride would be a good friend to Brian during a defining time in both their lives, and via his later marriage to Val would come to understand some of the emotional carnage Brian had wrought. He uses the phrase 'charming but manipulative' of Brian.

Friendship with him had its drawbacks, such as embarrassment when seeing ex-girlfriends, or having to cope with his unreliability. The cause, says Graham, was that 'Brian was a very instant person. He lived in the here and now, so if he wanted to make love, that's what he'd do. He never thought about the consequences. If he hadn't been so fertile it wouldn't have been such a problem!'

Brian Jones was typical of a particular generation of men who'd rejected the repressive morality of the 1950s but retained many of that era's misogynist traits. Barry Miles, who'd define, participate in and document much of the sixties counter-culture, encountered Brian many times and remembers, 'He did have a horrible attitude to women. But that was a very common thing in those days – the way most people behaved. There was a lot of misogyny over that decade.'

Through 1960, then, Brian laid down many of the lifestyle traits of his future band. More significantly, over the next twenty months he built the foundations of their music, too, discovering crucial touchstones from Jimmy Reed to Robert Johnson, Elmore James to Slim Harpo. While his future bandmates continued their studies and played music at home for fun, Brian immersed himself in a journey deep into the heart of the music he loved.

By the late spring of 1960 Brian had given up hope of placating his father – ophthalmology, you might say, wasn't something he'd ever really focused on – and over the summer he returned to Cheltenham. By the autumn, many of the grammar school girls and boys had turned their backs on him, as had his parents. It was the making of him. While scraping together money from a variety of jobs, he turned to music as his only salvation. Here, rather than always giving less than he promised, he was happy, indeed motivated, to give more.

In those first months back in Cheltenham, when he stayed with his parents in Hatherley Road, his income was erratic: he worked in Boots the chemist, did a spot of van driving, and later did a stint in the architects office at the County Council. But by the end of the year a large part of his income was starting to come from gigs and music. As his obsession with the blues grew, he also developed a nomadic, rent-party lifestyle that would have been familiar to the musicians who kicked off the genre in Mississippi fifty years before.

Brian had kept up his friendship with Phil Crowther, and when Phil left school that summer the pair spent hours working on songs at Phil's dad's newspaper warehouse. Phil was more of a rock'n'roll fan; Brian, dogmatic in so many ways, enjoyed working across genres, figuring out songs by Eddie Cochran, Little Richard, King Curtis and Duane Eddy alongside the usual jazz numbers. When Phil teamed up with a local ex-Boys Brigade turned skiffle band to form what would become the Ramrods, Brian tagged along. Given that the band already had a guitarist, and that was Phil's main instrument too, Brian switched to tenor sax (he'd also owned an alto at one point). He made plain this wasn't his main gig, but he put the effort in. 'He knew what he was doing,' says drummer Buck Jones, 'no question about that.' Barry Miles, then at the art college, remembers he had a greasy rock'n'roll King Curtis or Earl Bostic style 'all figured out'.

He impressed his fellow band members, especially considering the sax was just a sideline; they'd also seen him depping on guitar with Bill Nile at Filby's basement on the odd occasion, and knew of jazz dates over in Bath that he'd played with Harry Brampton, another ex-grammar school boy. Brian remained good mates with Phil throughout his Cheltenham chum's short life (he choked to death on his honeymoon in 1964) and, according to Buck Jones, Brian was laid-back and supportive. But bassist Graham Stodart remembers a perfectionism that sometimes gave way to frustration. 'We all liked him. He was a brilliant musician. But he wanted things to be absolutely perfect. And it's when things weren't absolutely perfect that he would show his darker side. We didn't see it an awful lot but he could get a little moody if things hadn't gone the way he'd liked.' The odd black look, the occasional depression when things weren't moving on, would recur later. But in 1960, such moods were fleeting.

Harry Brampton had bumped into Brian at Sid Tong's Record Shop, where he worked in late 1960, and the clarinettist had persuaded Brian to join him on guitar for a series of Wednesday-night shows in a Bath pub, augmenting a five-piece band every week for four or five months. The material was simple – 'the usual stuff, Just A Closer Walk With Thee, Royal Garden Blues, all that kind of thing' – but Brian was unfazed by being asked to turn up at short notice. 'He was a confident guy,' says Brampton. 'In those circumstances as a musician you encounter your share of jobsworths, but he was always a pleasant guy to be around.' With the regular shows with the Ramrods, and in Bath, plus numerous sessions dropping in with visiting and local bands, Brian was already rated, says Brampton, as a 'serious musician'.

In his music, Brian was applying all the focus that was lacking in his efforts to find a conventional career. Back home his relationship with Lewis and Louisa was at breaking point, but in other respects this period was often a blissful one. Away from the straight kids at school he had a wide group of friends who met regularly at the cinema or at barbecues up at Kemton Hill. Around September, one of his musician acquaintances bumped into a fifteen-year-old girl named Pat Andrews and told her how his friend had lost touch with the Cheltenham scene after stays in Germany and London. A few days later, Pat turned up for a blind date at the Aztec coffee bar on the high street, and in the alcove, behind the Chianti bottles and mugs, saw a striking, golden-haired 'angel. I couldn't speak. I literally couldn't speak. There was this light coming from I don't know where . . . I don't remember what he said, I was so focused on this angelic blond hair, but we agreed to meet again, and started going out for walks.'

In those first weeks, spent wandering in the hills around Cheltenham, in its coffee bars, and even around the railroad tracks, Pat's fascination with the teenager who was blessed with immense charm and an enchanting imagination grew. 'He would tell all sorts of stories, he could be amusing, he could capture you with card games, he could do magic tricks. And of course when I sat there and listened to him playing, I was transported into another world, another realm.'

In those early days, Brian lived up to that first angelic impression, and Pat became a little besotted with him. But she noticed some worrying traits, too. 'I'd been going out with this German boy for months, then he'd gone back to Stuttgart. He used to write me all these letters, and one night in the Aztec, Brian asked, "Do you have any cigarettes?" So I look in my bag and of course forgot the letters were in there. Brian pulled them out, saw the pictures, and got really upset, grabbing everything. I was shocked, going, "They're mine, don't tear them!" We'd only been going out a week. And I thought, bloody hell, this is someone who's really jealous.'

Some days with Brian were bliss, spent fooling around on carefree walks. But there were dramas, too, with even darker undertones. In particular there was a Wednesday afternoon when Pat was helping Brian get his clothes ready before they went on to a Jazz Night at the Rotunda. Pat had met Brian's parents a couple of times, found Lewis polite but withdrawn, but was convinced that Louisa looked down on her. Pat had taken it upon herself to iron Brian's shirt, in the Jones family front room. Louisa walked in.

'She just lost it,' says Pat. 'I think she was upset I was ironing his shirt, as that meant [intimacy] . . . She got really cross, and this happened really quickly, but Brian's guitar was on an armchair nearby, and she went to grab it.' Brian leapt in front of the guitar, his mother screamed at him, and he slapped her across the face.

Today, sitting in a coffee bar in Crystal Palace, Pat is anxious to point out, 'It was not a big slap. It was a slap to bring her out of her hysteria, which it did.' Brian's ex-girlfriend is keen that 'no one should judge him too harshly'. Yet it was immediately obvious to her that there was something dysfunctional about the Jones family. In the following months, Brian confided in Pat and spoke of what happened after his sister Pamela died. 'Brian's mum told him that if he didn't behave, he'd be sent away – just like his [dead] sister,' says Pat.

Just a few weeks after the ironing incident, in December 1960, the fault lines in the Jones family relations split wide open when Lewis, Louisa and Barbara went away for Christmas and left Brian's bags in the drive. Long before Andrew Oldham manufactured the Stones' image as icons of outrage, Brian Jones had passed irrevocably beyond the boundaries of the decent, aspirational middle class.

Those who knew Brian well often observe that he'd plead ignorance when he'd destroyed a relationship, or make unconvincing apologies. That didn't happen after this formative, fundamental split. There was no looking back; he seemed hardened to his parents' rejection, barely mentioning it to others. Instead, all the energy he'd spent dealing with his earnest, uncomprehending parents was channelled into music. Two friends would become Brian's main accomplices as he abandoned strait-laced society: Dick Hattrell, the son of a successful Tewkesbury solicitor, and

John Keen, the former Cheltenham Grammar School boy whose parents had been friends of Lewis and Louisa.

Dick was a Filby's regular who'd also bumped into Brian during jazz shows at Bishop's Cleeve Village Hall and the Waikiki (also known as the Barbecue) on the Queen's Circus, and finally got talking to him one night at the Rotunda. Brian was moving fast; 'he was already frustrated by the jazz scene,' says Dick. 'He knew I read *Jazz Journal*, so that first night he said to me, "Can you write me a complete discography of Muddy Waters?" The following week, I gave him a list of everything Muddy had recorded, on various labels, not just Chess, and he was delighted. Then it was, "Can you dig out some information on Elmore James?" I said yeah, no problem. And so on.'

Dick was enthusiastic and skittish, like a young puppy-dog. Although six years older than Brian, he'd always remain the more junior member in their relationship, partly because he didn't play, partly because he was unassertive, ready and willing to follow Brian's whims. Dick's father was a pillar of the establishment, and when Dick's partying and love of jazz became the talk of Tewkesbury, his dad, politely enough, gave him his marching orders. This happened just at the time when Brian had outstayed his welcome at his current abode, a room rented from Pat Andrews' brother. Brian had found a flat in Selkirk House, an impressive, stucco-fronted building at 73 Prestbury Road, and talked Dick into sharing the large space. Together, they developed a lifestyle that would have been pretty familiar to Brian's musical heroes. 'We had a great life,' says Dick. 'We'd survive by holding rent parties, like in the old New Orleans days. When trad jazz bands were playing in Cheltenham, we'd encourage them back for a few beers to let their hair down. We'd buy a load of beer and stuff to eat, encourage the musicians to play in the flat, then charge an entrance fee, which all went towards the rent. Then we'd take the empty bottles back the next day and get the money back. We had some good times.'

The pair usually got up around noon, then wandered into town, most often to the Barbecue, which hosted jazz shows in the evening. Brian was the one who'd usually venture out to shows and persuade musicians like Eric Allendale, and many others, back to the flat. His charm and focus were incredible. Teenage disenchantment played a part in this lifestyle, but only a minor part, says Dick. 'It was a lot deeper. He wanted to be a good musician. He was on a musical journey.'

Brian had turned his back on Cheltenham society, as it had on him, but there was a major payoff: this was the making of him as a musician. In those months, spent constantly practising on a Hofner f-hole archtop he'd acquired, he moved far ahead of most of his peers.

It was most likely on Monday, 18 April 1960 that Brian had first met John Keen, whose band was playing at Filby's basement. Like Dick, Keen was several years older than Brian; he'd recently returned from the Merchant Marine and had made his name locally fronting Bill Nile's Delta Jazzmen during Bill's National Service. Kind, self-deprecating – although he had a formidable reputation on the Cheltenham and later the London 100 Club scene – and incisive, Keen is also the most valuable early observer of Brian Jones that we have. He came from a similar background, and his latter-day second career as an educational psychologist allows him valuable insight into interactions within rock'n'roll bands. Keen may have spent more years on the planet and seen more of it when they teamed up, but he insists that 'Brian was streets ahead of us. He was very skilled musically, very impressive on the guitar. We couldn't understand the chordal things he knew. My skills weren't far advanced compared to Brian.'

The pair spent much of 1961 working together; Keen got to know a different side of Brian from Dick, and Brian's later flatmate, Graham Ride. They all witnessed Brian's moods, but with Keen, the nineteen-year-old showed minimal self-indulgence. There was plenty of messing around – that almost telepathic banter you develop in a little band, plus the endless pursuit of women – but when it came to music, Brian was super-serious. 'He really knew what he wanted to do. It was really impressive, his focus. He was ambitious, and he felt like a fish out of water in Cheltenham. He had no interest in the business side, so I did the fixing. Brian's main interest was the music – and if it didn't sound right, he would say so. So quite often, although he was three or four years younger than me, he was the leader. I realize these things now, but I didn't realize when I was younger.'

Keen, along with Graham Ride, was Brian's closest collaborator in 1961 – although Brian turned up at many shows independently, and towards the end of the year linked up with a new circle in Oxford, a common destination for many Cheltenham teenagers who were into jazz and the Campaign for Nuclear Disarmament. Along with other pickup musicians and soon Graham Ride on sax, they played shows either as John Keen's Jazz Band or the Brian Jones Blues Band, depending on who had arranged the gig. Their set included classics like Tin Roof Blues, St Louis Blues, Memphis Blues and Careless Love, which always went down well with the audiences at Filby's. The group ventured out to little village pubs in the Cotswolds like the Royal George in Birdlip and the Bear Pools in Stroud, house parties in Evesham, or played back home at the Barbecue. For bigger shows, when he was supporting touring acts like Acker Bilk at the Town Hall, Keen would book a six-piece band, with a banjo player, and Brian would stay at home. 'Banjos are over,' he'd tell Keen. 'A band with a banjo in has no swing.'

Brian had long grown tired of the 'Purist Jazz' movement and instead searched out the work of Freddie Green, the guitarist in Count Basie's band. 'Listen to this guy,' he'd persuade Keen, 'how his chordal work makes the whole band swing!' Inspired by Green, Brian studied deeply the intricacies of big band guitar playing. 'He didn't differentiate between traditional jazz, mainstream jazz, modern jazz and blues,' says Keen, 'he kind of drew out of all of it, while the blues evolved into his main interest.' Although rock'n'roll had spluttered into self-parody in both Britain and the US, Brian was still enthused by Elvis, Little Richard and Chuck Berry, too, showing other guitarists how to play Chuck licks. He was also listening to Charlie Christian, Benny Goodman's visionary guitarist. 'There was a lot of knowledge that simply wasn't around then,' Keen continues. 'It wasn't in books, so how would we know? But Brian had his fingers in all sorts of pies.'

Although Dick Hattrell or John Keen would often tag along, Brian had the confidence to take off on his own, turning up at a gig at the Town Hall or at the club above the swimming baths and talking older, more experienced musicians into letting him share the bandstand. After one show at the Town Hall, bandleader Kenny Ball sat with Brian and was almost gushing in his praise: 'You're so young – how did you learn to play like that?' Keen, who was there that evening, sat by, without interrupting, content to bask in the reflected glory. The same happened with Alex Welsh's band at St Luke's Hall, where Brian contributed a forceful, propulsive rhythm guitar over several songs as the older musicians gave him looks of approval. 'They were definitely appreciative,' says Keen. 'A bloke that young, out in the provinces – they were obviously surprised.'

Keen reckons that in 1961, including a couple of dozen shows with their own band, Brian notched up 'well over a hundred' gigs and guest appearances. Add in his stints with Bill Nile, the Barn

Owls, and earlier minor slots at Filby's basement, and it's obvious that the young guitarist was accumulating experience much faster than most of his contemporaries.

His rapid, obsessive quest to search out new music had intensified from the summer of that year when new housemate Graham Ride arrived on the scene. Graham had discovered the work of Leadbelly a couple of years earlier, and like Brian was aware of Chicago blues via the pioneering work of Chris Barber, who had ventured out to the Chicago South Side in 1959 and brought innovators such as Muddy Waters and Sister Rosetta Tharpe to Britain, all in the face of opposition by the British Musicians' Union, which attempted to keep out 'foreign' performers. Graham had moved to Cheltenham from Liverpool and was playing clarinet in a local band when he first met Dick and Brian, in May. During their first afternoon together, Graham listened to the pair enthuse about music and argue about who'd been stealing food from the fridge – a typical day at Selkirk House. Graham moved into the flat later that summer, bringing along a copy of *The Blues*, an EMI/Vee Jay compilation featuring Elmore James and Jimmy Reed that would become a cornerstone of Brian's little world.

Graham and Brian became good chums. Graham was more forceful than the easy-going Dick and rarely suffered from Brian's moods, but right from the off he noticed the tensions around the young guitarist. It wasn't difficult. That summer the pair bumped into Brian's sister, Barbara, on the Promenade: the fifteen-year-old, who looked quite a bit like her brother, seemed anxious, as if she'd been forbidden even to talk to him, and walked off after exchanging only a couple of words. Brian would never mention his parents, either to Graham or to John Keen, whose parents knew the Joneses well: 'If the subject ever came up, he'd avoid talking about it, but you got the impression he wanted to escape their influence, any way he could.' Pat Andrews, who spent most of that summer with Brian, believes Brian's estrangement from his parents, never really resolved, would go on to cause real psychological damage: 'All he ever wanted was for them to say well done. It was all he wanted, but he never got it.'

Graham was well aware of Brian's faults, but he liked him; he was smart, well read, enthusiastic and focused. The manipulativeness, he says, 'didn't affect [me]. I don't think he ever put a charm offensive on me. Yes, he charmed money out of me, cos I paid for more cigarettes, more drinks. But that's par for the course, a part of growing up. You're away from home and mates are pretty important.'

In fact Graham came to enjoy that slight sense of chaos; he and Brian would laugh about the encounters that characterized Brian's life. Around May or June, Brian had confided in Graham and Dick, telling them that his girlfriend Pat was pregnant. For most of that summer, says Dick, Brian was well behaved – 'he stayed faithful to Pat at this point' – but there would be no reward. Later that summer, Brian and Graham were ambling up the Promenade, headed for the Waikiki, when Brian let out a sudden curse. He'd been spotted by Pat Andrews' mum and sister. The mum marched up, launched into a tirade of abuse, and smacked Brian with her brolly. Graham, too, had to dodge the blows, but the mum's switch of attack gave Brian the chance he needed and he ran off at full speed, laughing, with Graham bringing up the rear.

Graham, John and Dick were all close witnesses to Brian's messy life, spent on the edge of penury. He was always cadging cash. Many other frequenters of Cheltenham's coffee bars found themselves suddenly cornered by Brian, fixed by his boyish, apologetic smile, and were somehow compelled to hand over a few shillings for a cup of tea or a sandwich. But for the trio, who were involved in the music,

Brian's commitment and focus always outweighed his flakiness.

It was the autumn of 1961 when the obsessions that shaped Brian's life finally cohered into a musical manifesto. He'd heard a lot of blues, but it was the sound of Jimmy Reed and Elmore James, along with the Muddy Waters records he'd already discovered, that became his lodestone. Thanks to the Stones, these giants of electric blues would become celebrated, and their influence would pervade the sixties and seventies. But in 1961 they were mysterious figures whose lives and musical output had to be pieced together from disparate sources.

First of all, Brian fixed on the music of Elmore James, a shimmering, glossy, thrillingly electric sound unlike anything he'd heard before. He played Coming Home from Graham Ride's Vee Jay compilation over and over, working out that he was using a slider or bottleneck, with the guitar tuned to an Open D chord. Brian started experimenting with a steel and brass tube he'd found in a Cheltenham junk yard; later he found a glass tube that did the job better. Once he'd nailed the tuning, he focused on the sound. 'I don't know how he did it: he converted a reel-to-reel tape recorder into an amplifier,' says Dick Hattrell. 'He plugged his guitar in there, an acoustic with a DeArmond pickup, and he was playing as close as he could to the style of Elmore James. If you didn't know it was Brian you'd think it was a record of Elmore James.'

Brian unleashed this new sound on the public towards the end of 1961. That first performance was likely in a pub in one of the outlying Gloucester villages Birdlip or Painswick. Using a Vox AC15 amplifier he'd persuaded John Keen to buy on hire purchase, Brian Jones kicked off a new era in musical history. There was no other electric slide player in the UK, and quite possibly no such white player in the US (Elvin Bishop had yet to venture out to the Chicago clubs). Brian's use of amplified blues guitar came within a couple of weeks of Chris Barber's first experiments in electric blues, with his recruitment of guitarist Alexis Korner. Barber had played a crucial role in championing the blues form, but Brian was about to take up the baton and take the music somewhere completely new. Few other people in the UK, apart from John Lennon and Paul McCartney, were working out how to fuse together such different strands of music into a coherent whole.

One other cornerstone of Brian's music was hoisted into place in 1961 when he brought home a copy of Robert Johnson's *King Of The Delta Blues Singers*. This album of sixteen tracks compiled by researcher Frank Driggs would become a key artefact of British blues, regarded in mystical terms by Keith Richards, who'd hear Brian's copy at Edith Grove (where they lived in a flat together). Brian played the album over and over at Selkirk House. Having followed the work of *Jazz Monthly* writer Paul Oliver, a pioneer in the research of early blues, he'd also bought a copy of Oliver's landmark book, *Blues Fell This Morning*, soon after its publication. 'He wasn't only playing this stuff,' says Keen, 'he was reading about it too. It was fascinating.'

Johnson's music would become the leitmotif of Jones's life. The bluesman's short existence was shrouded in myth, and did indeed seem to draw on some dark power. Johnson was the man who told his fellow musicians, like Son House, that he'd learned his fiendish guitar skills at the Crossroads, an intersection of two roads in the desolate depths of Mississippi where he'd met a 'Black Man' who took his guitar and retuned it. The Black Man was, scholars suggest, a representation of the old African god Elegua, or Legba – a manifestation of the Devil. This was a potent tale for Brian, who instantly recognized the value of Oliver's groundbreaking research.

There was substance to the Crossroads myth. Robert Johnson had undoubtedly spiced up the tale to impress fellow musicians and shock God-fearing Christians: his friend Honeyboy Edwards heard the story from Johnson and qualified it with the words 'Robert was a big bullshitter'. Yet Honeyboy and others felt the presence of the Devil in Mississippi where in the 1930s a black man on the road with a guitar was subject to summary imprisonment, or worse. Musicians who didn't 'Yassuh, Nossuh' the white man – in other words abase themselves like children – often found themselves looking down the business end of a lawman's Colt. Many were ostracized by their families simply for choosing the blues, the Devil's music, over God-fearing gospel. Brian was a pioneer, perhaps the very first British musician to pick up on the potency of Johnson's myth and music. For comparison's sake, at the time when Brian was immersed in the world of Robert Johnson, hitching round the South West to find someone who would let him share a stage, Mick Jagger was enchanting mums in the front rooms of Dartford singing songs by Buddy Holly.

In later years it was important for those who survived Brian, like Charlie Watts, to dismiss him as a middle-class boy from Cheltenham, with some nasty ways: 'He was a pretentious little sod. He was from Cheltenham. Does that sum it up?' Some of it was justified; much of it was that Confucian twist: we hate a man who does us a favour. Brian Jones was responsible not just for the musical inspiration of the Rolling Stones, but their dark magic, too. He was the Stone with something of the dark about him. There were other aspects of his personality, like his sexuality, that also seemed portentous. Barry Miles remembers that in respectable, polite Cheltenham there was a bookseller who furnished clients with the works of the Marquis de Sade – works that would be devoured throughout the period of sixties counter-culture Brian helped inspire but which in 1961 were esoteric indeed. 'Brian knew of de Sade,' Miles confirms, 'even in Cheltenham, I think.'

*

Cheltenham ... that supposedly pretentious provincial town turned out to be a centre for a range of beautifully nefarious activities. Thanks to its role as a hub of trad jazz it would also host a pioneering blues performance, when Chris Barber, who had worked with Muddy Waters on live dates in 1959, decided to try his hand at electric blues with the aid of Alexis Korner.

A fascinating figure who would become a key influence in Brian's life, Korner boasted a complex Austrian, Jewish and Greek heritage, had lucked into a job with the British Forces Network in 1947, and had discovered the blues, via Leadbelly, a couple of years later. Within a year he was playing guitar in a trad jazz band with Barber, who had begun his own journey into the heart of jazz and blues thanks to a discarded biography of jazz clarinettist and dope-head Mez Mezzrow that he'd found in a USAF rubbish dump. The pair reunited in 1961 and were destined to become regarded as the two key British patrons of blues, despite their generally incompatible personalities. 'Chris led a jazz band and Alexi really didn't like traditional jazz,' says Korner's wife, Bobbie. 'Chris was an amazing businessman and Alexi was an appalling businessman. They just were not at all similar.'

For all their differences, Barber and Korner would prove crucial catalysts. Brian had followed Korner's work religiously in the pages of *Jazz Journal*, and when Barber's band was booked into Cheltenham Town Hall on 10 October 1961, Brian was ready. This was his chance to penetrate the heart of the country's embryonic electric blues scene.

He enrolled Dick Hattrell and John Keen as moral support, and when Barber announced the segment of his set that featured Korner, 'Brian and I were shouting our heads off!' says Dick. 'I think we were the only two people there who had heard of him.'

Brian found it easy to hustle his way backstage where he went straight for the main man, Barber. They discussed mutual acquaintances, says Barber, probably meaning Bill Nile. 'He knew a lot about the business, and knew what he was doing. I thought he was a very nice guy. Serious about music. But I let Alexis do all the talking with him, he was the bluesman there.'

The trio took Korner to one of Brian's favourite clubs, the Patio. 'It was then that Alexis told us he was forming a new band, playing the music of Muddy Waters,' Dick recalls. 'And that they'd be starting at a new club. And we said, "We'll be there."' It was also at this meeting that Brian told Korner he intended to move to London and play blues. Korner's reaction was illuminating. According to John Keen, the father of British blues reckoned Brian's scheme was a madcap one. 'He told Brian, "Don't go to London! It's no good, you'll never make it there, it's all too commercial – this blues style is never going to be popular." Brian took absolutely no notice. In some ways he was so confident and strong-willed.'

Despite his conviction that blues would never become mainstream, Alexis Korner, then thirty-three, would become Brian's most important patron. Chris Barber, with manager Harold Pendleton, was a business powerhouse who established key venues like the Marquee and the National Jazz and Blues Festival. Korner, in contrast, was more of a father figure. He established a bohemian household in an apartment on Moscow Road in Bayswater, west London, along with his wife Bobbie, herself a key early blues fan and supporter, and writer friend Charles Fox. And among the first younger visitors to Moscow Road would be Brian Jones and Dick Hattrell.

Korner was proprietorial about the music he loved, which caused fallings-out with supposed rivals like Chris Barber and Paul Oliver. Younger musicians, though, brought out the best in him. He would always be a sympathetic paternal figure in Brian's life. 'Alexis was a really nice bloke, in the sense that he took Brian seriously,' says Keen. 'Some people would write off a nineteen-year-old who had passion and interest but maybe didn't know what he was doing. Alexis realized Brian was utterly devoted to the cause.'

From the outset Brian worked assiduously on his relationship with Alexis Korner. He and Graham Ride had recently moved to 56 Bath Road, a smaller apartment nearer the town centre, after an argument with their old landlord over money disappearing from the gas meter. The pair hated the new flat – it was too small for rent parties – but there was a handy phone box nearby that Brian had learned to hack. By tapping out the correct sequence of clicks he could dial Korner's London number for free. Soon he discovered that Korner would be back in Cheltenham late in October, and once again he and Graham talked their way backstage at the Gaumont, where Brian had seen that lacklustre Bill Haley show. The pair then made their way to the Waikiki with Korner and Sonny Terry and Brownie McGhee, two bluesmen who'd managed to evade the union ban on US musicians by billing themselves as 'entertainers'.

Brian was at ease with Brownie and Sonny, whose eyesight was so bad that Brian and Graham had to read out the Waikiki menu for him. Sonny settled on steak and kidney pie, and the Mississippi bluesmen tucked wholeheartedly into British comfort food while Brian kept the conversation going. 'He just turned on the charm,' says Graham. 'He was good at it, knowledgeable, and [he] could talk.' It was one more stage in Brian's induction into Alexis Korner's extended family.

He and Dick Hattrell became regulars on the hitchhike trail into London. The trips were always gruelling, despite the kindness of the occasional truck driver who fell for Brian's spiel and stumped up the money for egg and chips at a transport caff. 'Oh God, it was awful, it would take so long to get there,' Dick recalls. 'But it was all worth it. When we got to Alexis's house, it was like we were living in the house of the Lord.'

Korner laid out his plans to Brian, how he was forming an all-electric blues band with Cyril Davies, the ornery harmonica player he'd previously worked with at the Barrelhouse Blues club. Cyril, a panel beater by trade, looked a bit like Lyndon B. Johnson but was Britain's first master of the 'Mississippi saxophone' – the amplified harmonica, as played by Little Walter and James Cotton. In turn, Brian made his own plans. For several weeks he tried to persuade a Cheltenham singer, Gordon Harper, to join him in an electric blues band. 'Gordon was a short-back-and-sides insurance salesman, and a good bloke,' says mutual friend Ken Ames. Harper enjoyed playing Bill Broonzy-style blues at the weekend – and thought that was as far as that music would take anyone. 'You'll never get anywhere with a blues band,' he told Brian. 'Not commercial. It's a specialist market.'

It was the standard refrain of 1961. Brian Jones, the mad, bad boy of Cheltenham, was the only person who challenged this received wisdom, which came not only from outsiders but from insiders too. Even his new patron, Alexis Korner, persisted in taking the same line. Brian saw R&B (as he termed it) as popular music that just happened to be made by African Americans. But Korner and his circle loved the music precisely because it was *un*popular. 'We always thought it was exclusive and esoteric,' says Bobbie Korner. 'I guess we thought we were into something the vast majority would never understand. There was an arrogance [to that attitude]. We were tribal.'

It was Brian Jones alone who had a vision, that raw electric blues could appeal to the youth of Britain rather than only to a narrow circle of bohemians. He was undeterred by the fact that others didn't see it that way, and broadened his search for like-minded souls. The Oxford scene, which he'd ventured into with a small coterie of CND supporters like Harry Washbourne and Barry Miles, looked more promising, especially when he bumped into aspiring blues fan Paul Pond, who'd recently moved to the city and had formed 'what I thought was the only blues band in Britain'.

Much like Brian, Paul Pond – soon to be known as Paul Jones – had discovered the blues via jazz, and was taken with the Chicago blues sound, harmonica players like Sonny Boy Williamson 1 and 2, James Cotton and Junior Wells. Again like Brian, he had been forced to spread the net wide in his attempts to form a blues band: 'I had two renegades from a trad group on bass and drums, I had a sort of a mainstream-cum-early-modern-jazz guitar player . . . and a saxophone player who was out-and-out modern jazz.'

Paul Jones would become Brian's next musical collaborator, after John Keen. The date of their first meeting is vague, but almost certainly Paul first bumped into Brian in Oxford around October 1961, via the Cheltenham–Oxford art school or CND connection. Paul took to him immediately: 'He was very talkative, very loquacious, very opinionated. About blues and everything. And I liked him very much; he seemed to me my sort of bloke. First of all, he was really good. But although he was so good, he didn't rub your nose in it.'

Paul was the first peer who really understood Brian's musical explorations. Brian had already gone beyond figuring out the electric slide: he'd mastered blues harmonica. Paul had struggled trying to emulate Little Walter and Sonny Boy; Brian showed him that the secret was to play 'cross-harp', using a harmonica a fifth up from its nominal key. Other musicians jealously guarded such trade secrets; Brian shared his knowledge. 'It was like he'd opened doors to an unseen kingdom. The fact he unlocked the secrets of the harmonica was amazing. I was off and running. So I would always like him just for that. Then we started to play together, and that was that.'

Brian began to hitch to Oxford on Friday nights. 'This wasn't every week, but it happened more than once. He or I would find some party, and we'd go off, him with his guitar, and we'd jam or not depending on how open and generous the mood was.' Paul bumped into the future Eric Clapton and his band the Roosters that same autumn; Clapton describes himself as having 'the accelerator down' over this period. But it was Brian Jones who was travelling the fastest, says Paul Jones: 'He was so single-minded, and definite. And also he could *really* play. At that stage I didn't know anybody who could play that well. No one – not Alexis, for that matter.'

Like John Keen, Paul was impressed by Brian's drive and single-mindedness. He was evangelical in his belief that now was the time to form a blues band. Alexis Korner had already made the first move, unveiling an early version of Blues Incorporated, his Chicago-style electric band, in Croydon on 19 January 1961. The event had proved satisfyingly controversial: the band was supporting Acker Bilk, and one trad jazz fan in the audience yelled 'We came to see a jazz concert!' before scuffles broke out. Korner, it turned out, was shaken by the episode. Brian loved the controversy, which was duly reported in *Jazz News*. When Alexis told Brian, during their regular talks, that he was planning to open a club in Ealing that would showcase his band, and electric blues in general, Brian became even more driven. 'We've just been mucking about till now,' he told his new mate Pond. 'We need to take things seriously. First of all I'm going to leave Cheltenham and move to London. I'm starting a band, and I'm going to be rich and famous. Do you want to be my singer?'

No, Paul Pond informed him. 'My theory at the time, my reason for saying no, was I had exactly the attitude of Alexis Korner. This is niche music. I will always love it, I will always play it, but it won't give me a living.'

None the less, the duo made a tape together, which they sent to Alexis Korner, aiming for a slot at the opening of his club in March 1962. While they waited to hear, Brian continued with his other plans, working on ideas with Graham Ride, playing the odd jazz circuit show with John Keen, writing letters to the London music press, and telling his friends that once Korner's club opened he'd move to London.

Brian Jones's move to the capital would have far-reaching consequences. His vision of blues as mainstream youth music and his deeply felt evangelism would ultimately redefine the world's cultural landscape. So far, so noble. But like new hero Robert Johnson he had to keep moving, for there were plenty of outraged townsfolk on his trail. He wasn't just heading for London, he was escaping Cheltenham.

The consequences of Brian's alley-cat sexuality were starting to multiply in his home town, as were his offspring. Any support Brian gave Pat Andrews during her pregnancy was intermittent; not for one moment did the two address the implications: 'We didn't talk about it. He knew I was innocent . . . maybe he was a coward.' Like others who came after her, Pat was star-struck by Brian. She loved him, still does in a way, although she also uses words like 'crafty', 'conniving' and 'chancer'. Brian stayed mainly faithful to Pat, but by the autumn of 1961 he'd acquired another girlfriend, whom Graham Ride refers to as Gee.

Over the next decade, rumours would continue to circulate about Brian. (Years later it would turn out he'd had yet another affair around 1959, with a married Surrey woman, who in turn had a child, Belinda, who in this case stayed with the family.) Often they underplayed the magnitude of his old-fashioned philandering, as in the story about the pregnant Pate's girl who turned out to be two pregnant Pate's girls. Exactly the same applies to rumours that Brian faced a legal threat from the outraged burghers of Cheltenham – for it wasn't one threat, it was two.

Dave Jones, who'd briefly played with Brian, was working as an articled clerk for Rowberry and Warren Green, a prestigious law firm located on the Promenade, when he heard about the rumpus caused by his old grammar school friend. 'Rowberry was a very well-known solicitor in Gloucester. And he was asked to write a letter on behalf of the parents of a girl, who I recall was under age.' The Rowberry and Warren Green letter was finally sent on behalf of several concerned citizens. There was no specific legal threat, for there was little legal sanction they could take. 'It was more, "What are your intentions?"' remembers Jones. 'I think this letter involved three different fathers. Then later it turned out there was *another* big law firm, Watterson Moore and Co., on Royal Crescent, who'd independently written a letter, from different parents, along the same lines.'

Jones recalls the two law firms arranging a meeting with Brian in a local coffee bar – with inconclusive results. 'I don't think he gave a damn. Not to say he was heartless or shallow – he wouldn't have gone down in my book as a bad guy. He was a healthy eighteen-year-old [*sic*] lad going out with a number of girls. Sequentially, although there was some overlapping.'

Brian wasn't intimidated, but the letters were more evidence that 'things were hotting up'. As in the case of Val, Brian made intermittent attempts to be responsible. When Pat finally gave birth to his fourth child, Julian Mark Anthony – the Julian after Cannonball

Adderley, the Mark Anthony to signify strength – on 23 October 1961, Brian appeared at her bedside with a huge bunch of flowers. He'd pop into the hospital often, when Pat's mum – and her umbrella – weren't around, and sold several of his treasured albums to buy her a mohair skirt. Yet for much of the time, he simply disappeared. When he and Graham Ride were thrown out of Bath Road early in 1962, he even managed to keep the location of his new digs quiet. He confided some of his plans to Pat, about the move to London when Alexis Korner's new club opened, hinting they could make a new start in a new town – but it was always vague, always keeping her hoping.

That sketchiness affected other people, too, mostly friends he'd borrow money from. He'd do it with charm, and a kind of sincerity. But it rankled with many that they were expected to subsidize his lifestyle when they were also short of cash. Barry Miles remembers being touched for £2 – 'and my entire student grant was £100 a year, so that was a lot' – but there were bigger sums, £20 or so, owing to Pat's brother, and probably more still to Dick Hattrell. Whether or not he'd had a calling to the blues, Brian would have had to move out of Cheltenham anyway, simply to find a new crowd to cadge from.

For all that, his friends loved him, and respected his bravery in taking off for London. John Keen and Graham Ride couldn't imagine leaping into the void like that, although Dick, who still received an allowance from his dad, volunteered to take the train to London with him. The Thursday before Brian left, Graham struck lucky at the Cheltenham races and won £18 – timely winnings, for they allowed him to buy Brian a farewell Chinese and lend him £20 for his train fare and to help him find his feet. 'We'd had a great time,' says Graham, 'in a world of our own, doing our own thing.' 'He told me he was going to catch this train, the weekend of 20 March 1962,' says John Keen. 'I felt he'd be back soon. How little did I know.'

Brian Jones left for London as a young man with a chaotic lovelife but a disciplined, honed sense of musical direction bolstered by the experience of all those live performances. It was this sense that he was already a fully developed musician that simultaneously impressed and intimidated Mick Jagger, Keith Richards and Dick Taylor when the trio first saw Brian on stage at Ealing in late March 1962, the night he appeared with Paul Jones, aka P. P. Pond.

Dick Taylor would later become famous as the temporary Stone who went on to form the Pretty Things, the Stones' R&B rivals. Taylor's is the most tantalizing view of the band in its embryonic state, untouched by bitterness. He recalls Brian's inspirational qualities, and his moodiness, but most of all he remembers the way Brian's musical investigations went far deeper than anything they'd encountered: he'd studied the styles of Elmore James, Robert Johnson and Muddy Waters, and worked out their secrets – powerful and arcane knowledge in the spring of 1962. Knowledge that would sustain the Stones for decades, to the present day – to a more profound extent than any of the band's present members acknowledge.

Paul Jones is one of many who recall how generous Brian Jones was with this knowledge. Taylor remembers it too, and unprompted points out one of the telling quirks in the Stones' story. A few people today, Marianne Faithfull in particular, theorize that Brian's death left his old bandmate Keith free 'to *become* Brian' – to take his persona, adapt and improve it. What only Taylor seems to have noticed is that Keith's trademark guitar style – his Open G tuning, a blues tuning with a distinctive country lilt – comes from Brian too. Curiously, for at least the last thirty years Keith has been describing how he took the style from Ry Cooder, a guitarist he met in 1968. 'Brian used that tuning for things like Feel Like Going Home and I Can't Be Satisfied,' says Taylor. 'Keith watched Brian play that tuning, and certainly knew all about it. Why he says he got it from Ry Cooder I don't know. It's strange.'

Strange indeed that Keith would credit an outsider rather than his own bandmate for a distinctive technique that he'd seen him use, live and in the studio – a technique he would eulogize over several pages in his life story, detailing the notes, the sound, how the Open G tuning got back to the sound of old blues players, how it 'transformed my life'.

It was Niccolò Machiavelli, in his book *The Prince*, who suggested we often resent people who open doors for us, who leave us with a sense of obligation. It would take a Machiavelli to disentangle the internal politics and feuding within the Rolling Stones over the next few years.

3

A Bunch of Nankers

THE TWO BOYS who would become Brian Jones's best friends, his brothers, were pretty late starters. Keith Richards was a shy rebel whose musical career seemed to have peaked at the age of eleven when the Dartford Tech school choir performed at St Margarets, Westminster, in front of the Queen. But he became a fairly well-known figure at Sidcup Art College, strumming I'm Left, You're Right, She's Gone in the cloakroom next to the office of the laid-back headmaster. 'He came out of the office once,' says Dick Taylor, who was his classmate, 'and said, "It's good you play guitar – but could you lower the volume please? A picture just fell off my wall."'

Skinny, gawky and lovable, invariably dressed in a purple shirt, Wrangler denim jacket and skinny jeans, Keith hung out with Dick, who'd moved to the more arty Dartford Tech from the grammar school. Keith knew Dick was going to regular weekend practice sessions with Mick Jagger, an old acquaintance from Wentworth Primary School, but was too shy to ask if he could come along, until he bumped into him at Dartford train station. Along with Bob Beckwith – guitarist and later a stalwart of the Keighley Labour Party – and harp-player Alan Etherington, they practised in the Beckwith and Taylor front rooms. Their repertoire was the usual staples: Buddy Holly, Chuck Berry, Bo Diddley, a bit of John Lee Hooker, plus Mick's hokey take on La Bamba. Dick Taylor and Beckwith's tastes were more hardcore blues, Keith was into Chuck Berry and Scotty Moore. The group made a demo for Alexis Korner on Beckwith's little Grundig tape recorder that was, says Dick, 'basic, and that's being kind', but they did have something special about them that entranced Mrs Taylor. 'Contrary to all the stories that Mick learned to dance from Tina Turner, he danced all the while. He was unstoppable. My mum used to come in with Jaffa Cakes and tea so she could pop her head around the door and watch him dancing, cos she thought he was brilliant. My sister, too.'

Like Brian, the young Mick Jagger was charming, but this was charm of a different species: he seemed younger, sporty, cheeky rather than fey, and was always nicely spoken. Mums loved him.

When Mick, Keith and Dick arrived at Korner's club in Ealing not long after it had opened, reputations were already being made. Brian Jones was asserting himself with an almost hypermanic energy that irritated some of the older musicians. The scene around Alexis Korner was always fluid, as was the line-up of his band, which relied on a constantly evolving cast of singers. Long John Baldry was a regular guest vocalist, as were Andy Wren, Art Wood, Brian Knight and Paul Jones. At first, Mick was too intimidated to get on stage; it took a few weeks for him and his friends to realize 'we could do that', says Dick Taylor. For most of the musicians present, Elmo Lewis, as the young slide guitarist called himself, remained the most significant guest, the one person whose playing and execution matched, even bettered, that of Cyril Davies. But as the weeks passed and the audience grew, some had their eyes on another band member. 'I was in the pub down the road and a girl I knew came up,' recalls Korner's bassist Andy Hoogenboom. 'She asked me, "Is that really crazy guy singing with you again?" I knew immediately she meant Mick. She really wanted to see him, and I simply thought, wow.' Eventually, Mick Jagger became a regular second vocalist – as much as anyone was a regular with Alexis Korner.

And so it was that the battle for supremacy in the future Rolling Stones got started.

Bobbie Korner was a close observer of that little gaggle of musicians who assembled in 1962. Mick she found pleasant, but different from the others: 'Mick was nice, but he wasn't warm. But then, he wasn't running away from a family, like the others were.' Keith she found lovable, especially the time when her husband apologized for taking Mick away from the Blue Boys and Keith replied, 'He's so good, he deserves anything he can get.' But it was Brian that she and her husband found the most fascinating. 'He had this fey thing about him, he was attractive and he was charming, a nice boy. But most of all he was very willing – willing to put in a bit of a slog, which a lot of them weren't.'

The more hardened musicians around the scene also built up a respect for the ambitious young slide guitarist. Drummer Ginger Baker had followed a similar route to Brian, building up experience with a string of trad and modern jazz bands, and finally started guesting with Alexis Korner alongside bassist Jack Bruce at the end of June. He remembers being persuaded by Korner to back Brian, and Mick, for an interval slot at Ealing. 'I liked Brian. He was cool – the real musician in the Stones. Mick, we used to take the piss out of, playing with the time signature and throwing him off. It was

Brian who'd be shouting "One, two, three!" in his ear, pulling him back in!'

Brian was good at keeping up appearances after he'd taken refuge with the Korners, but in reality things were getting desperate – all the more so when Pat Andrews discovered where he was living, got a coach to Victoria station, and arrived with their son Mark, as he was now known, at his fleapit new lodgings in Finchley. Brian stood leaning against the fence 'with a face like the hangman's just arrived', Pat remembers. Pat soon established herself, finding a job at Boots which allowed them to move to a flat in Powis Square, where they attained a temporary, somewhat skewed domestic harmony. Brian took jobs at Whiteleys department store, and later the Civil Service Stores, to pay the bills, and soon became notorious around the musicians' scene for petty thieving from the tills. The Stones would later enjoy trading stories of Brian's larcenous nature, but according to Pat, he had no choice. 'He wasn't a bad person. How can I put myself in Brian's position? He desperately wanted something. He's thinking, "I've given up my parents, burnt my boats, I have to go forward – if I don't, all that heartache will be for nothing." He had to do it.'

Brian was easily the pushiest of the young musicians around the Ealing scene – so pushy it bugged some people. He placed an advert for musicians in *Jazz News* on 2 May but really the ad served as much to publicize his arrival on the scene as to recruit musicians, for everyone who turned up at the jam sessions he organized, initially at the Bricklayer's Arms in Soho, came from Alexis Korner's circle.

Yet Brian had a very different attitude about bands to his mentor. Korner favoured informal, fluid, jazz-style line-ups, under his umbrella. In 1962, bands were passé, but Brian wanted a gang. Right from the start he wanted musicians who'd stick together – to champion R&B, to become stars, to prove his parents wrong. That was why early singers like Andy Wren simply didn't work out. The ideal recruits, as Bobbie Korner suggests, didn't have a family, which is why Brian's first choice, pianist Ian Stewart, was so perfect, so resonant.

Stewart – Stu – knew Alexis Korner from before the Ealing opening and had been playing in little informal jazz and skiffle bands at pubs and parties for a year or two. Some time before meeting Brian at Ealing, Stu got a clerical job at ICI, and could be found many weekends at Bridport in Dorset where he and his friend Hamish Maxwell would take walks, fish for mackerel, and visit the two local pubs. Stu and Brian would be a great combination of opposites – 'they had a common purpose' according to Hamish. Stu was born in Pittenweem, Fife in 1938, although he spent most of his childhood in Sutton, Surrey. By his teens, he was already crafting his own piano style from a mix of jazz and blues. But unlike Brian, Stu was anything but driven. Although he had a genius for seeming unfazed – by fame, by musicians' bullshit – he lacked confidence in his playing. In private 'he'd put himself down, he didn't think he was good enough'. Yet Stu hid his insecurity behind a lovable dryness and humour.

When Brian first teamed up with Stu, the pianist's propulsive left hand, banging out sixths, took care of the whole middle and bottom end of the sound, and Brian had a band. 'Stu started the band with Brian, and Stu's as important or more important – that's my opinion,' says Stewart's friend and Stones engineer Glyn Johns.

Paul Pond continued to regard blues as an enjoyable hobby rather than a career, so by April Brian was approaching other singers from Alexis Korner's pool of talent, with Andy Wren the first one he tried out. By May, when Korner and Cyril Davies started playing Thursdays at the Marquee club, the pool widened.

During the interval of one Korner set early in May, Brian approached Geoff Bradford, who'd played in a duo with Davies and often depped for Blues Incorporated, and Bradford brought along singer Brian Knight, who also worked for Davies' panel-beating business. This seemed the most stable line-up for Brian Jones's Blues Band, and rehearsals went on for some weeks. Keith, who'd done a couple of interval sets with Mick at Ealing, was the next to turn up.

Today, Keith still waxes lyrical about that meeting at the Bricklayer's Arms, an old-fashioned, lavishly tiled pub just off Berwick Street. He remembers the beautiful summer evening, Ian Stewart in a pair of Tyrolean leather pants (a charming detail unique to his telling) and the dodgy friendly hookers who hung around. Stu knew well the work of Johnnie Johnson, who co-created Chuck Berry's sound. Keith was impressed by Brian, maybe intimidated, but these days he fixes on Stu as the engine room of the band. 'It was Stu's band,' he says, the sigh implicit rather than audible, 'still is.' The phrase says everything about Keith – the soulfulness, the down-to-earth quality, and also the possessiveness. And the need to attribute ownership of the Stones to an unassertive character rather than the man who actually formed the band.

Third-hand accounts suggest that this short-lived line-up fell apart after a fight between Keith and Geoff Bradford. The story is, says Bradford, 'just cobblers'. Although impressed by Brian's technical abilities, Bradford wasn't that keen on electric slide, and wasn't that keen on Brian. 'I don't know why,' he says. 'Why don't you take to someone? I just wouldn't have picked him as a friend. Kind of a spoilt boy.' Nor did he like Chuck Berry, so he and Brian Knight drifted away, and the choice of singer seemed to narrow down to the Dartford boy who had first plucked up the courage to speak to Brian: Mick Jagger. Mick had probably been on the radar right from the beginning. Keith himself reckons Brian didn't want both the Dartford boys, but that Mick told him, 'I'm not doing it if Keith's not doing it'. Pat Andrews reckons Alexis Korner advised Brian, 'Take one, don't take them both', knowing that Brian would lose control of his band. In any case, immediately he'd settled on Mick and Keith, Brian recruited a third Blue Boy, Dick Taylor, who'd been playing the drums in the Bricklayer's Arms sessions. 'Brian knew I played guitar. And one night at Ealing he said, "Why don't you play bass?" So I went into a shop in Soho, bought an Emperor bass, and off we went.'

With Dick switching to bass, the band was short of a drummer. Brian had mentioned to Charlie Watts as early as April that he was forming a band, and the group even managed to entice him to practice sessions, even to the odd gig, over the summer of 1962 – 'at least a couple of times' reckons Dick Taylor – but Charlie was committed to Alexis Korner and reluctant to quit his job in graphic design. Their eventual choice, Tony Chapman, responded to another ad Brian placed in *Melody Maker*.

The band began to assemble a selection of songs that included mutual faves like Muddy and Chuck Berry, Brian's Elmore James showcases, and Bo Diddley – a Mick and Keith fave. Keith and Mick had heard a little Jimmy Reed but Brian, says Keith, unleashed a whole bunch of his sides they'd never heard before. If there was any rivalry in those first sessions, it was probably over the harmonica: Mick hadn't sussed out cross-harp, so Brian showed him how. Outsiders who watched the band remember Brian dominating the sound; insiders remember him defining something more important: the vibe. 'He was more worldly-wise than us, most definitely,' says Dick Taylor. 'But very soon we started laughing, cos he was really good at making stupid faces. There was a hell of a lot of humour, particularly from Brian. That was why everyone got on well.'

The Bricklayer's Arms was a wonderfully sleazy hangout, right by Soho's walk-up brothels, and the blues songs spilling out into the red-light district attracted a gaggle of girls who excelled in their own laconic humour. 'I've been having trouble with me minge' became a band catchphrase. Or there'd be long monologues, Brian or Dick impersonating oily 'artists representatives' who insisted the band should stick to country and western, buy suits, and go on a tour round US Army bases. Someone, Dick or Keith, drew a cartoon lampooning each band member. Mick posed with a huge, phallic microphone; Brian was marked 'Elmo Lewis' with a straight blond fringe; Keith was depicted with pinpoint pupils – the result, the band reckoned, of his nicking his mum's period pills; Dick was pictured with a huge bass and straggly boho beard; while Stu sat by the piano, plaintively asking, 'Can we play some Jimmy Witherspoon?'

Above Tony Chapman, though, was a huge question mark with the words 'probably in Liverpool'. The drummer's lack of commitment and frequent absences were a niggling concern, which is probably why when the suggestion of the band's debut at the Marquee club came up, Mick, the only future Stone with a phone, called up a pro drummer, Syd Paine, who advertised in *Melody Maker*. Paine suggested a younger substitute, Mick Avory, who turned up for one rehearsal. Avory didn't really take to any of the band, bar Stu, nor did he want to play electric blues. 'I was more interested in jazz so couldn't see myself doing it for a living,' he says. Although he offered to play the gig if necessary, he heard no more, so his career with the band, oft discussed, lasted for just that one rehearsal. 'I know that completely contradicts all the previous accounts of what happened and is not as interesting,' Avory comments, drily. 'That's the trouble with the truth.' (Fifty years on, Keith Richards still reckons Avory played his band's debut gig.)

The band had been talking to Alexis Korner about a guest spot at the Marquee for a week or two when they heard that Blues Incorporated had been offered a BBC session on *Jazz Club*, on Thursday, 12 July. Mick hoped he might be guesting with Korner on his band's radio debut, but Korner started sounding character-istically vague, before suggesting that Brian's crew could fill in for the Marquee date along with a band fronted by Long John Baldry. Up to that point they'd thought of themselves as the Brian Jones Blues Band, reckons Dick Taylor, but now they wanted something tougher, sexier for a name. As he stood by the upstairs fireplace at the Bricklayer's, Brian suggested 'The Rollin' Stones' (as they'd officially style themselves for the next year), a line from the Muddy Waters song Manish Boy. Stu thought it sounded corny. The rest of them went for it.

There is a faint, maybe snooty smile on Brian Jones's face as he swoops a bottleneck up his fretboard, coaxing glossy, glistening streams of sound from his acoustic guitar, all distorted by the add-on pickup and cheap amplifier, for his signature song, a long-forgotten number called Dust My Broom. To his left, Ian Stewart cheerily pounds out a sequence of sixths with his left hand – they anchor the band, holding down the bottom end, but the beer in the glass sitting atop the piano looks less secure, shaking and foaming. In the middle, Mick Jagger is moving a little jerkily, one of the girls in the audience thinks, but he too has a knowing, cheeky grin, like it's all a joke and only he and his mates know the secret.

The audience was a mixed bunch, older trad jazz fans plus a good number of younger kids. As we know, one girl in that audience understood the significance of that show more than any other. Here was black culture, the music of Elmore James and

Jimmy Reed, making its first entrance under that stripey Marquee. The Stones' first gig, on 12 July 1962, was not just the debut of a legendary rock band, it marked the beginning of an irrevocable change in popular culture. This was the first time a young, white, European audience encountered black R&B not as something foreign and exotic, but as their own; the first time that music largely ignored in its homeland was reforged, ready to spread across the world. This was the moment that finally made sense of Brian Jones's confused life. It was 'very exciting and very raw', Cleo Sylvestre remembers. Both Brian and Mick, she thought, oozed sex appeal.

'It was brilliant,' says Pat Andrews. 'We had become important. All of a sudden, we're not satellites of our parents or our elders.' The band themselves were modestly encouraged. 'It got a pretty good reaction,' says Dick Taylor, 'but we weren't aware that history was in the making.'

Keith, Mick, Dick and the others chatted excitedly afterwards about how the show went, how it felt. Brian hardly participated. He was lost in thought, working things out: 'OK – so what are we gonna do in a week's time?' Pat still remembers that perfect time, when Brian's mind 'was always ten feet in front of what was actually happening'.

Over the rest of that summer, the key elements that would define the Rolling Stones' fifty-year career were mapped out – namely, the music, the subject of care and devotion, and the first suggestions of nastiness, a struggle for top-dog status that was pretty shocking in its ferocity.

In the first twelve months, Brian was the unrivalled boss. Recently, in his book *Life*, Keith Richards mentioned how he 'assume[d] the mantle of musical director' towards the end of the year – a claim that his friends recall differently. 'There was no question about who was in charge,' says Dick Hattrell, who moved into the Edith Grove flat with Mick, Keith and Brian that autumn. 'You see, where Brian scored was he just worked damn hard. He'd listen to a record, practise and practise until he got to what he considered somewhere near that sound. In the early days in Edith Grove – oh my God, what a hellhole – they'd come back from a gig, [and] Brian would say to Keith, "That was a load of crap. We've got to go over and over it again until we get better."'

James Phelge, another flatmate, sums up the later Edith Grove period, when Keith was 'musical director', even more unequivocally: 'If Keith did something wrong Brian would fuckin' tell him! And Brian could play harmonica really well, so that was another string to his bow. Keith could play Chuck Berry stuff, but so could Brian – so Keith certainly wasn't as indispensable as he says now. I think it's just the fuckin' drugs talking – he gets confused.'

Occasionally, Keith waxes lyrical about the summer of 1962. Although the band was still only managing the occasional interval spot at the Marquee, Keith was the first to throw in his lot with Brian, leaving Sidcup Art College and moving in with him, initially into a flat Brian had found in Beckenham (Pat had returned to Cheltenham with Mark, although she continued to drop in on her elusive, unreliable lover). The thought still inspires warm memories, of magical days spent 'toe to toe, working out guitar weaving'. Brian dominated the band vibe as well as the music – the funny voices, the piss-taking, the arrogance to try and do something different. Mick – and, for that matter, Dick Taylor, and doubtless Tony Chapman – saw their band as an engaging hobby. Keith saw them as 'waving our little blues flags for a year or two'. Brian was the one with no escape route – a predicament which defined both his strengths and weaknesses as a leader.

Dick, one of Mick's posse, liked Brian's humour and drive, but remembers his obvious vulnerability, too. 'The thing was, after a while you used to wonder which Brian Jones you'd get. As in, what mood: whether it's "We're gonna conquer the world" or "Wow, is it ever gonna happen?"' Many other people remember Brian's moodiness from that summer – even, some say, outright despair. 'He was very vulnerable,' says Billie Davis, the singer who had at one point rented a flat adjacent to Brian and Pat's at Powis Square. 'He was working at a record shop, trying to get his thing together, and it was very hard. I remember most of all the fish paste sandwiches, horrible things that he'd make so he could get through another day without money. He had a very dry sense of humour, but I also remember him being very lonely and down.' Keith, in contrast, was less bothered by setbacks – 'after all, he had his mum, who would turn up to bring round food and collect his washing,' comments Dick Hattrell. Together, Brian Jones and Keith Richards became the engine room of the band, incessantly working up their sound.

Keith and Brian's relationship deepened from September, when Mick returned to his Economic History course at the London School of Economics, and Dick Taylor decided to resume studies at Sidcup and focus on winning a place at the Royal College of Art. Stu was as dependable and cheery as ever, but still maintained his desk job at ICI. Keith was the only Stone to give up on his other options. He wasn't fixed on fame or glory, like Brian. But he was the first to join him in turning their backs on the conventional careers their parents had mapped out for them.

Mick remained close to his dad, Joe, who was forthright but reasonable, and unlike Lewis Jones had no objections to his son pursuing his hobby as long as he didn't neglect his studies. The idea of courting his disapproval was unthinkable; besides, Mick's student grant was the band's most regular source of income. It allowed them to rent that first (and most infamous) shared flat, at 102 Edith Grove in Chelsea. By September, Brian, Keith, an occasionally absent Mick and a string of guests, sharing two rooms (with Brian commandeering the best bed), had embarked on their journey to local notoriety.

Dick Hattrell was one of the first companions to join Brian's rag-tag crew at Edith Grove. He'd just returned from Territorial Army summer camp with a cash bonus which the band were ready to help him spend, and remembers their increasingly desperate straits as the winter of 1962 took hold. 'The guys were literally starving to death, no exaggeration, so I decided to stay for a few days. They couldn't afford milk, so when I heard the milk float in the morning I'd get up and pinch a pint. I used to buy potatoes cheap from local growers, then a few cans of baked beans, to help them survive.'

Dick was sweet, loved hanging out with musicians, and was eager to please. Too eager, maybe: as Brian and Keith built up their us-against-the-world mentality, Dick became the butt of their humour, and began to see a side of Brian he hadn't seen before. 'He had a very changeable, almost split personality. He could be really nice, pleasant and friendly. Then at other times he could be a right bastard.'

Dick and James Phelge, who joined the household later, remember long hours of Brian and Keith playing together, working out textures and voicings. The collection of albums they'd assembled as source material was basic, says Keith, 'Not big. We had our Robert Johnson, that I heard for the first time at Edith Grove, Muddy at Newport, the best of Muddy Waters, Howlin' Wolf, some Slim Harpo, and most of Chuck Berry's and Jimmy Reed's that were available. That was the basic diet.' Mick was away at the LSE most days and was often a spectator when he returned, watching intently and thinking as Brian and Keith worked on a song, or laughing in disbelief at their antics. For this was the winter of 'nankering' – taking the piss. James Phelge became a master: 'A nanker was a person we regarded as a jobsworth, people who can't deviate from the script. So it was a parody of those people's attitudes.'

Brian had been taking the piss out of nankers for years – by now, rebellion was intrinsic to his psyche. Keith, in contrast, was 'absolutely not someone you'd find at the centre of a rebellion' according to Dick Taylor, 'but he was definitely his own guy'. Keith's upstart image was for the time being confined to sitting in a prominent place in a bar or shop scattering cigarette ash, or else picking his nose and ostentatiously flicking the bogeys around. Such obnoxiousness was their way of dealing with establishment figures, and with rejection, which seemed omnipresent. By the end of 1962, the band's most regular gig was the Marquee interval slot, filling in for Cyril Davies, who'd now split from Alexis Korner. Davies was taciturn and famously grumpy, although he was help-ful enough to suggest to his bassist, Rick Brown, that he fill in for the upstart band now that they lacked a bassist. Brown enjoyed the set, but found it all 'a bit Heath Robinson'.

The Flamingo, a long-established R&B club on Wardour Street where Korner now headlined regularly with his own band, was another possibility, but their first show there was shaky. The gangster-backed club had long been the haunt of off-duty American GIs; they were a tough crowd, and didn't seem to take to the Stones' R&B. Brian was shaken. 'He was virtually in tears,' says Cleo Sylvestre, who'd followed the band since the summer, 'saying, "Cleo, do you ever think we'll make it?"' Cleo had got to know Mick, Keith and Brian well, and considered Brian 'the most sensitive' of the Stones. Yet in public, the sneer, the aggression, masked his worries.

Alexis Korner kept his eye on the Stones that year. Like others, he saw the British music scene changing – and as the Beatles' take on American R&B threatened to take off that winter, he worried his own purist vision would become outdated. Korner had never envisaged playing blues the way the Stones did – 'for him, blues was like the Bible, and you don't fuck with the Bible', says Pretty Things vocalist Phil May. Yet Korner was open-minded enough to appreciate the band's power and energy. He and Bobbie liked Mick, but it was Brian they most admired. One night Korner was in the audience at the Marquee watching Brian play when the guitarist suddenly swung round, a casually evil look on his face, and brought his guitar right up to his face, inspiring a sudden shiver of panic, excitement and sexual tension. Bobbie shared the sensation with her husband: 'I remember the way he would step forward, and snap a tambourine, staring at you. Very aggressive – a real come-hither thing. It was incredibly sexy.'

Ginger Baker also recalls Brian's aggression, his instinct for firing up an audience. 'Brian was doing all the showmanship. Jagger was just standing there and singing, Brian was running into the audience with his guitar. Mick got it from Brian, bit by bit. I was watching with Jack [Bruce, bassist]. We weren't terribly impressed with the music – but it was so raw, there was obviously something about it that would take off.'

The band inspired a gamut of reactions from their audiences. Some girls, like Cleo, were fascinated by Mick, others found him 'constrained', says Janet Couzens, another Ealing and Marquee regular – 'it took time for him to develop that confidence'. Brian, though, was 'the one in control – more confident. He'd have a slight smirk on his face, as if he knew he was sexy. And he was definitely sexy.' Couzens, like many, couldn't know for sure – the Rolling Stones might well burn out in a year or two – but she was convinced they were the harbinger of something significant, that 'what was happening was changing society in a way we hadn't known before'.

Harold Pendleton, manager of the Marquee and a key figure in the birth of British blues and rock music, was no uncritical fan. 'Bear in mind,' he insists, 'when they started, the Stones were rubbish! Nothing like what they were later!' But he is certain that the main elements of their notoriety were established long before their celebrated manager Andrew Oldham appeared on the scene, and he is unequivocal about who was responsible: 'Brian Jones was the genius of the Stones. It was his extremely brilliant idea that they should be the opposite of the Beatles; that they should lurch on stage in street clothes, all leery. A deliberate marketing ploy.'

Pendleton claims only a passing acquaintance with the band's music from their Marquee dates – 'We didn't have a [alcohol] licence, so I was always coming back from the pub just as they finished their set.' But he met the band often throughout 1962, and was in no doubt about who was in charge. 'Brian was clearly the leader. It wasn't Mick. Brian called the tunes, Brian called the shots.'

He made a powerful impression on the Marquee boss. Witty and acerbic, Pendleton has a hilarious way of dismissing mediocrities with withering put-downs. Not Brian, though. Brian was a force to contend with. 'An evil genius' is how Pendleton describes him. Asked to elaborate, he adds simply, 'It's just from meeting, and speaking to him, I got the impression he was not a nice person. The rest of them, Mick for instance, were reasonably nice people, even when they pretended to be urchins. Brian Jones was coldly, cynically evil.'

Coldly, cynically evil. This description could apply to many in and around the Stones in the years that followed. But in the early ones it attaches itself most often to Brian, the boy his fellow pupils believed had something of the night about him. He liked cats, people remember, responded to them, their sensuousness and narcissism. People loved him in the way they'd love a cat, for its charm, elegance and intelligence – people like Ginger Baker, not known for his patience with time-wasters. 'He was a cool guy. We really got on well.' Doggy people, no-nonsense dependable types like Ian Stewart who liked pubs and blokey talk, sometimes came to hate him for that feline selfishness, the way he loved keeping people on edge.

The worst some friends, like John Keen, recall of Brian is that when he didn't want to do something, he simply wouldn't do it. James Phelge well remembers Brian's maddening unreliability. Any arrangement you'd made with him would be forgotten the moment something more interesting came along. 'It's like me saying to you, "Come over." I go all the way over, finally I'm there. And Brian would say, "Sorry, I've got to go out now." That's what Brian was like. He would say, "Let's go somewhere." We maybe get halfway and it's, "I've changed my mind, I've got to go over to Linda's, I'll drop you off here."'

This distracted youth could bristle on occasion. From his teens, Brian had mimicked yokels and straights, laughing at them – it was an integral part of the Stones' us-against-the-world gangster mentality. But when Brian felt threatened – for instance, when he felt his fellow Cheltonian Dick Hattrell's guileless behaviour meant that he too would be labelled a provincial bumpkin – then the nasty side of the wannabe gangsterism could surface. 'He could be the sweetest person ever,' Dick recalls, 'then, just like that, click of the fingers, he'd lose his temper completely and be the most horrible person you could ever be with. Then three quarters of an hour after that he'd say, "Why is everyone looking so glum?"'

That winter of 1962/63 was harsh, and the two-room apartment was freezing. One night in January, Dick missed his lift to the gig with Stu in the pianist's van. As the long dark night dragged on, he left his normal place on the living-room couch for the relative warmth of Brian's bed, and drifted off to sleep. Some time later he was shaken awake. Brian's face was right in front of him, contorted with rage. Struggling to register what was happening, Dick saw that Brian was holding two electrical wires in front of his face. 'Two hundred and forty volts,' he spat at his old buddy. 'Let's see how you like two hundred and forty volts through you!' Terrified, Dick ran from the room and out of the house, and ended up on the front doorstep, shivering in his underpants in the freezing cold, listening to Brian and Keith cackling with glee through the first-floor window. It seemed like hours before the pair relented and let him back in. Even today, Dick is mystified by Brian's behaviour. 'I don't know why he did it. Maybe he thought it was something sexual. I can assure you it wasn't.' Brian did apologize, as he always did, and Dick forgave him. But why did he put up with such treatment? Dick replies, 'I don't know. I guess I just liked musicians.'

Keith, who shared in the bullying, would later cite their treatment of Dick Hattrell as evidence of Brian's mean streak. Which it was, but Dick's naive name-dropping and general behaviour did, in fairness, often affect people that way. Characters on the Cheltenham scene 'were very mean to him' according to Jane Filby. 'He'd been saying he was friends with Acker Bilk one time, then when he fell asleep someone scribbled in biro on his face. He often got teased – it was a different world then.' Although Dick learned to be more careful of Brian, he none the less remained anxious to please. Throughout that winter Brian was intent on buying an electric guitar to replace the acoustic with a pickup. Dick half-volunteered and was half-persuaded into funding the purchase, and he ventured into Bill Lewington's shop in Soho with Brian to pick out the Les Paul-shaped Harmony Stratotone that would be used on all the Stones' early recordings.

For all the unpredictable behaviour, Dick loved being part of the crazed Stones circus. He felt he belonged, but although he says he was offered the job of road manager, he didn't have the physical stamina to stay at Edith Grove: 'I couldn't live like that. Really, my health was broken.' As 1963 dawned, Dick returned to his native Tewkesbury, to be replaced by the much less pliable James Phelge. The new housemate, who instinctively understood, 'You could never be in a situation where you didn't give as good as you got,' would witness how, as the long-awaited thaw came and spring took hold, the Stones' prospects finally started to blossom.

Some of the change came with the departure of Tony Chapman, the drummer who'd had a question mark over his head since the summer, who finally disappeared, presumably back to Liverpool. For several gigs before his departure he'd usually worked alongside Colin Goulding on bass, but by December 1962 the band had fixed on a far more potent rhythm section. Rick Brown (aka Ricky Fenson) and Carlo Little, both of them from Cyril Davies' band, took the intensity up a notch: Fenson had mastered walking basslines, and Little not only swung but added another level of aggression, propelling the band forward. They continued to help out the band, mainly at the Marquee but also at the Flamingo – but there was a big problem. With Davies, they made £40 a week. There was no way the Stones could match that, so Brian didn't even raise the subject of Fenson and Little joining permanently. 'We didn't seriously consider it even for one microsecond – I don't think we even discussed it,' says Fenson, who went on to join Lord Sutch's band. 'We were on a good living wage with a working band. The

Stones couldn't even guarantee us £10 a week. Why would we want to join them?'

Instead, it would be a friend of Fenson's and Tony Chapman's who'd make up half of one of the greatest rhythm sections in rock'n'roll. Bill Perks turned up for a rehearsal at the Wetherby Arms on 7 December and stayed on the scene, dropping in to see the band members at Edith Grove. The potential bassist obviously found the scene 'distasteful', says James Phelge, but according to Bill he was 'sucked into something that had its own momentum'. Bill made his debut, with Chapman on drums, on 15 December. It was a decent show, but the pair didn't match up to Ricky Fenson and Carlo Little. For just a few weeks, as the band played the Marquee, the Flamingo, Ealing (where they'd now taken over as headliners) and other odd gigs, they flipped between the two rhythm sections.

Then the drummer Brian had first spoken to back in May found his interest piqued. Charlie Watts still lived with his mum and dad in Neasden, which happened to be close to Carlo Little, and the word spread around that part of town that Little and Fenson were a hot ticket with the Stones. Suddenly, the idea of Brian's band seemed more attractive to the quiet, modest drummer who'd practically handed the role in Alexis Korner's band to Ginger Baker, convinced he was a better player. 'He's quiet, yet assertive,' insists his Korner bandmate Andy Hoogenboom, 'in both his demeanour and his playing.' Baker, who'd seen the band with Tony Chapman several times, reckons he helped broker the deal. 'I said, "You're OK but the drummer's fuckin' awful! Why don't you get Charlie?"'

Charlie Watts and Bill Perks – who'd soon try out the name Lee Wyman before settling on Bill Wyman as his stage name – debuted as the rhythm section at the Flamingo on 14 January 1963, according to Bill (Keith Richards reckons it was 2 February). It took a few weeks for everyone to decide it worked. Bill was a good bassist, but

Keith and Brian wondered whether he was 'a bit of an Ernie'. Keith would remain pretty much undecided on that point for fifty years. As for Charlie, Keith's recently rediscovered diary revealed he initially compared him unfavourably to the raw power of Carlo Little. But eventually, says Keith, he realized that 'he never hits 'em hard but he comes out with a more powerful sound than some guy ramming his fist through the drums'. It had taken a while, ten months, but over all those occasional rehearsals and shows Charlie had finally come to believe Brian's line that 'R&B was going to be a big part of the scene'.

There was no overnight revelation when the new line-up began to play, but as the band strung more shows together over January, February and March, their sound changed, and with it the sound of British blues. Alexis Korner still played a lot of slower blues numbers, watched intently by an audience that hardly moved; the Stones were more up tempo, even without the inclusion of the Chuck Berry and Bo Diddley numbers that Korner wouldn't touch. James Phelge watched the band as they progressed from Marquee interval slots, to Ealing on Tuesday nights, and finally on to Richmond's Station Hotel. 'That period is when the Stones took over,' he says. 'The Marquee, when they first went, sometimes there'd be seven people downstairs and you had plenty of room to wander around. Then with the Richmond thing, there was one big space, and now people weren't standing around watching, everyone was dancing. The whole place was a dancefloor. Then at the end you're getting three hundred people and could hardly move.'

Phelge, an aspiring drummer himself, would become part of Stones mythology thanks to his outrageous antics at Edith Grove, which included miking up the toilet, greeting visitors with underpants on his head, and other imaginatively twisted shenanigans. He was the closest, most intimate observer of the band in their pre-fame days. He understood immediately that any weakness would be seized upon. 'It wasn't like a competition,' he says of their behaviour, 'but you were gonna get swamped by those guys if you tried to meet them on equal terms – they were gonna run you over.'

The internal dynamics were ever-shifting, with just a couple of constants: the nankering – the ceaseless mockery of outsiders – and the strange, elusive behaviour of Mick Jagger, who'd watch, quietly observing and making mental notes, careful not to commit himself. Initially created by Brian as a shared language, nankering had by now become so highly developed that the slightest look or change in intonation cracked people up within seconds. The nankering look was a vacant leer; for fuller effect he'd pull down his eyes and pull up his nostrils. The nankering voice was an officious or wheedling tone. 'You'd change to a yokeling, retarded kind of voice,' says Phelge. 'You'd take on the persona, to parody people's attitudes, people who say, "I can't let you do that, it's more than my job's worth" – people who can't deviate from the script.' It was a way of challenging authority – and of testing outsiders. Nankering bonded the band, but it was dangerous. Brian was the master, in control, with Keith 'in awe of Brian', says Phelge, while Jagger often 'felt left out – you know, three's a crowd'. But on one occasion, Phelge was looking at an official document with Brian's full name on it, and the proliferation of middle names – Hopkins, why Hopkins? – caught his eye. When Brian noticed what was going on, he rushed over and snatched the paper out of Phelge's hand, his face so contorted that Phelge was momentarily shocked. A few hours later, Brian sidled up to him again, studiedly casual: 'Phelge, do me a favour . . . don't mention the name. You know how people will take the piss.' Phelge, as it happened, didn't mention it again – but he was struck by Brian's visceral terror of humiliation.

Outside isolated glimpses of vulnerability, Brian's command of the Stones seemed unchallenged. Although he soon started to disappear with Linda Lawrence, a tall dark-haired sixteen-year-old from Windsor he'd met at the Ricky Tick Club on 11 January, he and Keith played 'incessantly' at Edith Grove, working out interlaced guitar parts, harmonica and guitar parts, even vocal harmonies. When the two engaged in their more crazed antics, Mick would simply look on. The singer had his own little circle of college friends, girls too, and did his homework at the LSE library more and more often as Brian, Keith and Phelge dominated the vibe. 'He'd always stand back and not leap in on anything first,' says Phelge. 'If you were taking the piss, he would take the piss. Occasionally he might take the lead, but he was more of a follower at that stage.'

Keith, still a bit skinny and spotty, didn't openly defer to Brian; rather, he listened intently as Brian mapped out manifestos and the pair worked on the music. Occasionally, Mick would sit in on rehearsals in the flat, but not often. 'To be honest, I didn't rate his singing in the flat,' says Phelge. 'Without a microphone, Mick was just dreadful.' The band's future manager, Andrew Oldham, would later allege that Brian schemed to sack Mick, but others remember he was zealous in his loyalty to the band's singer. One typical example was the time Mick was suffering from laryngitis and couldn't make a gig at the Station Hotel. 'He called me up, said, "We're singer-less,"' says Paul Jones. 'Then when I arrived, it turned out he'd also rung Andy Wren and Art Wood. Which was a very cunning move. I realized it was Brian's way of showing you need three people to fill in for Mick Jagger.'

As the band emerged from the winter, their confidence grew. Linda Lawrence, who had just left school and was drawn to the beatnik lifestyle, had first seen them in January and was overwhelmed by their power and confidence, especially the radical sound of Brian's electric slide guitar. Brian walked over to her after the show, and bought her a soda; 'he was calm . . . deep. I instantly felt close to him.' Soon she was regularly getting the train into Soho to see the band at the Flamingo. With Charlie on drums, and Bill, and an increasing number of shows lined up, Brian was focused and re-energized. On 10 March, the Stones played Ken Colyer's club at lunchtime, and Richmond's Station Hotel (at that time a new venue) in the evening, booked by aspiring film director Giorgio Gomelsky, who would become a key supporter. The music had indeed shifted up a gear. Buoyed by a bigger, younger, hipper crowd, Mick started to look less serious, less self-conscious. He started to laugh. At times, he and Brian would be on maracas together, giggling at each other over long rhythmic freakouts that brought the standout songs, like Bo Diddley's Pretty Thing, to a frenzied peak. At other times, Brian and Keith's guitars punched out intricately synchronized riffs in quick succession, without ever losing momentum; while, for the first time, Charlie unlocked the secrets of the laid-back, gloriously greasy Jimmy Reed boogie, leaving tantalizing spaces in the hi-hat rhythm, the crisp snare sound ringing out clearly on the two and the four. Stu continued to stomp away on the piano, filling out the rhythm part, while Bill pumped out basslines that locked in with Charlie's skipping rhythm. Even in these early days, the band had a lightness of touch their imitators would never quite master. 'But they never got cocky,' says Janet Couzens, who had followed them from the first Marquee shows, 'just more confident.'

Only a few weeks after finally establishing their definitive line-up, the Rolling Stones walked into their first professional recording studio, IBC, an impressive establishment spread over four floors of an elegant Georgian terrace house opposite the BBC's gleaming white HQ on Portland Place. In later days, the Who and the Kinks would make their breakthrough recordings here; in early 1963, though, IBC had only just started breaking into British rock'n'roll, thanks to an enthusiastic young engineer named Glyn Johns, a blues fan who happened to be friends with Stu. Johns was really just an upstart kid, he explains, 'but the new owners very kindly let me go in on a Sunday and record things. It was the only way I could learn. So the word got out there was this young lad giving free studio time.'

The Stones were the first band to use Johns' after-hours service. He had seen them play many times, at Ealing and at the Red Lion in Sutton, Surrey. He also owned albums by the acts who inspired them, like Jimmy Reed and Bo Diddley, but from the outset he was well aware this was something very different. 'It sounded really authentic – and bloody great. For one thing, they had youth on their side. Jimmy Reed's original stuff was far more laid-back, and they had more energy, absolutely.' These songs, including Bo Diddley's Road Runner, Muddy's I Want To Be Loved and Reed's Baby What's Wrong and Bright Lights, Big City, were staples of the live set. There were no drawn-out technical discussions; Brian simply sorted out what songs were played, in what order, the tempo, the density of the sound. 'He had a complete grip on it,' says Johns. 'He was very much the leader, quite specific about what they wanted or didn't want to do.'

British blues had finally arrived. In their first recording as a band, the Stones captured a sound that would take others years to master. There was a dirty, sexy swing to the music, along with a snotty attitude that would come to define their early work. The interplay between the two electric guitars was as finely honed as the great Chicago teams like Willie Johnson and Hubert Sumlin, and on these very early recordings Stu's piano adds a rollicking, exuberant extra strand to the melodies. The vocals are a little bland, over-treated with doubletracking, but the tracks marked out the Stones as a band ready to make their mark on the world. The first time their music hit tape, it was pretty much all there.

Sadly, even as their music came together, the rifts that would tear the band apart began to open.

In the early history of the Rolling Stones, the character of Mick Jagger seems slight, thin, only sketched in. He was a dutiful son, an earnest, nicely spoken music enthusiast, a boy who was, almost uniquely in his circle, fleeing no family traumas. But in one respect the Mick Jagger of legend was already being formed – his pursuit of women with a cheeky, seductive persona. Cleo Sylvestre is one of many who sum up his appeal in this way: 'energy and warmth and naughtiness all combined'.

Mick was, say their friends, a bit in awe of Brian as the Stones came together, deferring to him, paying close attention as Brian unveiled the secrets of cross-harp and listening even more intently whenever he passed on tips about how to bring a woman to orgasm. 'I was sitting nearby one night,' says Linda Lawrence. 'Mick really wanted to have that connection with women, and I heard Brian saying things to him, like how to make a girl get excited sexually, how to touch a girl and other things. I really thought Mick liked Brian, a lot.'

Mick did indeed like Brian, but his respect was always mixed with rivalry. Mick was competitive with other males when it came to women. And in the Rolling Stones, it was natural that he would be competitive with Brian, too.

The earliest – and, it turned out, deepest – rift had started in the wee small hours of a Friday night in the summer of 1962, when Brian and Pat were still living in Powis Square. The doorbell rang, and Brian answered the door to see Mick standing there. He explained he'd been singing with Alexis Korner, had missed the last train home to Dartford and needed a bed for the night. The couple showed Mick to the couch, where he bedded down. It was only a few hours later that Brian got up – he had an early start, for the half-day opening of the Civil Service Stores on the Strand. He was wary about leaving Pat alone with Mick, she says today, but had little choice.

After Pat had got up and tended to Mark, she boiled the kettle and made a couple of cups of coffee for her and Mick. There was only one place to sit in their tiny living room – on the sofa. And it was as she sipped her coffee that Mick put his arm round her. 'I laughed him off, said, "Don't be silly" or something like that,' she says. 'I was so embarrassed, I basically didn't even know what to do.'

Half a century on, Pat is adamant that Mick's pass at her, quickly rejected, is as far as it went. And half a century on it still matters, thanks to Keith and Mick's claims that the Stones singer did indeed seduce her. 'Mick came back drunk,' Keith wrote in *Life*, 'found Brian wasn't there, and screwed his old lady.'

We all know about playground boasts, like the ones Mick started spreading about Pat a few months after their supposed fling. They're meant to assert superiority, to help in the pursuit of top-dog status, and also to demean the women in question, make them mere chattels. Mick had sat back and observed Brian, so he knew how to play him, dropping hints to worry the Stones' leader before laying out the tale in its entirety a month or two later, at a time when Pat was back with her parents in Cheltenham and unable to give her side of the story. It was around April 1963 that Pat discovered Brian believed Mick's claims, and the consequences for her were devastating. 'Brian and I had agreed, in London, we'd always be best friends. Then suddenly I never heard from him again. Brian was never vindictive like that. Then I realized Mick had done this, spoiled the years his son could have had with his father. I felt such great sorrow.'

Most people, even Marianne Faithfull, who suffered at his hands, agree that 'Mick is not a bad person'. Maybe that competitive sexuality was instinctive. But as one contemplates the emotional carnage of that moment, Mick's claim that Brian's problems stemmed from the fact that 'He was so very jealous – that was his character failing' is as perfect an example of his coldness as you could ask for.

Mick enjoyed the naughty thrill of messy affairs. This was messier than most. Perhaps his boasts were aimed at destabilizing Brian's friendship with his old primary school pal Keith. If so, they succeeded beyond his wildest dreams, because in his attempt to reclaim his top-dog status Brian fixed on Keith's girlfriend, Sal, who was fifteen and still a virgin.

Pat heard this messy story from Sal during her final visit to Edith Grove, later in 1963. Sal and Keith had been an item for months, a sweet, romantic, quiet couple who'd hold hands like little kids. But then they had a tiff. In a game of sexual oneupmanship which would become a band trademark, Brian charmed Sal into bed. Pat already disliked Mick, but now, witnessing Keith mute, Mick a 'sexual predator', and Brian concealing his relationship with Linda Lawrence but engaging in revenge sex, she was disgusted by the lot of them.

Sitting in a picturesque pub overlooking the Thames, Pat shows little self-pity as she recounts this sad tale. But there's a sense of damage running deep. She's been one of the most vocal champions of the legacy of Brian Jones, leader of the Stones, even though she's one of a string of people whose lives were irrevocably damaged by contact with the band he founded. Every few months there are new newspaper headlines, or flurries of gossip on the Web, that cement her status as another of Mick's sexual chattels, just another stupid girl. Although her affection for Brian endures, her revulsion at the 'sexually predatory atmosphere' around the Stones remains visceral. It's something of a shock to realize that a band notorious for messy internal battles is even messier and nastier than you thought.

4

I Can't Be Satisfied

IT HAD BEEN a long two years since Brian was thrown out of the family home. A couple of people, Ian Stewart among them, reckon that throughout that time he'd been writing to his parents, trying to convince them he was doing something worthwhile with his life. It's likely there were moments of doubt – although he rarely mentioned his mother, Brian was too much like his dad to escape his influence completely – but flatmate James Phelge remembers no such backwards glances. 'Brian would *never* mention going to see his parents. He would have these mood swings, maybe because he had some issue with them. But he would join in, we'd have fun, staying up all night.' As the two years of hard graft, petty thieving and an almost desperate search for like-minded musicians finally seemed to be paying off, new supporters flocked around. Things were about to happen fast, yet it was only Brian who retained a sense of urgency, desperation almost, as the breaks started to cascade.

The tracks the band had recorded at IBC were a near obsession for Brian. He had brought back an acetate that must have worn out within weeks, so relentlessly did he cue it up. There were setbacks: IBC's owners, George Clouston and Eric Robinson, had promised to shop the tapes around their record company contacts but none of them nibbled at the bait. Yet there were enough enthusiasts around the west London scene to keep their momentum going, most notably Giorgio Gomelsky, whose ebullience had helped build a scene around the Station Hotel (soon to be billed as the Crawdaddy Club) from a standing start. He and Brian huddled together, making plans, starting with a film based around the band. Within weeks they had an encounter which held out some tantalizing possibilities.

Brian had been keeping tabs on the Beatles from at least the previous autumn. As it turned out, the Stones' open championing of purist blues, now regularly advertised in *Melody Maker* and else-where, had caught the Beatles' attention, probably via Gomelsky, who'd enthused about the band at a filming of the ITV pop music show *Thank Your Lucky Stars*. 'We'd heard about this blues band, and we were into American blues, so we turned up at the Station Hotel,' says Paul McCartney. 'And there they were.' All four Beatles, clad in long leather coats and peaked caps, stood at the back of the hotel, huddling around each other as the Stones finished Bye Bye Johnny so the crowd wouldn't recognize them as they filed out of the venue. Pat Andrews had dropped in to see Brian, and ended up directing Paul, who was driving the band's van, back to Edith Grove. There was little self-consciousness – the Beatles had only just finished their first nationwide tour, promoting Please Please Me, their first bona fide hit – and the two sets of musicians chatted comfortably. Paul spent most of the evening talking with Jay Reno, an aspiring Philadelphia songwriter who was hanging out at Edith Grove, while John asked about Brian and Pat's baby – perhaps the name Julian stuck in his mind when it came to naming his own son, born that August. All four Beatles listened as Brian played them their demos, including a version of Come On recorded at IBC, as well as some of his beloved Jimmy Reed. Brian and Mick were the two Stones the Fab Four took note of. 'Brian was the multi-instrumentalist, like John, Paul and George were,' says the Beatles' friend and road manager Tony Bramwell, 'which they liked.'

A few days later, on 18 April, according to legend, Brian Jones had his own eyes opened when he, Keith and Mick tucked guitars under their arms and snuck into the Beatles' show at the Albert Hall. Brian was transfixed. 'This is what we like,' Bill Wyman remembers him saying. 'This is what we want!' The yearning for fame and recognition was hardly a new addition to the Brian Jones psyche, but the Beatles were showing him the prospect was real. Not too long after that, an encounter with a cranked-up, skinny, self-mythologizing nineteen-year-old PR offered the chance of making it happen.

Andrew Loog Oldham had heard about an up-and-coming R&B band called the Rollin' Stones when he was pitching some PR ideas to *Record Mirror*'s Peter Jones at De Hems, a musicbiz hang-out in Soho. Despite smarting after Jones turned down his two stories, he none the less was intrigued by Jones's mention of the band and decided to check them out in Richmond. 'My reaction,' he says, 'was basically: this is what the preparation was all about. I am saying hello to the rest of my life.'

Right from birth, Andrew Oldham was an intriguing, contradictory character. His mother, Celia, was an enigmatic woman; he was never quite sure whether his dad was Andrew Loog, an American airman shot down over the Channel in 1943, or Alec, a Jewish businessman who kept his mum as a long-term mistress and regularly took the young Andrew to dinner at the Ivy.

From the time he was 'young and unbearably precocious', Oldham's was a curious personal chemistry, both novel and old-fashioned. His savoir faire and camp cool came straight from private boarding school. Wellingborough, an ancient establishment in Northamptonshire, benignly overlooked his love trysts with pretty schoolboys but frowned upon his obsession with rock'n'roll. He performed once as a singer, a cover of Tell Laura I Love Her, its maudlin melodrama a touchstone of his personal taste. But even at fifteen he was drawn to management, once turning up on the doorstep of Shirley Bassey's husband and manager Kenneth Hume to ask for tips. Oldham's life would always be defined by inspired leaps of faith and hubristic missteps. The young man realized – astutely – that designer Mary Quant was the embodiment of Swinging London style even before such a thing existed, and a brief summer spent window dressing in her King's Road shop morphed effortlessly into a career in PR. By the spring of 1962 he'd hung out with Phil Spector and worked PR for Brian Epstein and impresario Don Arden – who sacked him after Oldham sent out a press release promising riots and ripped-up cinema seats during an imminent Sam Cooke/Little Richard tour. Oldham was looking for the hustle of his life – and when he walked into the Station Hotel on 28 April 1963, a day when Giorgio Gomelsky happened to be in Switzerland for his father's funeral, he found it.

Oldham's memories of that fateful evening are heavily homoerotic. When the nineteen-year-old walked out of Richmond train station, Mick Jagger and his new girlfriend, Chrissie Shrimpton, were having an argument in an alleyway to the side of the Station Hotel. As Oldham walked by them, he remembered later, Mick gazed at him; Oldham took in the narrow waist, the lips and a look that said 'What are you doing with the rest of your life?'

He watched the band play a form of music he didn't quite understand; but he did, he would declaim, understand the erotic appeal of Mick Jagger, who was 'the hors d'oeuvre, the dessert and the meal in between'. The others were just the supporting act to Mick's urchin sexuality – Bill a stony monument, Charlie a neat suit, Stu an incongruous chin and bad haircut, Keith a source of barely understood riffs, and Brian a blond presence who looked hungrily around the room, Oldham reckoned, seeking sex, adoration and validation. How many of those initial impressions, described in his entertaining, contradictory memoirs, were the product of hindsight and revisionism is open to question – but a fair guess would be most of them. The Stones' story is full of unreliable narrators. Oldham's own account is engaging but full of blanks, a situation he explains with the statement, 'I only remember what I want to remember.'

Most of the revisionism applies to Brian, and Eric Easton, the agent who also visited the Station Hotel and became the Stones' co-manager. In earlier accounts, Oldham mentioned that, like most people in the audience, he saw Mick and Brian as twin beacons, commanding attention. In his three volumes of memoirs, Oldham progressively downgraded Brian; he has kind words for notorious thugs and criminals but none for the Stones' founder. Asked if that's reasonable, he replies: 'An older cunt in a school in the next barrio does not interfere with your life. But if he's the same age and going to the same school, then fuck him. He may be able to score brilliant goals, but you cannot rely on him.'

The reason for the rancour is simple: the idea of another leader is anathema to the Oldham creation myth, that he was the originator of the Stones' snottiness and outrage. Yet, for all the narcissism and contradiction, Oldham *was* a crucial force in breaking the Stones. Brian Jones seemed to realize his potential when

Oldham went over to introduce himself the following Sunday night, accompanied by Easton. By Tuesday they were discussing a management deal in Easton's office.

Eric Easton – the forgotten man of the Stones story, once he was pushed out in favour of the far more predatory Allen Klein – was central to the deal, an established agent who was calm, dependable and knew the ropes. As Brian and Mick listened to the pair map out their case, it was the combination of Oldham's energy and Easton's experience that won them over. Oldham would later mock Easton as a one-time theatre organist and small-time agent who entirely lacked vision – but it was Easton who had the money and the know-how. As Harold Pendleton puts it, 'Eric Easton was a run-of-the-mill manager, calm, cold and efficient. Loog Oldham was a temperamental chancer and a fellow who understood artistic people. The combination of the two was better than either of them apart.'

But if Oldham was cut-throat, so was Brian. He had got on well with Giorgio Gomelsky, who was a big ball of energy, acting as a de facto manager. At Easton's office, though, Brian assured Oldham the band had no long-term commitment to the Crawdaddy's owner. The decision was brutal but realistic. He 'ran a great club – [but he] wasn't really a manager type' says James Phelge; Pendleton, who booked Gomelsky's later protégés the Yardbirds into the Marquee, remembers he was famously temperamental: 'if you wanted to cast somebody in a film as a mad genius you would have picked Giorgio. He filled the part beautifully. But as to efficiency, of being a good manager – he didn't fit the bill at all.'

Gomelsky was the first friend thrown under the bus to serve the Stones' ambition. He wouldn't be the last.

As the most focused band member in those early months, Brian was the most enthusiastic about the new managers; that spring of

1963 he remained the Stone with whom Oldham and Easton would huddle and share plans. Keith was concentrating more on the music, and Mick was still attending daytime lectures at the LSE, bringing his coursework home in the evenings. Jones and Oldham shared a similar ambition, manic energy, extreme narcissism and an obsession with gangsters. 'It was one of the most distasteful things about the Stones,' says Jeff Dexter, the band's first stylist, 'this posh boys' fascination with tough guys.'

For all his inconsistency, Oldham had one all-encompassing skill: he knew how to seize the day, keeping up the momentum. The Station Hotel show and the IBC tapes were enough to convince him the band were his Beatles. But he was concerned to discover that, in return for studio time, the band had signed over a contract option to Glyn Johns' employers, George Clouston and Eric Robinson. It was Brian he fixed on to extract the band from the deal.

For Brian Jones, this was a cinch. He was already a master of wheedling money out of people – and this time he had £100, provided by Easton, to buy back the tapes. He put on his best apologetic tone, explained that he had found the music business all too commercial and unpleasant, and offered them a cheque so they wouldn't lose out. The pair agreed to his oh-so-reasonable request, then within two or three days found out that the band had been signed to a major record deal. Glyn Johns was yet another man stitched up by the Stones. 'No one even talked to me about it,' he says today. 'There's gratitude for you. Bastards.'

Oldham's speed and aggression were vital. It turned out that even as Brian was negotiating with IBC, Dick Rowe, the most maligned record company executive in history, was attempting to atone for his biggest failure by pulling off his biggest coup.

Rowe, head of A&R at Decca, was doomed to go down in history as the man who turned down the Beatles with the infamous words 'groups of guitarists are on the way out'. In fact that phrase was probably fabricated by Beatles manager Brian Epstein, while the decision to reject the Liverpool group was taken by Rowe's assistant, Mike Smith. The extent of Decca's mistake only truly dawned on 4 May 1963, the day From Me To You became the band's first number 1 hit. Rowe didn't mess around. The next day, by chance, he was up in Liverpool judging a talent show alongside George Harrison. The Beatles guitarist bore no grudges; instead, he told Rowe about the blues band he'd seen at the Station Hotel. One week later, Rowe turned up in Richmond to find the hotel packed, 'like the black hole of Calcutta. I'd never seen anything like that. It was incredible.' Rowe knew Eric Easton well, and called him immediately; the deal was signed a few days later.

Easton was the man Rowe respected, a steady pair of hands he could rely on. But it was the upstart Andrew Oldham who gave an adrenalin shot to the negotiations, bullshitting Rowe, insisting on a tape licensing deal and even, with insane chutzpah, insisting he produce the band himself. The experienced Decca man reflected later that he actually relished the thrill Oldham brought to the talks: 'He drove me. He was exciting and had tremendous flair.'

Oldham's first session as producer to the Rolling Stones would become infamous – the way he seemed to think that electric guitars plugged directly into the mains socket, or didn't realize that the four-track recording had to be mixed down to mono. Engineers are often disparaging about his talents: Glyn Johns, for instance, simply remarks, 'His abilities? I have no comment on them.' As a producer, Oldham was reliant on the talents of others, like arranger Jack Nitzsche, and George Chkiantz, engineer on Oldham's greatest post-Stones hit, the Small Faces' Itchycoo Park. Yet, as Chkiantz points out, 'Andrew had the best ears. He knew a hit when he heard one.' In the case of the Stones' debut single, Oldham's role was mainly to inject excitement, some buzz, into the process, insisting the band record quickly. He was content to stick with a song already picked out by Brian at IBC, a stripped-down, simplified version of Chuck Berry's Latin-flavoured Come On, dominated by Brian's harmonica.

Glyn Johns is insistent that the new Oldham-produced version was 'exactly like [the one] I'd done'. Yet the two weren't identical. On the IBC sessions, Ian Stewart's piano adds an insistent, jiggling, almost funky counter-melody; on Oldham's recording, the pianist is virtually inaudible. The band's new co-manager had already decided that Stu was one Stone too many, with a face that didn't fit.

The sacking of Ian Stewart was the third time the snake had entered the Rolling Stones' little Garden of Eden, but this parting was tougher than Gomelsky's and Johns'. Stu was the first Stone to join Brian's cause, and his departure would leave enduring damage. Oldham's demand that he be booted out was issued just a few days after the recording of Come On, and had the force of cold, hard logic: Oldham knew he was selling sex, and Stu's 1950s hairstyle and Fred Flintstone chin could never fit the bill. He also insisted that from now on, the band use the name the Rolling Stones.

Friends remember different versions of Stu's sacking. Glyn Johns says it was done in his earshot, at Decca studios, and delivered brutally; 'I went in and told Andrew what an arsehole he was'. James Phelge, meanwhile, recalls Oldham instructing the band to inform Stu, a task which Keith and Brian put off for a few days – so it's likely they never did the deed and simply left it to Oldham to deliver the news.

Stu's reaction was complex. On one level 'he wasn't bothered at all', says Johns. Stu showed little ego or vanity. But another close friend, Keith Altham, says that in quiet moments 'it was obvious that he was deeply hurt'. Yet the resentment that festered was not directed at Oldham; it was Brian's attempts to soothe the humiliation that provoked the enmity. 'Don't worry, Stu,' he'd told the pianist, 'we'll see you all right. You'll have a sixth of everything.' Brian was known for making promises he couldn't keep. This was one of his most ill judged. His attempt to placate Stu came from the band's continuing need for him to help out on piano; in addition, they offered him the job of road manager. Stu's dry humour would sustain the Stones for decades, as he opened dressing-room doors the world over and alerted the band with phrases like 'you're on stage now, my little three-chord wonders'. Yet the humour never really extended to Brian. From that point on, Stu essentially hated him.

The psychology and logic behind Stu's sacking are all the more complex and fascinating when we include the perspective of Stones confidant Keith Altham for he believes that Mick was involved: 'Mick must have realized that one into six was not as good as one into five in terms of shares. I suspect that Andrew and Mick made the decision.' Stu quite probably knew Mick was responsible, but his resentment centred on Brian because he had made a promise he wouldn't keep. And that was ultimately Brian's problem, says Altham: he lacked the true killer touch. 'Brian could be duplicitous, but Mick was capable of being duplicitous *and* cunning. Brian wasn't terribly good at cunning. People saw through it quite quickly. Brian wasn't good at being bad. Mick was.'

With the hostility generated by Stu's sacking, plus the fall-out from the main members' sexual games, the thrilling prospect of a break-through was laced with darker feelings. But the long-term repercussions of the band's fragmentation were far from anyone's mind as summer arrived. Come On was released on 17 June 1963 and became a hot song in the London clubs, but it was a slow burner. Oldham's first attempt at marketing the Stones was a failure. His plan was to make them 'hipper but smarter than the Beatles', says Jeff Dexter, a nascent mod and future mainstay of Swinging London who was called in to help style them: he took them down to Wardour Street to get custom shirts made, plus 'those dodgy houndstooth jackets and pants. But that's what Andrew wanted.' Brian was 'more careful with his choices than the others. Although Charlie was already buying nice shirts.' Brian and Keith conspired to mess up Oldham's nice new suits – 'so all that bollocks of how Andrew made them the anti-Beatles, that was just an accident,' Dexter concludes.

Oldham's misstep was obvious even to his band's greatest rivals, who were sitting in a hotel lobby on 13 July watching TV for the Stones' appearance on *Thank Your Lucky Stars*: 'John [Lennon] was shouting out, "What have they done?"' remembers Tony Bramwell. 'They were wearing tweed jackets, and houndstooth shirts, whereas when we first saw them they were in jeans and striped T-shirts!' Oldham was smart enough to drop the suits and roll with Brian's vision of the band as anti-heroes. 'Andrew didn't get everything right – he was naive, just a hustler,' says Keith Altham. 'But he was a very good hustler.'

Oldham later boasted about how he bought Come On into the charts – a tradition as old as rock'n'roll. Still, by 11 August, when the Stones headlined at the third National Jazz and Blues Festival at Richmond Athletic Ground, the key event in the jazz calendar, established by Chris Barber and Harold Pendleton, it was obvious that, in the south at least, an unstoppable momentum was building.

It was one of Brian's old trad jazz friends, on the bill that Sunday afternoon, who noticed – to his mild chagrin – that 'things were about to change'. John Keen had played with the River City Stompers to a modest crowd in one section of the large field, then noticed a large queue building up further over. 'They were all youngsters, teenagers, and there were a lot more people than in our part of the ground, and you could see something was going on. So I wandered over, trying to work out "Why aren't they listening to *us*?"'

The stage, in front of which stylish teenagers were queueing patiently, was packed with impressive new Vox amplifiers, shiny square Reslo microphones, and a neatly dressed group of musicians; in the midst of them Keen recognized the distinctive blond barnet of his old guitarist. Stepping over the ropes that sectioned off the younger kids, Keen walked towards the stage. When he spotted him, a delighted, smiling Brian Jones beckoned him over. 'This is my rhythm and blues band!' he proclaimed proudly, before calling over Mick and Keith to introduce them to his old Cheltenham chum. They both deferred to Brian, asking how long they had until showtime. Brian was effervescent, bubbling with happiness. Keen took in the suit and the buzz of excitement, impressed and confused at how the arcane music Brian had championed back home barely a year before could already be attracting such a crowd. 'It was the birth of a phenomenon. Before you'd had serious music, jazz, and you had pop music, Cliff and the Shadows. And suddenly this fringe music was about to become massive, and you could see already it had significance and status.' Brian told Keen he was playing only his beloved R&B, no trad jazz numbers thrown in to please the crowd. His manner was joyous rather than boastful as he explained how he'd found a bunch of like-minded souls, and finally an audience that appreciated what he did. 'He was in his element,' says Keen.

The trumpet player was pleased for his old friend, but there were pangs of jealousy, too, as he looked at all the attractive women waiting to see Brian play, and the realization dawned that the traditional jazz to which he'd committed himself was now the music of the past. All the ambition, the focus that Keen had seen up close the previous year had, it seemed, paid off.

This appreciative audience had built up steadily – slowly at first, all via word of mouth. Come On was in fact the opposite of a hustled hit: it sneaked its way into the UK Top 50 on 22 July, took a full two months to haul its way up to number 21, and nearly as long to drift out of the Top 50. With Eric Easton now booking the band on the ballroom circuit, the Stones made their first tentative steps out of London, starting with the Corn Exchange in Wisbech, north Cambridgeshire, in late July. Soon after the Richmond festival performance, on 23 August, the band made their first appearance on the recently launched ITV programme *Ready Steady Go!* (it would become the definitive sixties British music show). Throughout this time Mick Jagger was still a student at the LSE; it wasn't until the end of the summer that he decided not to re-enrol for the September term. Brian, says Linda Lawrence, was delighted. Not until later did he, or anyone else, notice that this was a fated turning point in his own life: even as success and fame beckoned, he would be manipulated into a minority position within his own band. As James Phelge points out, 'it just broke the wrong way when they left Edith Grove.'

Although the nankering vibe at Edith Grove had been established by Brian, Keith and Phelge, with Mick only dipping in and out of the camaraderie – sometimes joking with the others, sometimes earnestly studying his textbooks – Brian also was occasionally aloof, disappearing with Linda or telling the others to sod off when she arrived. He could be snooty, too. Already the others had started to mock his obsession with shampooing his hair, which he was starting to grow longer, figuring it was his most striking asset. Even before his photo was being reproduced in teen magazines, he was an obvious narcissist. 'I remember he was, not a control freak, but he was very fastidious as a person,' says Paul Jones. 'I never knew anyone who was more fastidious about his appearance, his hygiene, or his clothes. He told me he picked girl-friends on the basis of how well they would do his laundry! And for some people that's quite hard to live with on a daily basis.' However much he'd slummed it at Selkirk House or Edith Grove, Brian was at heart a sybarite. Hence, when the band members finally decided to leave Edith Grove for plusher pads, he opted at the last moment for home comforts and moved in with Linda and her parents, at 90 St Leonards Road in Windsor. Mick found a flat for himself and Keith at 33 Mapesbury Road, in north London. In the months since he'd first signed up the Stones, Andrew Oldham had been living with his mum, Celia, with whom he'd always maintained a complex, strained relationship. It wasn't until the autumn that Oldham asked Mick and Keith if he could move in with them. 'It was decided that way, and I don't think Brian even thought about it,' says Phelge, who stayed on in the Edith Grove flat but continued to hang out with the band.

The happy, fulfilled musician whom John Keen had seen at Richmond was at a new summit – finally vindicated, with the music he'd been championing for nearly three years now at a tipping point. 'This was his band – his realization of the dream,' says Bill Wyman. Yet, in a cruel twist, this moment was also the one, Bill adds, when 'he proved the most vulnerable'.

Brian was still comfortably the top dog of the Stones in August 1963. The first threat to this status came on the 27th of that month when exhaustion caused him to miss a show at the Ricky Tick Club. This first obvious bout of ill health lasted only two nights, but by early September he had developed a rash, with 'blotches all over his face', says Bill. The Stones coped with Brian's absence by bringing back Stu on piano, miking the instrument up to fill out the sound.

Bill Wyman would speculate in his memoir, *Stone Alone*, that Brian suffered from a mild form of epilepsy. It's an intriguing possibility, which we'll never be able to confirm, but what's undoubtedly true is that Brian's health problems stretched back eight years or more, to when – as neighbour Roger Jessop remembers – he dropped out of the school cricket team because he was 'extremely asthmatic'. What's most telling about Jessop's recollection is not the fact that Brian resented his condition, it's that he also 'resented himself'. Brian was now on the brink of achieving musically what he'd been looking for, and again his physical weakness was jeopardizing everything.

Linda Lawrence remembers the summer of 1963 as a joyful period. Brian loved being in the bosom of a family, enjoying cooked breakfasts, chatting about music with Linda's mum, borrowing clothes from her brother: 'He had a direction, and was doing what he loved.' But as the band's schedule intensified and Brian succumbed to nervous rashes or bouts of asthma, she noticed, like Dellar, the resentment of his own frailty. 'I only realized slowly. But then he started talking to me, about how he wouldn't live past thirty. He just didn't feel his health, his body, was in good shape.'

Brian's main response to his physical shortcomings seemed to be a form of self-loathing. A secondary response was recklessness. He was a daredevil driver. In 1964 he took delivery of a sleek, phallic Jaguar E-type, took it for a spin with Linda, and lost control. The sports car rolled over but miraculously Brian and Linda walked away unhurt. (The drama inspired Linda's dad to go out and source Brian a solid, safe Humber Snipe.) Another time, Brian and Linda were enjoying an idyllic afternoon boating in Windsor when Brian spotted some fast water, like rapids, running up to a sluice gate. He steered the little motorboat straight for it, laughing manically as Linda spotted the danger and screamed. 'It was child's play, daring, seeing how close to the edge he could take it. And it was scary.' Actions without consideration or fear of the consequences – Brian seemed to relish the panic, the energy, that unleashed. As the pressures on him intensified over the coming years, it was always hard to predict whether he'd respond with depressive, self-hating torpor or slightly crazed escapism.

For all the minor portents, though, Brian and his band were managing to ride the wave. As they approached the end of 1963 there was the niggling need to come up with a second single that would capitalize on the modest success of Come On, their decent but unadventurous debut. After a couple of studio sessions failed to gel, the solution fell into their lap. Mick and Keith were driving down Charing Cross Road in a cab and spotted Paul McCartney and John Lennon window shopping. They shouted mocking greetings at their friends and rivals.

'Hey, hey, give us a lift!' Paul and John yelled in reply.

The taxi pulled to the kerb, the pair stepped in for a natter, and Mick mentioned that the band were looking for some new songs.

'Ah, yeah, sure,' Paul responded. 'We got one. How about Ringo's song? You could do it as a single.'

The gift of I Wanna Be Your Man was as big a coup for the Beatles as it was for the Stones, helping them gain part-ownership of the success of their rivals. 'It was a throwaway,' John Lennon would later tell *Hit Parader*. 'We weren't gonna give them anything *great*, right?' Although in later days they would be closer, Tony Bramwell says, 'I'm not sure exactly how much the Beatles actually *liked* the Stones in those early days, but they did make us all realize there was a world way beyond Chuck Berry and Bo Diddley.' Brian

Jones, in particular, opened up that world for the Beatles, who continued to regard him as the lead Stone.

As a result of the mix of friendship and rivalry, the Beatles sent their road manager to sit in on the I Wanna Be Your Man session and keep tabs on the Stones. After the comparative luxury of Abbey Road, Bramwell was shocked by the grottiness of the studios the Stones worked in. 'We'd hardly been outside EMI, which was like a laboratory; the Stones usually worked in Regent Sound [on Denmark Street in London], which was tiny, ropey, and looked like someone's front room.' For the main recording at De Lane Lea, Andrew Oldham had disappeared: the manic energy of the summer had been succeeded by a black depression, which he sat out in Paris. The much-maligned Eric Easton oversaw the session, which meant Brian dominated the recording, doubling Mick's vocals and layering slashing electric slide all over the track.

It's no coincidence that the one early Stones recording for which Oldham was absent is the song on which Brian is omnipresent; his feral guitar, even his backing vocals, would be toned down on future recordings, just like Stu's piano had been. I Wanna Be Your Man was a mess, but touched by genius; its trebly distortion and sneered vocals would form the prototype for a whole generation of American garage bands. In retrospect, the single's cranked-up aggression was a huge leap forward for British rock'n'roll, radically different from the Beatles' impeccably clean Abbey Road recordings. It would be years before other players – notably Eric Clapton with the Bluesbreakers – mastered the same sound. Although Mick Jagger would attract a lot of press attention when the single, released that November, became a success, Brian remained the undisputed architect of the band's sound. In interviews for the *New Musical Express* and *Melody Maker* he stood out as the one with a mission, a manifesto, and as 'the most intelligent member of the group', says *NME* journalist Chris Hutchins. 'And, I thought, the least star-struck.'

Tony Bramwell – who had grown up with George Harrison, known Paul McCartney well as a kid, and joined their tiny crew as Brian Epstein's assistant at his record store chain, NEMS, and then the band's road manager – continued to keep tabs on the Stones and report back on what he saw. He liked the Stones, organized a welcome party for them at the Cavern, and ended up accompanying them on several dates of their first major UK tour, with Bo Diddley. It was Brian he hung out with, and mostly reported back on. 'I just liked Brian. It was Brian's band, and he was a very, very good musician. He looked great, he was cool, he didn't fuck around on stage – maybe he shook his head a bit. He was the leader; Mick and Keith hadn't established themselves as [anything] other than a singer and second guitars.'

That late '63 tour was manic, with hysterical crowds, a generation of kids who felt like they'd been waiting for this moment all their lives; who felt, like Ealing regular Janet Couzens, 'We were off into the sixties and there was no going back. There's been this tedium before, that emphasis that you don't go beyond your station. But now we had confidence in what we felt.' The Beatles were a beacon of hope, of freedom; the Stones entering the fray proved a tipping point. The genie would never go back in the bottle.

The band's set was based around Come On, their magnificently upbeat version of Route 66, Fortune Teller and Money. On dates with Bo they'd drop their crowd-pleasing versions of his songs, but none the less, even the shorter version of the set proved electrifying. Half a century on, when we've had plenty of time to assimilate the sound of electric blues, those songs still have an energy and exuberance that will never be rivalled. There would be many great

Stones tours, but for some observers, including the Animals' singer Eric Burdon, who would become Mick Jagger's leading rival in 1964, this one was the greatest: 'I remember them as a club band, and that's the way I want to remember them, that's when they were at their best.' He recalls Keith as an impressive rhythm guitarist, the foundation of their Chuck Berry-style songs – but both Keith and Mick were 'in the shadows. Because on the side is this blond-haired Aryan dude on guitar, and you couldn't help but look at him. He had this magnetism about him, you couldn't escape it. But it was twisted.'

Maybe Burdon's take on the band is tainted by his rivalry with Mick, but in his view, Brian 'was the one. The one wanting to stretch out and be inventive.' The pair hung out in the London clubs, talking sometimes about Elmore James and Howlin' Wolf, but mostly about girls, and in the following years they'd become drug buddies. Burdon liked and respected this blond-haired pioneer. Yet there were parts of Brian that Burdon, and many others, simply didn't understand. 'I knew him,' says Burdon, 'and yet I didn't know him.' Burdon didn't, for instance, know about Linda Lawrence (she came on few tour dates), and says, 'I didn't ever see him with a girlfriend. He seemed to be obsessed with hookers, which was strange. And I'm not sure I ever spoke to him properly, not close, except when we were high. It was strange, hard to explain.'

There was nothing hard to explain about the first step in Brian's downfall. It all came down to money. A staggeringly small amount of it: five pounds. In context, it was trivial, ludicrous, especially looked at from the perspective of today, when for decades Mick Jagger and Keith Richards have banked most of the band's performance royalties while keeping their sidemen on a salary.

The Stones' trip to Liverpool to play the Cavern was on the

surface a celebration. The Beatles were away and had arranged a party for the Stones, attended by Cynthia Lennon and other friends of the Fab Four. But the sense of camaraderie was shattered when Stu discovered, during the stay in Liverpool, that Brian was earning an extra fiver compared to the rest of the band. The deal, Oldham would later relate, was organized in secret by Eric Easton – for whom the Stones' co-manager was already gunning, accusing him of shady business practices.

The sum would become so proverbial that it could have made a good Bible story. For one thing, Bill Wyman's records show it was a tiny proportion of their overall earnings: each band member was by now making £193 a week. Yet that five pounds was symbolic: for Stu, already disenchanted with Brian, it embodied Brian's slipperiness; for Keith, it was a betrayal of their gang mentality; and for Mick – well, it was five pounds. The extra fiver marginalized Easton and Brian – and Oldham used it to his advantage.

James Phelge was probably the only insider with no axe to grind. He'd heard Brian boast about the extra money earlier that year. 'I thought he was fucking joking, but it turned out it was true.' To Phelge, that stupid fiver marked an irrevocable turning point: 'They just weren't really friends after that.' Brian's pettiness would be paid back with nastiness: 'There was a period where if the van was ready for the next gig and Brian wasn't there, they would drive off and fuckin' leave him. And it really did seem to stem from that five quid.'

So, the slow decline of Brian Jones started with a five-pound note. Over the next few months his leadership would remain largely unchallenged, but the incident was like the point in an affair when one first notices a lover's flaw: it's never possible to go back to that first, carefree relationship. From now on, Brian would be on the back foot, pitched against the Jagger-Oldham-Richards troika.

Anyone who's been in a band will know how it's impossible to overstate the resentment, hatred even, that one member can inspire once you get it in your head they're not pulling their weight or not being fair, even when you know that hatred isn't rational. Worse still, although the Christian tradition suggests that adversity makes us better people, that's rarely the case. More often it makes us bitter, or prone to self-pity, emotions to which Brian Jones would increasingly succumb. As the games of sexual oneupmanship, misogyny and nankering showed, the Rolling Stones could be a vicious gang. And, as Brian's ex-bandmate and educational psychologist John Keen points out, 'Gangs, of animals, of children, do tend to pick on the vulnerable creature in the pack. It performs a kind of group bonding. You see it happening at secondary schools. Brian could be difficult – but I know what he was like, and he didn't deserve it.'

In spite of the slowly deepening rifts, the months into the spring of 1964 shot by in a blizzard of adrenalin and thrills: the Bo Diddley tour was succeeded after only the shortest of breaks by January's 'Group Scene 1964' package, and then a third set of dates, propped up by Jet Harris and Brian's old friend Billie Davis. The band was at a peak: distorted guitars, songs played at breakneck speed, Mick stoking the frenzy with his urchin come-ons while Brian channelled a uniquely dark energy, often goading the crowd into stage invasions, relishing the panic it created. 'You realized it was probably out of control, but there was nothing you could do about it,' says Keith. 'But it was exhilarating fun.'

There was an ever-present buzz of rutting sexuality, Mick, Brian and Bill competing to recruit teenage girls, while Andrew Oldham spent much of the time gazing at Jet Harris, who loved camping around and during one particularly debauched night in Manchester sneaked into the lobby stark naked, popped a lampshade on his head, and stood immobile in the corner waiting to see who'd notice. Brian loved the buzz, loved hanging out with all the musicians, sometimes with Mick or Keith, although Mick in particular was usually seen huddled with Oldham. He also loved the camp undercurrent. It was probably on this tour that he first made friends with Michael Aldred, the *Ready Steady Go!* interviewer. The pair would camp it up together, swapping clothes and sashaying around. 'The whole thing was utter chaos,' remembers Billie Davis, 'and it escalated throughout the tour.' Brian seemed happier travelling with Jet, Billie and the other musicians on their coach rather than in his own band's van. 'He always seemed to be worried,' says Billie. 'He was certainly in control of the music, but the whole thing was madness, exhausting, and he seemed frail. And it was constant; there was no let-up.'

When the frenzy did let up, as the third tour came to a temporary halt on 2 February, Brian was optimistic, buoyed up with enthusiasm about sessions for the band's debut album – so much so that he invited Tony Bramwell, the Beatles' aide, to some of them.

Every studio engineer who'd worked with the band up to that point had recognized Brian as the custodian of their sound, the one person with an innate understanding of how their live energy could transfer on to record. Their manager claimed to be overseeing the band's records, but that night Oldham was nowhere to be seen as Brian asked the engineer to roll the tape and the pair listened to a guitar part. Brian plugged his shiny new distinctive pale green Gretsch into his AC30, ready to make it sound better, just a bit funkier, just a bit dirtier; his concentration was intense. As the tape rolled, Bramwell realized that Brian was replacing the guitar part being played by Keith with one of his own; later he saw him patching up the odd bass guitar part or other detail in much the same way. The trade term for this is a 'sponge job'. In later years, Keith Richards boasted about how he'd done this to Bill Wyman and guest guitarist Ry Cooder – but as far as Bramwell could tell at that point, Keith had no idea that the same thing was being done to his own efforts.

Bramwell got no sense of any internal conflicts as he watched Brian record. Brian seemed focused, in control, happy. This debut album was his baby. Away from the growing competition, thinking purely about how a guitar line should sound, he was relaxed, with none of the growing angst that Billie Davis had seen. Bramwell's experience was something another friend, John 'Hoppy' Hopkins, noticed. Hoppy knew Brian from the Oxford CND scene before they both arrived in London, he photographed the Stones several times and bumped into Brian around the city. In one sentence, Hoppy crystallizes what would become the new reality from 1964: 'I'd see Brian a lot, but I don't think I ever saw him smile, apart from when he had a guitar in his hands.'

All Brian's ambitions centred on the album; he was obsessed with making it work. 'I think it's good . . . I hope it's good enough,' he told his friends, as if the record was a vindication of his life so far. The album was for him the ultimate personal statement. There were few concessions to commercialism for, as Bill points out, Brian 'wanted fame and fortune but didn't want to sacrifice his musical integrity to get it'.

Through the spring of 1964, as the Beatles' iconography was set in stone in *A Hard Day's Night*, the Stones were defined week by week in the *New Musical Express* and *Melody Maker*, which followed their every move and sketched their contrasting characters: Mick was businesslike; Bill was boring; Charlie was the jazzbo; Keith the nice guy. Mick scored a good number of interviews, almost always in conjunction with Andrew Oldham, who now sported a shaggy, distinctly Rolling Stones haircut and loved seeing himself in print. But Brian Jones was the visionary, the one in charge of the music, and also, according to *Melody Maker*'s Ray Coleman, the 'deep . . . the most expressive Stone'. Inescapably it was Brian who had the sense of mission, to spread the gospel of R&B. 'I think I've finally proved to those people who said I was always doing the wrong thing that I've been right all along,' he told people like Coleman. And when, on 10 April, the *NME* gave the 'fantastic' debut album by the Rolling Stones a laudatory review, it was Brian, alone, who explained its genesis and hoped that 'people will accept it . . . as good R&B'. He seemed unassailable, the most musically talented Stone, 'and also the one the girls liked best', as Robin Pike, his old schoolmate, who turned up for several shows, remembers.

But the band's increasing exhaustion and occasional squabbles seemed to affect Brian more than the others. In those early months of 1964, with Mick, Keith and Oldham mostly holed up at Mapesbury Road, Bill out in Penge, and Charlie still living with his parents, Brian had precious few confidants. One of them was Nicky Wright, a fast-emerging photographer who worked mainly around the King's Road fashion scene, for Dezo Hoffman's studio, and who for a brief time became the Stones' main photographer (he was soon shouldered aside by Oldham and replaced by Gered Mankowitz, another great photographer who happened to be the son of *Expresso Bongo* writer Wolf Mankowitz). He'd seen the band many times throughout 1963 and hung out with Brian in west London, mostly talking about clothes, girls and cars. It was Wright who designed and photographed the debut album cover, a stark, evocative image that showed Brian in the foreground in sharp focus, a searching gaze directed at the camera, and Mick set somewhat behind and to his left, while a sullen Keith, Charlie and

Bill brought up the rear. This reflected Wright's perception of the band.

Wright liked Keith and Charlie, but Brian became his closest friend and he shared his excitement as their following grew, and enthused with him about the making of the album. Brian liked fame, he liked women, but the recording of their first LP was something more important, Wright knew, something that promised a longed-for justification. Wright often saw Brian, Mick and Keith take the piss out of each other, and heard jibes about Brian being a short-arse – all normal band behaviour, he reckoned. Never once did Brian signal any worries about internal power struggles – until the winter of 1963. Wright had a small cottage in Whitehill, Hampshire, in the grounds of his family's house, where Brian turned up regularly in his green Humber Snipe to take refuge. As they drank late into the night, Brian would become 'more and more morose', says Wright, 'complaining how he wasn't being listened to.' When they smoked dope together, Wright found Brian playful and funny, but alcohol, he realized, unleashed something darker. One night, sitting in the tiny kitchen with Wright's brother Patrick, Brian shouted, 'This will show them!', grabbed a knife and started to draw it across his wrist. A mêlée ensued during which Patrick punched Brian on the chin to put him out of action. The golden-haired Stone went out cold.

Brian's mood didn't improve, and later that night the drama escalated into pure farce. Still apparently intent on ending it all, Brian decided to jump out of his bedroom window. 'The silly sod was so drunk he'd forgotten the window was on the ground floor,' says Patrick. Nicky and Patrick heard a rustling sound, ran outside, and realized Brian had fallen into a large bush just below the window. But they could find no trace of him there nor in the gardens surrounding the cottage. Nicky, says Patrick, became panicky and phoned the local police station to warn them that 'a famous rock star is mentally deranged and rampaging through the countryside'. Eventually a portly sergeant arrived with several uniformed officers, and they were about to search the grounds when Brian emerged from some nearby shrubbery.

As Brian approached, Nicky worried how the sergeant would react to what was indisputably a criminal offence – wasting police time. He had reckoned without Brian's charm.

'I'm so sorry, officer,' he said, his handsome face a picture of sincerity. 'I've been an absolute cunt.'

Taken aback by the rock star's humble behaviour, the gruff sergeant gathered up his officers and left.

Nicky Wright doesn't claim to be an objective observer – he has no love for Andrew Oldham – but he sees Brian not as a flawed character but as a man who, when attacked, turned on himself. 'Things got to him.' If he'd been more politically astute he would have formed alliances within the band rather than outside it. But he wasn't. As his grip on the band started to loosen, so did much of his fragile self-esteem. Although Nicky stayed firmly on Brian's side in 1964, Patrick came to dread his visits. 'Initially I think we were all fairly thrilled to have a rock star staying. The novelty wore off as we realized – Brian sucked. He was forever belly-aching that no one understood him or the pressure he was under. It became very boring.'

The elusive warm English summer had finally arrived, and were were few more beautiful places to experience it than Surrey, home to Eric Clapton, Ringo Starr and James Phelge.

Phelge, whose name famously adorned many of the Rolling Stones' songs before Mick Jagger and Keith Richards managed to lock them all down for themselves, is a living embodiment of the

Stones' lost camaraderie. The man who famously greeted the Stones with his underpants on his head, or pissed on them as they made their way up the stairs at Edith Grove, was, in those early days, more integral to their rebel, outcast vibe than their manager, or even their rhythm section. Fast-talking, wiry, he's still an engaging raconteur, reclining in his easy chair facing a window that looks out on to a leafy garden. The font of stories seems bottomless, punctuated only by regular cigarette breaks, each tale highlighting a fluid, ever-changing situation in contrast to the rather static, repetitive versions you hear from today's surviving Stones.

Most of the band's circle have been split into factions for decades, like rival religious sects; Phelge pre-dates that split, so is one of the most objective observers of their genesis. His stories are from an era when five musicians dreamt of success rather than argued over the spoils. When Keith or Mick discuss Brian, they have pat answers; Phelge describes a more intriguing human who was powerful but vulnerable, resourceful but unreliable. At one point, as we continue to grapple with the issue of why Brian Jones became irrevocably sundered from his fellow Stones, he utters a simple, resonant truth: 'Brian was never satisfied.'

What drove Brian Jones forward, what inspired him to champion his beloved, obscure R&B, was dissatisfaction. A teenager's claustrophobia, the sense that there had to be something better – this was at the root of his rebelliousness; and given that the Stones inspired Dylan, Iggy's Stooges and others, his frustration and angst were the inspiration for the sixties counter-culture. Brian Jones, as much as any single figure, helped destroy the rotten, complacent establishment.

Yet a horrible irony would underlie this profound achievement. Brian invented the Stones, hot-wired their music, out of this sense of dissatisfaction. But success didn't ease his frustrations, it confirmed them. For as Phelge observes, 'With Brian it was never good enough. Because it wasn't perfect. Then because it wasn't perfect, he'd find fault all the way through.'

Brian Jones's life up to the spring of 1964 had been a quest for vindication. Thereafter it was a tragedy, for vindication brought no happiness, only sorrow.

5

How Many More Years

THE FATES OF Andrew Oldham and Brian Jones were always closely intertwined, and never more so than in the beautiful autumn of 1964, when all their bravado and bullshit seemed to be paying off. Brian had finally exported his beloved R&B to its birthplace – a cultural realignment that would have profound and long-lasting implications. Where Brian saw America as the birthplace of the blues, Oldham regarded it as the home of the hustler, and he was just as keen to make his mark on the nation. Just like Brian, the moment he won was the moment he started to lose, as he signed his own Faustian pact.

For Brian, the timespan between his great triumph and the realization that his life had spun out of control would be dizzyingly short. At the end of 1964, the song that embodied his pioneering vision would top the British charts, yet its recording would mark a new humiliation, and by the following spring he'd be contemplating a future outside the band he'd formed.

*

As James Phelge noted, the key turning point in Brian Jones's life was the way that 'everything broke wrong' when the band moved out of Edith Grove. There was no masterplan that meant Mick, Keith and Andrew Oldham ended up living together at Mapesbury Road. But the trio's time in the flat marked Oldham's most crucial contribution to popular culture: he forced Mick and Keith to write together, triggering a complex relationship that has endured, with much griping and oneupmanship, for half a century.

These days we're all familiar with the character templates of the controlling Stones – Mick cool and managerial, Keith swaggering and piratical. Yet that view underplays the intricacy of their relationship, a mix of admiration and suspicion that stretches back to the time they bumped into each other on the platform of Dartford railway station with half an hour to kill, when Keith said to his Wentworth Road pal, 'I haven't seen you for fucking ages – and what's that under your arm?'

Today, Keith still recalls his boyhood affection for Mick, but it's mixed with a retrospective wariness owing to how Mick played on the authority he'd amassed thanks to being one year above him at school, and his being in possession of an impressive record collection. Keith's little stash of vinyl at that point consisted of 'half-price bullshit cover versions', so Mick's possession of the real thing was a big deal. 'He shows me these Chess records, and I was like, wow,' says Keith. 'He held sway over me for quite a while, [because] he was already internationally inclined, and had got it all together.'

Keith's almost puppy-dog respect for Mick endured for several years – until challenged by the arrival of Brian Jones, whose musical and sexual experience made both Mick and Keith look like wannabes. Today, Keith often indulges in cold-hearted mockery of Brian, but his influence lingers: 'Brian Jones was the first one to

'A clever bloke', and a 'devil'. Brian Jones (left), on the eve of his thirteenth birthday, in February 1955, with Colin Dellar, plus Colin's cat Hillary and dog Leo, Asquith Road, Cheltenham. Colin was a firm friend, until the pair fell out in 1956, the year Brian turned from an 'almost priggish' nerd into a teenage rebel.

Above left: Baby Brian, the oldest child in a family touched by tragedy when sister Pamela died of leukaemia. Her brief existence would become a family secret.

Above right: Brian's younger sister Barbara (centre, behind rabbit).

Centre: Brian dances at Filby's basement, a musical refuge from 1957 on.

Above: Brian still retained some of his dad's geeky traits, working on restoring trams at Crich, Derbyshire, in 1960.

Right: Brian with Valerie Corbett, his girlfriend from 1959 to 1960.

Above: Brian with Valerie, plus her father Ken and brother Derek, probably in the summer of 1959, on the River Avon near Tewkesbury. Val gave birth to Brian's baby – his second child – the following May, accelerating his estrangement from polite society.

Above: Brian's two key musical accomplices in Cheltenham, John Keen (trumpet) and Graham Ride (sax). The trio played together through 1961. 'Brian was streets ahead of us,' says Keen. 'His focus was incredible.'

Right: Alexis Korner's pioneering electric blues band, with Cyril Davies on harmonica and Charlie Watts on drums. Korner would be Brian's key patron, a father figure to the ambitious young bluesman.

Above: Early Marquee show by 'The Rollin' Stones'. 'There was obviously something about it that would take off,' says witness Ginger Baker. Brian was unquestionably the leader, Baker remembers; but the advent of co-manager Andrew Oldham (shown **below**, left, with Brian and Keith), would eventually pit Brian against 'the cabal'. According to his friend Scott Ross, 'With that triumvirate against him . . . he didn't stand a chance'.

Left: 'He would tell all sorts of stories . . . do magic tricks . . . I was transported into another world, another realm,' recalls Pat Andrews, mother of Julian Mark Anthony, born in October 1961. But Brian could also be 'conniving . . . a chancer'.

Right: 'He was calm . . . deep,' says Linda Lawrence, mother of Julian, born in July 1964. Linda also remembered Brian's addiction to risk, to 'taking things to the edge'.

Below: 'Mischievous . . . very, very sensual . . . kind of devilish'. Dawn Molloy became besotted with Brian through 1964. Their baby, Paul Andrew, was born in March 1965; Dawn was forced to give her son up for adoption.

Above: French actress and singer Zouzou, who stayed in Brian's Chelsea mews home in 1965. 'It was very fun . . . but he was up and down very often.'

Above and below: Arriving at Kingsway Studio, Holborn, 7 October 1963. Brian carries the sheet music for I Wanna Be Your Man under his arm. He dominated the session, in manager Andrew Oldham's absence. The single – tough, distorted and aggressive – would form a template for American garage rock.

Above: Brian Jones the dandy and narcissist, at Beau Gentry, LA, in June 1964. West Coast scenesters considered Brian the premier Stone, exacerbating the band's internal rivalries. 'Mick had this jealousy, that a lot of the girls liked Brian rather than Mick,' remembers one insider.

Above: May 1965: Brian introduces Howlin' Wolf to America, the fulfilment of his vision of blues as mainstream music for a white audience, breaking 'a boundary line which no one thought could be crossed', says Buddy Guy.

Below: Clearwater, Florida, 8 or 9 May 1965. Brian had fled the band just days before, his conflicts with Oldham, Mick and Keith 'beyond any kind of resolution', says Scott Ross. The stay saw Brian beaten up – and the genesis of (I Can't Get No) Satisfaction.

play me so much Jimmy Reed – and Robert Johnson. It's just that he couldn't handle he wasn't the guy writing the songs.'

Keith remembers the crucial time when he and Mick became the guys writing the songs as 'that night we got locked in the kitchen at Mapesbury Road'. It's a symbolic moment, for neither Mick nor Oldham remembers it that way. In fact the Stones had already written several songs as a band, including Little By Little and Off The Hook, all credited to 'Nanker Phelge'. Mick and Keith had also started working on ideas with Gene Pitney, one of Oldham's PR clients, in January 1964 as a duo. Oldham's innovation wasn't in getting the Stones to write, it was in marketing the Jagger-Richards brand as a rival to Lennon-McCartney. 'He was obsessed that it had to be a duo, like the Beatles,' says Oldham's PR partner Tony Calder. 'That's why it had to be Jagger-Richards. It was exactly the same with the Small Faces, where everything was Marriott-Lane, even though Stevie [Marriott] wrote all the songs himself.'

Slowly, the Nanker Phelge songs were dropped, while Mick and Keith continued to work at their craft. Many of their early efforts were shallow sub-Spector ditties, but they kept at it. Keith's magical moment in the kitchen came in April 1964, by which time Oldham had become obsessed with the luminously hypnotic Marianne Faithfull, 'an angel with big tits' whom he'd met at a party on 27 March. Marianne would become a key part of Stones mythology; inspiring the first great Jagger-Richards song was only the beginning of her legacy. Oldham kept badgering the pair to come up with a song for his new protégée. 'It was probably a desperate act on his part,' says Keith. 'But sometimes the mother of invention is necessity and as the sun was coming up in the kitchen, we had As Tears Go By. Six weeks later it's in the Top 10.'

That one song transformed both Andrew Oldham's fortunes and the balance of power within the Stones. It therefore marked the beginning of the end of Brian's dominance of the band. Yet while Oldham is always ready to put down Brian – 'the cunt in the barrio' – he maintains that, while Brian sensed the change in the balance of power, he never betrayed his feelings. 'Brian may have resented me, but he never showed it,' he says today. 'And if he did we never confronted or handled it. We were all too busy.'

When the Stones landed in New York on 1 June 1964, there was little inkling of the success that lay ahead for the Stones' writing team. Oldham arrived in the US full of big talk – but he, more than anyone, was aware their success was patchy, and unlike the Beatles, they were short of material. 'The Stones landed in America without vinyl legs. The lack of them in the UK was handled with balls and front. In America, except for the cities where they took to us like the Sex Pistols, it was embarrassing – until we got our hands on Time Is On My Side and It's All Over Now.' Oldham was adamant that cover versions of blues songs would not get them to the top of the charts. But during the very first appointment in their tour diary – a press conference with Murray the K's WINS radio show – Murray suggested the band cover the Valentinos song It's All Over Now, just released on Sam Cooke's label. 'Things happen in weird ways,' says Keith. 'It was Murray the K who said, "This sounds up your alley."'

The Stones' first days in the States were surreal. Their plane had touched down to five hundred screaming fans, and some wag had decided that the band should appear alongside a couple of Old English Sheepdogs. One of the first questions fired at them as they met the press was whether they ever washed. Cool as a cucumber, Brian stood up, raised his arms and retorted, 'Want a smell?' After a hectic day, and a couple of hours' sleep, it was on to Los Angeles, initially for a crushing disappointment when they were pilloried by Dean Martin on their first primetime TV show: 'their hair isn't long – it's just smaller foreheads and higher eyebrows'. But it didn't matter. The next day they hit the Strip, met up at RCA studios with arranger Jack Nitzsche – soon to be one of Brian's closest friends in the band's circle – and then came the Stones' first US performance, a brilliantly frenzied show at San Bernardino.

In the UK, the music press often focused on Brian owing to his role as the band's founder and spokesman, despite the way Oldham constantly pushed Mick forward. In the US, how the Stones got together was irrelevant. American teens loved Brian because he was the coolest. By October, the blond hair he shampooed religiously every day formed a perfect golden halo for those slightly sinister cheekbones, while his choice of clothing grew more and more distinctive, skinny stripey long-sleeved T-shirts or a slim-lapelled stripey jacket over a white polo neck. Brian would become the model for dozens if not hundreds of upstart garage bands across the nation.

In Hollywood especially, as teenage fan Ken Kubernik puts it, 'everyone was watching Brian'. Mick was popular – Americans loved his cheeky, earnest persona, and that he didn't wear the obligatory shirt and tie on TV – but nearly everyone on the LA scene focused on the saturnine Stone. 'Mick and Keith were considered bit players by everyone I knew, until well into the sixties,' says Kubernik. 'Brian was at the centre of everything, everyone wanted to ape his fashion; then there was the fact he was blond – there are all these tropes you can tie into it.'

There were many shaky moments during that first brief visit – mocking radio and press interviewers, half-full venues in Omaha and Detroit, Oldham's awareness that the Beatles had been there before them, with two tours and a massively influential movie under their belt. But all such memories and musings were erased by their visit on 10 June to the Chess Studio, at 2120 South Michigan Avenue, the home of the music they'd worshipped for so long. More crucially, with resident Chess engineer Ron Malo, they recorded those two definitive singles, It's All Over Now and the cover of Irma Thomas's Time Is On My Side. The recordings were a level of magnitude tougher than their previous work. 'The *sound* was the thing,' says Charlie Watts. 'It was such a great room and the engineer [Malo] was fabulous, a bit like [Dave Hassinger] at RCA. They had a much better idea of the sound of rock'n'roll.' The playing was on a new level, too, Brian and Keith's guitar parts meshing perfectly, Brian's chunky Gretsch arpeggios anchoring Keith's urgent guitar solo on Time Is On My Side.

Keith's curious memory from the first two days in Chicago is a vision of Muddy Waters, the famously regal King of Chicago, whitewashing the studio, paint splattered down his handsome face. It's evocative, but just that, a vision, for Waters was too proud a man for such menial work. Yet Keith's recollection that the Stones were accepted as equals, as buddies, by the Chess musicians is completely accurate. For Brian, the mocking American establishment were just another bunch of Ernies and nankers; it was the musicians who worked at Chess, like Bo Diddley and Buddy Guy, who became real friends. Dave Myers, who along with Willie Dixon was virtually house bassist at Chess, is just one of several who remember a strange bond with the Stones founder. 'He was a good guy, in a world of motherfuckers who thought we all came from the cottonfields,' he remembers. 'It's a strange world, where the only people who ever did anything for us were Europeans.' Like the musicians in Hollywood, Myers saw Brian Jones as key to the Stones. On TV shows like Mike Douglas's, where Brian joked alongside Mick, the Stones' singer was still often tentative; Brian was the cool, confident one, 'the deep thinker'. But even with the lousy quality of black and white TV in 1964 you can make out the heavy bags under his eyes.

*

Brian Jones wasn't the only one looking dark around the eyes. Andrew Oldham had already ducked out of the fray for a couple of weeks in the aftermath of I Wanna Be Your Man. A similar bout of mental exhaustion followed that summer of 1964. Oldham's stress levels, the delusions of grandeur, turned up the heat on the Stones' chemistry. He'd become enraptured with Phil Spector, bought a pair of identical shades and ramped up the tough-guy act he'd already learned from the impresario Don Arden. 'He could be a real bully,' says NME journalist Chris Hutchins. 'I received quite a few threatening phone calls late at night, which I believe were instigated by him.'

Brian was close behind Oldham in terms of stress levels. Up to this point he'd achieved some stability via his relationship with Linda Lawrence, to whom he wrote postcards throughout that first US tour. When Linda realized she was pregnant, right at the end of 1963, Brian had at first been solicitous. 'I thought we were so much in love, everything could be worked out,' she says. 'Brian talked about getting a house, my dad took me around looking at places, there was this feeling it might be OK.' But in the whirlwind of tour and recording dates, the idea kept getting postponed. Between the band's first visit to the USA in June 1964 and their third in April 1965 he would become more maddeningly unavailable, more maddeningly inconsistent – all the more so because from the summer of 1964 he became involved with another young woman, Dawn Molloy.

As Brian's stress levels increased, so did his drug consumption. His drinking had become heavier around the beginning of 1964; later that year his friend Dave Thomson remembered Brian drinking a bottle of whisky in an hour or two. Brian had most likely tried smoking pot earlier that year, too, but once the band hit the States they discovered a cornucopia of the stuff thanks to the musicians in Chicago, New York and on the West Coast. For Brian, just as it was a point of honour to have discovered the rarest Robert Johnson track before his bandmates, so it was with new varieties of dope. It affected his behaviour noticeably, and quickly. 'It became the thing among us,' says James Phelge. 'If Brian's taking drink or drugs then it's, Oh great, there must be some better drink or drugs. If Brian had some drugs and got smashed for twenty-four hours, then it was, Let's see if we can get smashed for forty-eight hours.'

There was another reason, beyond his competitiveness, for Brian's increasing drugs intake. He'd always been one to evade problems or difficult decisions – unlike Mick, who was far more decisive. From July 1964, as another string of British dates followed the first jaunt to the States, he had more and more reason to blot out reality. Phelge believes it all stemmed from 'that stupid five quid' and that it rankled more and more. Phelge remembers, 'It would be, We're going to eat over here, and Brian can eat over there, or they'd drive off without him. Then as Brian became more and more of an outcast, that was when he started smoking more and more dope, and drinking more and more.'

Some thought Brian deserved what came to him – Ian Stewart, in particular, came to heartily detest him ('Brian was Welsh, and Welsh people are very devious'). But when Stu died, tragically young, he was still close to the Stones, still bound up with all their multifaceted internal bickering. Plenty of others, as we shall see, saw a long, enduring process in which Oldham, Mick and often Keith set out to wear Brian down. In later years Bill Wyman would express his guilt that he hadn't stood up for the band's founder. His then-girlfriend, Astrid Lundstrom, agreed with this take: 'Mick and Keith got away with murder . . . because Bill and Charlie enabled Mick and Keith to go on being incredibly selfish.'

But in the studio, Brian still held many trump cards, and would continue to do so. As Gered Mankowitz, who joined the organization that autumn, points out, 'These guys are musicians, and musically, there is another language going on. If somebody strikes the right chord, as the expression goes, then for the duration of that shared experience, you can really tune in with someone – really like them. And that could still be true, even in the very last days.'

Increasingly insecure and occasionally paranoid, Brian was still conscious he was holding aces, and took to flaunting his differences from the band members – Andrew Oldham in particular. In the summer of 1964 he resumed his wandering – his whereabouts in Windsor were too well known – and began seeing Dawn Molloy, who lived nearby.

Naturally, for Linda Lawrence this was an unsettling, confusing time. She and Brian had driven to Cheltenham at the beginning of the year so that she could meet Lewis and Louisa. Brian's parents were polite but undemonstrative. The pair had arranged the trip in order to break the news of Linda's pregnancy, but in the frosty, repressed atmosphere of Hatherley Road they abandoned the scheme. Stressed by the meeting with his mum and dad, Brian succumbed to an asthma attack; he'd never address the subject of the impending birth with them. Worse still, when Linda's parents finally contacted the Joneses directly, Lewis sent them a callously cold letter which implied the Lawrences were attempting to engage in some sort of financial squeeze. Brian, as usual, sought to flee the aggravation, told Linda he'd been warned by Oldham to keep news of her pregnancy quiet and needed to sort himself out. Linda decided, 'If I could be patient . . . maybe he would come back to me' and continued to see Brian, even as she knew he was drifting away.

His new pad was a floor in a lofty Georgian house in Chester Street, a beautiful part of Belgravia. It was a dangerously provocative location, given that he shared the house with Phil May, Viv Prince, Brian Pendleton and his old bassist Dick Taylor of the Pretty Things – a band Oldham detested, seeing their hardcore R&B as a direct challenge to the Stones, according to Phil May. Unsurprisingly, the move emphasized his growing separation from the Stones – which in turn inspired a contradictory torrent of emotions.

In the early days, Phil May heard stories of Brian's treatment by Oldham and the Stones, but if he raised the subject with Brian, 'he would pooh-pooh it . . . He didn't even want me to mention it.' Brian found it easy to chat to May about all the subjects that interested him – French films, art openings – but essentially it all came back to music. The more friendly Brian became with the Pretty Things, though, the more guilty he felt about being disloyal to his own band. One night he vented his frustrations by melting a stack of Pretty Things records on the stove, hanging them on the wall and writing 'Fuck Off Pretty Things' in shaving foam on the mirrors. The Pretty Things had their own crazed inter-band relations – 'I remember one time I had Brian [Pendleton] up against the wall there,' says May, 'trying to strangle him' – but some of the Stones' internecine rivalries went well beyond that.

The situation could lead to cruelty, too. The choice of the Stones' follow-up to It's All Over Now was tough. That song had fallen into their lap, and marked new territory: it wasn't just the sound, its cynicism and put-down of uppity women would prove a template for the band's whole shtick. After initial objections, Oldham bought into the idea of releasing Little Red Rooster, the beautifully minimal Howlin' Wolf song written by Willie Dixon, which was a showcase for Brian's still-pioneering electric slide guitar. Brian was overjoyed by the prospect, mentioning several times to Viv Prince and Phil May that the band was headed for Regent Sound studio to record the song the next day. 'That's weird,' thought May, who'd just been chatting to Ian Stewart, 'I heard they were in the studio today.'

Stu picked up Brian in his van at the appointed time, and May and Prince went along for the ride. As they walked up the stairs to Regent Sound, and into the tiny studio, there was no sign of the rest of the band. 'But there was a note on the chair,' says May, 'saying, "Only play on these bits". They had done the whole thing, and left him to overdub. It was such a mean thing to do.'

For the first time Brian was 'frantic', according to May; 'it was unbelievable'. In later years, Stu, for all his anger with Brian, would say he was ashamed of the trickery, for which he blamed Mick. For outsiders like May, this was the first sign that the brutality Oldham and his favoured band member directed at rival bands and managers could also be turned on Oldham's least favourite band member. Yet Mick remained careful around Brian, rarely confronting him openly. Oldham, too, gave little away: 'he was hard to make out,' says Dawn Molloy, 'strange'. Hence Brian would be left guessing, never quite sure what was going on. Keith was different. With him the abuse was physical, to an extent that shocked outsiders. 'Keith would take the piss all the time,' says Dawn, 'but it was plain nasty. If something was going on, he'd pick a fight. They might be throwing things around – and he'd hammer it, throw things at Brian so it really hurt. He was nasty. It was very unhealthy.'

Ultimately, though, the struggles over who controlled the music were more damaging than the fights. 'Loogie, for me, was a bastard,' says May. 'Very good for them but a real bastard. Brutal. Jagger and Oldham were the absolute masters of that ruthless approach.'

*

That September recording session for Little Red Rooster was squeezed between more British tour dates, followed by another European jaunt with just a couple of days' breathing space after Paris for the band to ready themselves for some unfinished business: their second onslaught on America. The Stones still travelled as a tiny crew, but for this trip they were joined by a new recruit, road manager Mike Dorsey.

On 25 October, the band debuted on *The Ed Sullivan Show*; it was a raucous performance as they ripped through Around And Around and Time Is On My Side, the camera constantly cutting to the hysterical audience. Sullivan seemed to relish the chaos – the screams continued as he attempted to introduce the other acts – but a few days later the story surfaced that the outraged host had proclaimed, 'I promise you, they will never be back on my show.' The threat, soon withdrawn, generated vital publicity on the East Coast.

Just days later came an equally significant rite of passage on the West Coast: the TAMI show at the Santa Monica Civic Auditorium. It was a hip programme, and the Stones were up against the Godfather of Soul, James Brown, then at his peak. Brown was a pro, steeped in the gospel culture where a preacher could induce hysteria and fits in his congregation, honed by nine years of cut-throat competition on the chitlin circuit. The Stones, just one year into their pro career, fought back using Oldham's key tactics: bull-shit and adrenalin. Oldham held them back, keeping the crowd waiting – a delay that testified both to their terror at following Brown, and their snotty belief that they could do what they want, that the crowd could and would wait.

Toni Basil, part of the circle of the show's music director Jack Nitzsche and soon to be a renowned choreographer, was fast becoming a key member of the Sunset Strip cool crew – and also happened to be a doe-eyed, luminously attractive brunette. As the Stones delayed, pleading an equipment breakdown, she wondered how they could possibly follow one of the greatest performances she'd ever witnessed. But then the Stones walked on stage and hit the first chord, 'And I tell you, Mick jumped in the air and Brian did the most shocking thing I've ever seen – because I come from a vaudevillian family: Brian simply turned his back to the audience. Which was such a comment on where this group was coming from, breaking all the boundaries of how we ever thought music was performed.' Basil's reaction to Brian pretty much epitomized how the West Coast took to him. 'He was so extraordinary-looking,' she says, 'this blond hair, bright red sideburns, those green eyes, and he dressed so flamboyantly. And, wow, he was really a knockout.'

It wasn't just teenagers, like Kubernik's circle, or music scenesters like Nitzsche or Basil who loved Brian. LA's photographers and artists gravitated to him, too. Guy Webster, who shot *High Tide and Green Grass*, was typical in that 'I just got on with Brian the best'. Guy's father was Paul Francis Webster, the lyricist who'd written (for example) I Got It Bad And That Ain't Good. 'I was hip to the blues from an early age cos of my dad,' says Webster. 'I loved that they played it with this English twist. And Brian was the guy who championed all of that.' The band was likeable, but Brian was the one who 'reached out, who was easiest to get along with'.

The entire band launched themselves on to the LA scene, hanging out at RCA – the studio that Nitzsche told them put the dumps in London to shame – at the clubs on the Strip, like the Action, or the city's hip clothing outlets. But Brian was the one who'd go out solo, or accompanied by locals like Basil, Nitzsche and Wallace Berman, one of the city's hippest artists.

Berman, one of those iconic twentieth-century figures who

made it on to the cover of the Beatles' *Sgt Pepper* album alongside Adolf Hitler and Mahatma Gandhi, epitomized a distinct element of California cool. He was a cutting-edge collagist who'd already been sought out by London's best-connected gallery owner, Robert Fraser, who flew out to visit him early in 1964. Berman had hung with the Beats in the fifties, designed sleeves for Charlie Parker, and was friends with the actors Dennis Hopper and Dean Stockwell. Andy Warhol used to drop in when in LA, and filmed Berman alongside Hopper and Taylor Mead in *Tarzan and Jane Regained*. Yet Berman was unpretentious, an unerring judge of art, and kept a tiny house in a gorgeous location in Topanga Canyon.

After Berman was introduced to Brian by Toni Basil, his home, almost a one-room shack, became a regular refuge for the lonely Stone. Brian and his newest friend would sit talking, sipping wine, toking on joints, playing Berman's exhaustive collection of jazz vinyl, or Glenn Gould's latest interpretation of Bach, beyond the wee small hours and into the morning. Often, when Berman's son Tosh got up for school or his wife Betty was on her way to work, Brian would still be up talking. 'He went to my father's world to get away from Stones world,' says Tosh, who as an impressionable ten-year-old remembers Brian as a powerful presence. Mick, when Tosh met him, ruffled the youngster's hair; Brian, in contrast, treated him more like an equal, asking him questions. It was the same with Berman senior: endless exchanges of information, Brian asking him about his collages, the people on the art scene, who to check out, or sharing his take on Charlie Parker recordings. It was the same, too, when Brian ventured out to clubs with Toni Basil or Jack Nitzsche: he was the one searching out the unfamiliar, eager to learn.

Brian's nocturnal ramblings took him well out of the other Stones' orbit; he became more and more elusive, only occasionally allowing them into his world. When they did enter it, it was more disorientating and decadent than they were used to. Andrew Oldham remembers one long, sensuous night from that tour when he and Brian briefly bonded, in New York. Brian initiated Oldham into his world via a multiway carnality that echoes the sex games screenwriter Donald Cammell set up in *Performance*, Mick Jagger's film-acting debut. It was twenty-four hours that seemed to go on for ever, Oldham recalled later, involving three women and a supply of amyl nitrates: 'five became one, a sexual androgyny mystified, in one popper-driven phallic rush'.

During that same New York trip, Brian shocked the writer Al Aronowitz by mentioning his prowess with girls, and showing the respected scribe a dog leash he claimed he used in his erotic explorations. This wasn't empty boasting: Brian showed other people a leash, or chain, that he used in his sex games, including his old Cheltenham acquaintance Barry Miles, who of course remembers Brian being acquainted with the work of the Marquis de Sade. 'He was most definitely a sadist, one side of him,' says Miles. The side of Brian that wasn't sadistic was undoubtedly narcissistic – a condition hardly rare among rock stars, though Brian was an extreme example.

It was ironic that Brian bonded briefly with his manager in a whirlwind of sex and drugs for it was behaviour like this that would sever both of them from the band, as it exacerbated their tendency to manic depression. And sybaritic streaks don't mix with physical fragility. After his manic highs in New York and LA, Brian collapsed with exhaustion on his arrival in Chicago on 11 November; he was hospitalized and missed four shows. Stu, in particular, blamed the collapse on Brian's drug use and self-indulgence, and his contempt for the man increased. This was the second time the band played several dates without Brian – but this wasn't like the earlier time he'd let them down, for their success in the US was on a knife-edge. This time their resentment festered, and then spread. By the end of the tour, Brian was telling friendly journalists, 'I'm not on my last legs through ill health and I'm not leaving the band.'

At the end of November, Little Red Rooster, the record that embodied so much of Brian's vision, became a shock UK number 1. A few weeks later, recording at RCA in Los Angeles, Brian lit a fire under Mick and Keith's first proper Stones single. As Gered Mankowitz pointed out, in the studio, Brian still had the power.

It was the release of The Last Time on 26 February 1965 that formalized Mick Jagger and Keith Richards' assumption of power in the band Brian had created – a brilliant single, with gloriously arrogant lyrics set to an elegantly simple chord sequence and an insistent, unforgettable guitar riff. The single showcased Mick and Keith as snotty young geniuses. Which they were, although not as complete as the single suggested. The song itself owes much to a Staple Singers track Keith had heard back in Chicago, and the Staple Singers' version was based on an old gospel tune that they'd extensively reworked with a new harmonized chorus: 'This may be the last time, I don't know'. Mick and Keith's take on it lifted that line whole. The verse itself was a simple E, D, A chord sequence, rather like the Beatles' Rain, or hundreds of other songs. It was the spiralling, insistent guitar melody that made sense of the verse – and this line was Brian's. For all his irritating habits, he still had the gift of musical insight, making Keith and Mick's song sound better, twisting the knife in his own wound.

Brian's ability to reach inside a song and make sense of it would be commented on by many observers, people who worked closely with the Stones, like Jack Nitzsche and studio engineers Eddie Kramer and George Chkiantz (Mick and Keith have rarely, if ever, voiced such compliments). This makes his failure to write any songs with the Stones all the more puzzling. Gered Mankowitz expresses the view of many insiders when he says, 'He simply wasn't able to write material for the band'. Andrew Oldham suggests a simple reason: 'You can't write popular music looking down at it – and that's what Brian did.' Yet that's a nonsensical statement, given that Brian was probably the most eclectic of the Stones. 'He loved pop music as well as R&B,' says the Who's Pete Townshend, who became friendly with Brian from 1964. 'That's what appealed to me – I hated snobbery.' In reality, Brian lacked what other emerging songwriters, like George Harrison, possessed: a supportive environment. Eric Burdon, who didn't start writing his own songs until 1967, remembers how crucial that was: 'I needed some sort of enthusiasm from somewhere, cos I wasn't getting it from my band, and it turned out to be George Harrison who helped. I played this rough version of Sky Pilot, we talked, and that was the pat on the back I needed, to be more experimental. I needed that boost to my confidence.' James Phelge remembers Brian's first attempts at songs being met with retorts like 'that sounds like a bloody Welsh hymn!' In the early Stones material, Brian contributed countless key riffs and backing vocals; the course of his relationship with Oldham can be seen in the way these backing vocals are pulled down in the mix, after I Wanna Be Your Man, and then disappear completely.

Back in the winter of 1963/64, when Mick and Keith were working on their tentative compositions, Brian had come up with his own material, mysterious songs including Sure I Do and I Want You To Know, rumoured to exist as acetates. Brian contributed to the first Jagger-Richards songs – in particular it seems he wrote the haunting keyboard riff, played by Jack Nitzsche on the recorded version, on one of the Stones' first great original songs, Play With Fire. Thereafter he was simply cut out of the loop.

Why? Andrew Oldham's PR partner, Tony Calder, has the simplest explanation. 'Look – Andrew would have you believe he was the first one to realize Mick Jagger's potential. But I think it's simply that Andrew fancied Mick more than he did everybody else. Brian developed this thing that Andrew always favoured Mick – and he was absolutely right.'

In the very first days of the Jagger-Richards partnership there'd also be band compositions floating around, as well as the songs Brian had written more or less solo. 'There were definitely acetates of his stuff,' says Calder. 'I played one to Andrew and said, "This is not a bad song!" Andrew's response was "Fuck off!" And of course Mick wasn't interested in singing it. They were cruel. Cruel fuckers.'

The contrast with the Beatles was stark. John and Paul might patronize George, but they deferred to Brian Epstein, who was careful to run the Beatles as a partnership of equals. 'Brian was meticulous like that,' says Paul McCartney's friend Barry Miles, 'because he recognized, in part commercially, that each had their fans. In America, for instance, Ringo was the most popular for a while. They all had to have their time on a record, or in the films. But the Stones never had that kind of management style.' Oldham's shtick, in contrast to Epstein's, was to cut out other band members so that the 'Nanker Phelge' band credit was gradually wound down in favour of 'Jagger-Richards'.

Brian's own faults – his unreliability, his choice of accommodation and, as Phelge puts it, 'that stupid five quid' – were all reasons to reject his early attempts at songwriting. But it wasn't just Brian; in the wolf-pack's natural tendency to pick on the less dominant males, the lead Stones turned on Bill Wyman, too. The difference was that Bill rolled over, exposed his stomach, wasn't a threat. 'They did everything they could to unload Bill,' says Phil May, 'but he simply bit his lip and went through it. They tried to jettison him in the early days but he kept his head down and didn't make waves. Yet he was an integral part of the band!' In those early days, say May and Dave Thomson, the art student who became one of Brian's closest friends, it was Oldham who was most intent on cutting Brian out. 'I remember a journey back from Birmingham, and all the way back Andrew was, "It's time we got rid of him",' says Thomson. 'Mick was going along with it, and Keith was neither one way or the other. People talk about Brian's paranoia – but I was to find out his reasons were one hundred per cent genuine.'

Dawn Molloy, who was seeing Brian more and more often, recalls him as embattled but unbowed over that time. She particularly remembers Keith's hostility and occasional aggression, yet Brian's sense of humour – 'mischievous, kind of devilish' – sustained him. Dawn, who lived close to Chester Street, had become utterly besotted with Brian, who had used by now well-honed techniques to draw her in: he told her about Linda, how he loved her like a sister, his very openness a ruse. He knew how to talk, telling her about his childhood, asking about every detail of her own life, treating her as his own, fragile, valuable possession, and 'he was very, very sensual'. Dawn had no wiles to resist his power; but he was silly, funny, too. 'There were these funny things. For instance his hair kinks in a certain place, and he would get really annoyed by it. He'd always be meticulously clean, with clean shoes, and he couldn't really deal with a dirty hotel. Then he'd spend ages in the bathroom, inspecting himself . . . he used to get annoyed because underneath his hair, his sideburns were ginger.'

There was a childish, escapist aspect to Brian's naughtiness – he was 'devilish', but playfully so. But Dawn recognized the fragility, which meant he seemed particularly vulnerable to band rivalries and aggression. His psychological stamina already seemed insufficient. 'I was getting the sense he didn't like being in a pop group,' says Dawn. 'His mind was always going, he wanted to play music . . . it was sad there was no one there to protect him, to be his friend. I was sad for him sometimes. It was no fun.'

The pressures continued to mount into the spring of 1965 as the band completed a frenetic British tour, a brief trip to Copenhagen – where Brian saved Mick from electrocution by pulling out the plug on his microphone – and then to Paris, for three sell-out shows at the Olympia, opening Friday, 16 April.

Paris was fast becoming one of Brian's favoured haunts. It was in this city that another dark, heady element would be added to the already mind-bending Stones alchemy.

For the Olympia shows, the Stones shared a bill with the original Ziggy Stardust: second-string Brit rocker Vince Taylor, who had become massive in France and who would soon lose his marbles thanks to LSD, wander round Charing Cross Road obsessing about UFO landings and eventually run into a young David Bowie. Vince's percussionist was another wild child, Prince Stanislas Klossowski de Rola, the son of the painter Balthus – his impressive moniker usually shortened to 'Stash'. As usual, Brian was the reach-out Stone, and he got himself caught up in a wild weekend with Stash and an eclectic array of people that included Stash's model actress friend Anita Pallenberg, gallery owner Robert Fraser (yet another key figure in the Stones menagerie), French singer Françoise Hardy and the skinny, ravishingly elegant actress/singer Zouzou, all of whom wandered off to the Parisian nightclub Chez Castel.

Zouzou liked the look of Brian, but took pleasure in playing hard to get. As she took in his blond bob and languid charm, he fixed his gaze on her. 'I *love* that shirt,' he announced. 'Would you like to swap with mine?' He followed her to the toilet, repeating his request. The chat-up line had worked for Brian many times – it had won him more than a few girls and he'd also blagged quite a few shirts from boys too, for as an emerging dandy he reckoned he had a kind of droit de seigneur on cool clothing, borrowing choice items and never returning them. Zouzou wasn't impressed by the white acrylic polo neck that was Brian's current fashion staple 'but he wouldn't let me out of the toilets! So I said OK, give me yours.' Soon the two were staring into each other's eyes and murmuring quietly. Brian had obtained some potent grass from a source unknown which sent his imagination spiralling off into all kinds of bizarre, dark locations. 'I heard you had a cannibal restaurant [in Paris],' he asked a puzzled Zouzou at one stage.

It was a heady, confused rush of experiences. The atmosphere became headier still when the group moved on to a dinner party at the apartment of the writer and artist Donald Cammell, who would be a potent figure in Stones mythology, partly because he wrote the script for the movie *Performance.* A scion of the Scottish shipbuilding family, he'd hung out with the occultist Aleister Crowley as a kid, drawn beautiful illustrations for children's books in his teens, won a scholarship to the Royal Academy at sixteen and now, aged thirty-one, was a wannabe film director, arch manipulator and, some reckoned, an aspiring pimp.

It was at Stash's instigation, says the percussionist, that Anita Pallenberg was there. He had met her earlier in the summer: 'she was extraordinary – right from the first time I met her: I'd seen her asleep, looking dazzling. It was a very odd way of meeting some-body.' Brian was too engrossed in Zouzou to exchange more than a couple of words with Anita, but at Cammell's he ended up sitting next to Stash, who found him intense, charming, the Stone who could hold the deepest conversation. But he was also 'spooked', says Stash, who would become one of Brian's few true friends. The atmosphere in Cammell's exotic but sombre apartment had a marked effect on him. 'Who's that woman?' he asked Stash, pointing at Cammell's girlfriend, Deborah Dixon. 'She's so pale.' He repeated this over and over, his eyes flicking in her direction as he continued to spook himself, convinced that she was some sort of ghoul. 'It was an attack of the horrors,' says Stash. 'He was prone to it, especially when he was high. So he spent much of the evening terrified of this very, very beautiful woman.'

Zouzou also remembers the bizarre atmosphere, and Cammell trying to involve Brian in some kind of sex game with Anita, Brian laughing and putting Zouzou's hand on his heart, which was racing in fear or excitement. It was nearing dawn when he made his way back to his small hotel on the Rue des Capucins, with Zouzou in tow. When they arrived a small group of girl fans were waiting for him with their little Kodak Instamatics, and they managed to snap his photo – a blond, dark-eyed spectre in the Paris gloom.

Maybe the spooks were gathering. There was no rest before the band's third tour of North America, which opened in Montreal on 23 April, and it was after just a couple of days that Brian decided his endurance was at an end. With no one inside the band he could turn to, he decided simply to disappear. In a funk, pondering whether or not to quit, he took refuge with New York DJ Scott Ross, one of the Stones' most consistent champions on the East Coast. 'He was in a tail-spin. There was a lot of conflict between the three of them, Mick, Keith and Andrew on one side, and him on the other. A lot of backstabbing and a lot of criticism. He was the originator in that band, but with that triumvirate against him, he didn't have much of a chance.' Brian, it is said, was famously oversensitive. In *Life*, Keith blamed Brian's paranoia for his estrangement from the band, his belief that 'there was a conspiracy to roll him out. Which wasn't true at all.' Ross, a first-hand witness whose memory is in a good state, begs to differ. 'I like Keith,' he says, 'but I disagree. One time I was in a hotel room in New York, me and Brian in one room, and in the next there was Mick and Keith – both of them getting at him, ganging up on him. I don't think he was overreacting. He was simply outnumbered.'

With the Stones organization unaware of his location, Brian and Ross wrestled with his predicament while holed up in his apartment on West 85th, just off Central Park. The pair walked around the park, where Brian passed unrecognized, but Brian felt most secure simply sitting in the apartment.

'I can't play, I simply can't do it,' he informed Ross, with a blank finality. 'I can't record. It's all out of my control.'

'It's a big step, leaving the group. What do you want to do?' Ross asked him.

'I don't know.'

The pair discussed whether Brian should form his own band. 'He talked about doing bluesier music, but he hadn't thought it all through, it wasn't something he had nailed down. He just wanted out, to get away from the conflict.'

To Ross, who knew all the band well, 'I simply didn't know how to get it resolved. It was beyond any kind of resolution. I think that Andrew had poisoned the well of the relationship with Mick and Keith, and there was no chance of reconciliation.'

In the end, with no alternative, no way even to get home to Britain, Brian faced up to his demons and rejoined the band, in time for their appearance on *The Ed Sullivan Show*. But there was more resentment over his disappearance – 'attention-seeking behaviour' is what Andrew Oldham called it – which festered until the next crisis just days later, on 6 May in Clearwater, Florida. As usual, Bill and Brian invited girls up to their motel rooms after the show. In the morning, Brian's girl appeared in tears telling the band that Brian had hit her. The other Stones asked roadie Mike Dorsey 'to sort him out. And I did,' says Dorsey. Bill remembers Dorsey pummelling Brian's ribs, cracking a couple, but Dorsey describes a more sophisticated punishment: 'He used to wear a belt and an Indian collar. I held him by the collar and belt out the hotel window and said, "If you ever do that again, I'll drop you." '

This wasn't the first instance of violence. Although Brian had never hit her, Pat Andrews remembers one time when she was in physical fear of him, back in Cheltenham. 'I'd been talking to a couple of guys I knew from somewhere, and he got very jealous. He did want to hit me.' Pat ascribed Brian's extreme jealousy to insecurity – 'I couldn't figure out why he was like that . . . until I met his parents.' Linda Lawrence, Scott Ross and others insist that, if he did occasionally lash out in 1964 and 1965, his behaviour was no worse than his fellow Stones. 'It was normal behaviour, like teenagers pushing people's buttons,' says Linda. 'And they were all doing it, even though everyone talks now as if it was just him.'

Whether that explanation is true or not, Brian's innate tendency to jealousy and aggression was exacerbated by his drinking. Keith Altham, later the Stones' PR and a good friend of Ian Stewart, came to share Stu's dismissal of Brian's demons, drink and insecurity: 'It was that old thing – they're drunk and don't know what they're doing. But that's an excuse – and you can't go on excusing some-body for bad behaviour. I think there was a kind of selfishness about him that was part of his downfall.'

As Brian nursed his wounds, and his humiliation, there came a potent symbol of that downfall. For it was at the Clearwater motel that Keith woke up in the middle of the night with a tune in his head, put it on tape, then went back to sleep. Keith wasn't con-vinced by the song: he worried it was a one-riff wonder, or that it was a rip-off of another tune he'd heard. Later he mentioned it was

Martha Reeves and the Vandellas' Dancing In The Street. In fact the main riff was taken directly from the Vandellas' Nowhere To Run, as indeed was the rhythm, complete with the exhilarating, stomping, on-beat drums of the definitive take of (I Can't Get No) Satisfaction, which the band nailed at RCA on 12 May after an abortive first attempt at Chess. Brian voted for Satisfaction as a single, against the objections of both Mick and Keith, depending on who you believe.

The blaring fuzzed guitar line marked Keith's ascendance as a sonic innovator. There was subtlety there, too, the way the lead guitar riff elegantly morphed into a rhythm pattern – an indication of how, with endless practice, Keith was now outstripping Brian as a guitarist. More significantly, the lyrics, stripped down, cynical and subversive, marked Mick's ascendance as the band's spokesman, for their impact exceeded anything Brian, Mick or even Andrew Oldham could deliver in a press interview.

Satisfaction was the perfect encapsulation of Brian's problems: it brought money flooding in and, more importantly, a cultural impact of which he'd long dreamed, but at the heavy price of losing the leadership of the band he'd created. There are stories he hated the song so much that he'd play Popeye The Sailor Man during live renditions. That wasn't the reason, says Keith: 'Oh no, I used to join in with him. It was like, why not, they won't know the difference.' Brian's relationship with Mick was similarly conflicted. Brian remained essentially loyal even as Mick threatened to supplant him, never voicing his frustrations in public. But in one pivotal show, one that exemplified all his achievements to date, the frustrations spilled over. Still, the backstage bickering couldn't prevent the enormity of the effect Brian Jones had on the world.

It was on 20 May 1965 that Brian Jones built a bridge over a cultural abyss and connected America with its own black culture.

The founder Stone introduced Chester Burnett, aka Howlin' Wolf, on ABC's *Shindig!* and thus engineered an event that fulfilled just about every ambition of his twenty-three-year-old life. This was truly a life-changing moment, both for the American teenagers clustered round the TV in their living rooms, and for a generation of blues performers who had been stuck in a cultural ghetto.

Ken Kubernik, the West Coast teenager who was watching that evening, was one of millions of kids who knew names like Chester Burnett and McKinley Morganfield only from the writing credits on the first Stones albums. He was part of a generation that was 'primed' for this moment: 'Seeing Brian on that show, introducing Howlin' Wolf to a white teeny-bopper audience, it was like Christmas morning for us. The next day in school, that was all anyone talked about. I don't think there's been anything that radical on TV since then. This was a profound paradigm shift – the Stones in general, Brian in particular, introducing our own culture, back to an entire generation of baby boomers. We'd have had no possibility of being exposed to Howlin' Wolf or Muddy Waters without them.'

Brian was a figure unlike anything previously seen on American TV, introducing another man who was just as unfamiliar and strange. With his long blond hair and soft-spoken, sincere manner, he was a spectacle quite unlike any of the quip-firing Beatles, the only real Brits Kubernik's generation knew about. 'We started because we wanted to play rhythm and blues,' he informed interviewer Jimmy O'Neill, 'and Howlin' Wolf was one of our greatest idols.' More than any other moment, Brian hogged the limelight. He was the champion of the rarest R&B, the boy who'd given his life up for it, and he wasn't letting Mick take any of the credit. As O'Neill asked Mick to add a few words, the Stones' ex-leader interrupted, 'It's about time we shut up and we had Howlin' Wolf on stage!' and the camera panned to the towering presence of Chester

Burnett, asking America's teenagers, 'How many more years I'm gonna let you dog me around?'

To this day, there are those who can't quite believe that the USA's first exposure to hardcore blues on mainstream media was all due to a bunch of foreigners. It's a hard fact to stomach for many Americans. Of course, there had been champions of black music before, visionaries such as John Hammond and Alan Lomax; Paul Butterfield had started guesting with blues musicians like Smokey Smothers in 1963, recruiting Wolf's drummer Sam Lay to his band later that year. Butterfield's was a significant step, but it wasn't a breakthrough, like *Shindig!* All the Chess musicians, including Sam Lay and Buddy Guy, who played guitar on Wolf's immortal song Killing Floor, were well aware that this mass exposure to a white audience was epochal. 'It was the light at the end of the tunnel,' says Guy. 'There was a boundary line which no one thought could be crossed, and the Rolling Stones broke it by getting Wolf on that show.' Peter Guralnick, the dean of American blues writers, agrees: 'I've listed it as one of the Top Ten TV moments of all time, one of the most significant moments in cultural history – part of a wonderful movement that couldn't be turned back.'

The resonance of the event was underscored by the presence of the bluesman Son House at the recording. Brian walked over to Son's manager, Dick Waterman, to ask who the venerable gentleman was. When told, he let out a sigh: 'Ah, the man who knew Robert Johnson and Charley Patton.'

Kids like Buddy Guy had left the South at a time when its representatives, led by Georgia senator Richard Russell, were successfully filibustering attempts to prevent lynchings and introduce civil rights. It took the murder of John Kennedy and the masterly politicking of Lyndon Johnson to pass basic civil rights legislation, albeit in a watered-down form, in the summer of 1964. Brian Jones sat at Wolf's feet at a time when many restaurants in the South would have refused him service. For a hip English rock group to champion Chicago blues, uncompromising music aimed at a black audience, was a radical, epoch-changing step, both for baby boomer Americans and the musicians themselves. Fourteen- and fifteen-year-old kids like Ken Kubernik hardly understood the growth of civil rights; but they could understand the importance of a handsome English man who described the mountainous, gravel-voiced bluesman as a 'hero' and sat smiling at his feet. If any moment epitomized the life work of Brian Jones, this – in all its sexiness and purity – was it.

Later in the show, the Stones got to mime Little Red Rooster. For most of the time the camera focused on Mick. But still that slide guitar rang out, unmistakably the sound of change.

It's a quiet night, for once, at Buddy Guy's club on the edge of the old Chicago South Side, the swaggering, smelly area over which Wolf and Muddy once vied for leadership. The smooth face and wondering, uncynical demeanour of the city's one-time young Turk bely his years. There's something entrancingly optimistic about his story, of how a kid who grew up playing a diddley bow – a one-string guitar nailed to the side of a shed – grew up to earn the respect of the President of the United States. His life is filled with many moments of wonder, and the night that Howlin' Wolf was beamed into millions of American households – that light at the end of the tunnel – was one of the most significant. 'It was something we would never even have thought of,' says Buddy. 'The hairs were just standing on my head.'

There are all too few interviews on the record with Howlin' Wolf to reveal his feelings that evening. Wolf was a fascinating figure, an intimidating presence who studied at night school, hired classical music tutors for his band members, and tapped right into the deepest, most profound heart of the blues. Buddy was a confidant of the big man, and remembers how the event affected him. 'We talked about it later. He said about how the man next door don't know who I am – and here's some British kids from thousands of miles away.' Wolf was friendly with the Stones, but somewhat guarded. Only with the younger Chess musicians, like Buddy, did he reveal what a profound moment this was in the venerable bluesman's life. 'I know he was proud of what happened,' says Buddy, 'cause as far as the record companies or the news media or anything, we were all ignored until those kids came in.'

It was a mere three years since Brian Jones had set out to champion his beloved R&B. However embattled he was, this was something real. A movement that couldn't be turned back.

6

Paranoia Meter

S HOULD I STAY? Should I go? How many of us delay that decision until it's too late to matter?

It is no surprise that Brian Jones, a man who enjoyed confront-ation but hated making decisions, would end up being pushed rather than jumping from the Rolling Stones juggernaut. Yet his senses had told him the right moment to jump, right at the beginning of 1965. Only one thing seemed to stop him: the people who were pushing.

It was an impressive Chelsea mews flat, a prototype for how all rock stars' pads should look: Moroccan carpets, walls crammed with artworks, records stacked at the side, dandyish clothes draped over antique chairs, and a woman cached in a side room. Brian, too, was the prototype of a sixties rock star: languid, softly spoken, almost effete, a charming blond choirboy with something of the night about him.

'Sorry, did I keep you waiting?' he asked Chris Welch, clucking around him attentively and yelling 'Sorry for the mess!' as he disappeared into the kitchen, emerging minutes later with two cups of Earl Grey, no milk, before sitting down to talk.

They huddled around the fan heater, listened to a bagful of singles Welch had brought along, Brian recognizing most of the artists and producers after a few seconds and debating the merits of Geoff Love or Mike Leander as arrangers, or picking out what style of harmonica Stevie Wonder played.

Welch had become mates with both Mick and Brian over the two years he'd covered them for *Melody Maker*. They were joint leaders of the Stones, he reckoned. He liked the way Mick would deflect a tricky question with a joke, his ambition veiled behind the humour. Brian was very different, more anarchic, unafraid of voicing controversial opinions, riffing on how Londoners were too neurotic and how he'd like to live in Australia. But most of all he talked about life outside the Stones. 'I'm soaking in the feel of the business at the moment,' he told Welch, 'but I want to produce records. In America. Who would I record? Any sort of pop artist.'

Welch realized the remarks about life outside the Stones were the real point of the interview, which had been planned as a guest review slot – that the idea was being tested on him. He thought it was a good one. In the topsy-turvy English scene, change was exciting. But for Brian, someone else would ring the changes.

Not that the Stones were sundered by some evil masterplan. Andrew Oldham didn't set out to unseat Brian, as his PR partner Tony Calder points out: 'It wasn't hate. It was just that Andrew only had eyes for Mick, and Andrew's supreme talent was that he could manipulate Mick.' It was more the lack of a plan, the obsession with making it quickly before everything fell apart, that meant no one took much account of the long-term future. Except Eric Easton and Brian, who discussed what Brian would do when it all blew over. It was Easton who spoke regularly to Chris Welch: like quite a few journalists, Welch trusted him more than the volatile, aggressive Oldham. And in the spring of 1965, Easton set out to push Brian back into the limelight. 'That interview was set up to take the spotlight away from Mick and Keith,' says Welch. '[Brian] was aiming to set himself up as a solo figure. That's why he was talking about working as a producer beyond the Stones.'

Easton, the older, old-school half of the Stones' management team, was Brian's main confidant within the band. 'There was this camaraderie, and understanding between them,' says Linda Lawrence. Easton was the only man Brian could trust to help float the idea of a solo career. But within weeks of the meeting with Welch, Easton was history, as was any prospect of his support for Brian.

Staying with the Stones allowed Brian to craft, to define, some of the most beautiful pop records of the sixties, but it would come at a terrible cost. The Stones' complex, nasty internal dynamics have been debated for decades, Keith Richards and Bill Wyman, for instance, giving drastically different interpretations of Brian's conduct. Brian's mistakes were indeed legion; yet in hindsight, his inability to jump off the juggernaut as it built momentum was the greatest of them. If Brian had formed his own purist blues outfit in the latter half of 1965, using friends like Paul Jones or Steve Winwood as guest vocalists, introducing exotic instrumentation and Islamic or Indian influences into the mix, he would have been perfectly placed for the second blues boom, kicked off by albums like John Mayall's *Blues Breakers* (a Top Ten LP in 1966) and continued by Peter Green's Fleetwood Mac, a band that started with purist blues songs then branched out to write their own material.

Paul Jones, the man who turned down a job as singer in Brian's band, was well aware of Brian's shortcomings, his overemphasis on being leader of the pack, his fastidiousness. He too shares the sense that if Brian had retained control of his own band and he had joined up with him, Brian 'may never have become quite so rich, or quite so famous – but he might have still been alive'.

Without managerial support, Brian's fantasies of launching his own band withered away. Lack of confidence was undoubtedly a factor, and in an act of bitter irony, it seems his decision to stay was partly inspired by more open attempts to dislodge him. Whatever the mix of motivations, with Easton gone he would never jump off a juggernaut that was picking up speed.

Zouzou was now Brian's most consistent girlfriend, staying in the mews flat at 7 Elm Park Lane, just off the Fulham Road (Brian was the first Stone to fix on Chelsea, which soon became an obligatory rock star hangout). When she came over from Paris in the summer to stay with Brian, she found him upbeat, 'wonderful, making me laugh all the time. He really was joking, laughing, full of energy. He was drinking a bit much, that's the only thing I could say.'

Brian was almost indecently good at building a rapport, one of those people who bind you to them by insatiably gathering information. 'He would call me up, was very curious – he wanted to know, was I sleeping on my right side or my left side, my belly or my back, all these crazy things that don't mean anything; all about my parents, if I was happy.' When Zouzou stayed over, they built their own silly routine. Brian didn't have a cleaner, so they created little games to make the housework more interesting. 'I was the captain of a ship. I would give him orders: you do this, you have to wash this part, like this. So it was very fun.' Only Brian's morbid narcissism and mood swings spoiled their on-off domestic harmony. 'Sometimes he was very depressed because he didn't like his eyes, the bags under his eyes, and he's asking me, shall I get a [plastic] surgeon! Sometimes he was laughing about it – but he was moody sometimes. He could be very upset, cry like a baby. Then suddenly he's starting to laugh and joke. He was up and down very often.'

As 1965 rolled on, Brian's mental state became steadily more volatile. There are a couple of versions of when he first dropped acid, but there's no doubt that he was the first Stone to do so. It's possible he discovered the drug via Robert Fraser, the London gallery owner who'd become a key figure in his circle, but it's more likely he dropped his first tab on the way to a club on Sunset Boulevard on 16 May, just a few days before the *Shindig!* show. Even in an altered state, though, threats were omnipresent. 'He said the whole ground was covered with snakes,' recalls Bill Wyman. 'He jumped along the pavement trying to avoid them.' The snakes would become a leitmotif, says Marianne Faithfull, who was encountering the Stones more often from around this time. '[His] paranoiac condition worsened on acid. Everyone would be looning about, and Brian would be over in the corner, crumpled up.' Yet Brian seemed to embrace these horrors, savour them almost. He'd dropped acid again when the band hit New York a few days later, and became something of an evangelist, pressing others to try it. One of the psychedelic season's most committed spokesmen, Eric Burdon, remembers being turned on, probably at Brian's hands, at the New York club Ondine's on 29 May: 'I was in the middle of the dancefloor among a bunch of people when someone pushed by me and said, "Here, try this." It was a sugar cube, and I think it came from Brian Jones. It blew my head open; it was like going straight into [the Beatles'] Day In The Life. I embraced it fully. I thought it was a way of changing humanity.'

Brian was busy that weekend, hanging out with both Burdon and the Animals' guitarist Hilton Valentine, turning Valentine on to acid too. 'Brian asked if I had ever tried LSD. I told him no and asked him what it was. He said it was just like hash but stronger and proceeded to hand me a sugar cube. We both popped one in our mouths and went off to the club.' The guitarists were kindred spirits. 'Brian was shy,' says Valentine, 'like me. I did like him – he was the only one from the Stones that bothered to reach out.' Burdon and Valentine got on with Brian in a way that, if you believed the accounts of people like Andrew Oldham and Ian Stewart, should have been impossible, given their description of him as pretentious and selfish. Burdon, like Phil May before him, blames the Stones' competitive streak: 'There was the band, the Stones, and there was Brian, on the outside. I actually think he handled drugs well – I don't think he was an acid casualty. I just think Brian had his own reasons for opting out.' Yet as Valentine points out, the Animals (like the Pretty Things) weren't that different: 'It's just too much to expect five people to be with each other for extended periods of time without something blowing up. Eric and I were taking all kinds of acid and the others didn't like that, but we thought they drank way too much. Add our manager stealing our money into the mix, and *boom*.'

Boom. The Animals' own story was uncomfortably close in some respects to that of the Stones, with bitter feuds, a mysterious death and vanishing fortunes. But the Stones story is bigger, not least owing to the appearance of a manager who wanted to control not one band but the entire British scene, a rapacious outsider whose art was money and whose genius lay in knowing how to hustle a hustler.

Allen Klein was hard-working, aggressive and boasted gangster smarts that entranced naive Brits like Andrew Oldham and John Lennon. Lennon would famously fall out with Klein, and mocked his legendary BO in one of his finest latter-day songs, Steel And

Glass ('you leave your smell like an alley cat'). In contrast, Oldham still seems strangely enchanted by the man whose estate now controls all the music he made with the Stones. 'There is, and will only ever be, one Allen Klein,' he says.

Klein's upbringing was fractured, like Oldham's, but way less cushy. Born in Newark, New Jersey, in 1931, Klein was brought up in an orphanage, took evening classes in accountancy and made his way into music publishing via hard graft. By the time Oldham first encountered him, Klein was intent on securing at least a slice of the British invasion. Klein played the much younger Oldham like a pro, appealing to him on both a practical level – he could refashion the band's finances and truly break them in the US – and tapping into his fantasies: Oldham could become a recording visionary and a record company owner. Oldham took the bait, hook, line and sinker.

Within days of meeting Klein, Oldham appointed him as his business manager, then started persuading Mick and Keith to make him the band's co-manager. After several secret get-togethers between Klein and the Oldham-Jagger-Richards triumvirate, an agreement was presented to the remaining Stones as a done deal, and Eric Easton was summarily sacked (his lawsuits would drag on for years). 'I was the lone voice to express reservations,' Bill Wyman would say in *Stone Alone*. Brian also missed Easton, the half of the Stones management he could talk to. Jeff Dexter, who worked with both Oldham and Tony Calder, speaks for many when he says, 'Given what Andrew actually had at that time, it just shows how lacking in self-belief he really was. He'd always had that fantasy of trying to be someone else – and he looked up to the dodgiest American. To allow a cunt like that to come in and take it all . . . it's unforgivable.'

In trademark fashion, the news of the change was announced via

huge interviews with Oldham and Klein, who considered themselves just as press-worthy as their band. In August 1965, Oldham
used his regular *Disc and Music Echo* column to announce the
launch of Immediate Records, aided by 'my two friends, Mick
Jagger and Keith Richard [*sic*]'. Eric Easton attempted to retaliate
with his own half of the story, but was frozen out by the music
press. 'He was sad and despondent,' says Chris Welch, who interviewed Easton about the split but had his story spiked. 'News editor
Ray Coleman's ethos was, we only talked to winners, not losers.'
That ethos, Welch believes, was inspired by Oldham. 'As you can
see, the sixties wasn't all peace and love.'

Klein had offered Oldham the irresistible prospect of his own
empire: films, a record label, a bigger stable of artists. Although this
was bad news for Brian, Oldham's grandiose schemes did produce
some fringe benefits. Back in March, a striking woman had arrived
at a London party attended by Brian and Oldham. The woman,
born Christa Päffgen but who would be forever known as Nico,
marched up to Oldham and impressed him with her deadpan cool,
talk of her role in Federico Fellini's *La Dolce Vita*, and her friendship with Bob Dylan. Then she noticed Brian Jones staring at her.
'Let's meet up again, and talk careers,' he told her.

Maybe Brian met his match in the self-styled 'Nazi anarchist
junkie'. Four years older than Brian and several inches taller, Nico
had grown up in Berlin's post-war wasteland and was an ambitious
enigma, an expert in the art of evasion. She claimed already to be
experienced in the dark sexual arts, mentioning to many that she
preferred anal intercourse – 'I like it the Turkish way: my father was
Turkish' – yet in the package of notes she left for biographer
Richard Witts, she claimed that Brian Jones was the more decadent,
bedding her in a room with ceremonial candles, then dripping hot
wax on to her, using a loaded gun as a dildo, piercing her labia with

163

a brooch pin when he was high, and slapping or hitting her in sex games that went out of control, leaving bruises. It's possible that some of the stories were true. Zouzou, who knew Nico well, maintains, 'Nico, he was scared to death of. One time we were in the Ad Lib [club], he was telling me, "If you see Nico let me know right away, cos she will jump on me!" I said, "You're big enough to look after yourself!" So no way. Maybe she had [Brian] one time then, but of course he would not tell me.'

Nico and Brian did meet up again, in LA in May around the time of the *Shindig!* show. She remembered Brian talking of his fascination with Aleister Crowley, widely acclaimed as the 'wickedest man in the world', and one-time acquaintance of Donald Cammell. Nico later told a journalist, 'Did you know Brian was a witch? We were interested in these things. Mick knew and was his enemy.' At other times she changed her story, theorizing that Brian's fascination with the occult was merely a cover story for his sexual experimentation.

The pair used each other, twin masters in mendacity, but Brian was true to his word in that they did 'talk careers'. With Brian on guitar, alongside house producer Jimmy Page, Nico's recording debut, I'm Not Sayin', would be one of the first batch of singles released on Oldham's Immediate label, alongside the McCoys' Hang On Sloopy. The McCoys single was a huge hit that summer, whereas Nico's twee version of the Gordon Lightfoot song sank without trace. But the venture served its purpose: Nico's face helped make Immediate hip, and when Brian introduced Nico to Andy Warhol in New York that November, the single became her entrée to a job with the Velvet Underground.

Nico would talk often of Brian over the years. She painted him as a potent figure – 'he gave the best sex', she pronounced, better than Jim Morrison – but opined that he never reached his full potential. He was gifted and could have made his own music but was also lazy: 'I kept saying that, but he called me a nag.' In her telling, Brian's obsessive pursuit of carnal pleasures was enough explanation for his failure to branch out on his own. Yet somehow, in her story, that gives him greatness too: he was an untameable being who could never become, like Mick, a conventional careerist.

Nico's observations would get rolled up into Brian's mythology. Her unreliable memories suggest his fascination with the occult pre-dated his involvement with Anita Pallenberg, the woman who friends of Brian's like Marianne Faithfull and fellow dandy Christopher Gibbs agree seemed to 'know all about witchcraft'. Brian was indeed interested in Aleister Crowley, confirms Stash Klossowski, who also got to know him that year. 'Especially with psychedelics being involved, there was a definite all-pervading presence of the occult, and its potentiality.'

Brian's status as an 'adept', or some form of witch, was confirmed by the presence of a third nipple situated on his inner thigh, according to the film-maker and Crowley acolyte Kenneth Anger and at least one of Brian's lovers. It was Brian's dark powers, once he'd teamed up with Anita Pallenberg, that made him 'the occult unit of the Stones', Anger reckoned. Others, as we shall see, believe he had certain gifts of insight. But those close to him suggest that, rather than devoting himself to Satan, Brian fixed on a more nuanced and benign deity, namely the god Pan. The Greek god of fertility, half goat, half man, Pan was quite literally demonized with the advent of Christianity, but he was essentially a benevolent entity. To Brian, Pan embodied the spirit of rock'n'roll, says Stash, who explains how in Greek myth, King Midas was called upon to judge a contest between the stirring, syncopated music of Pan's pipes and the elevated, pure melodies of Apollo's lyre. It turned out, to Apollo's rage, that Midas couldn't resist the lascivious sound of the pipes. 'The rock'n'roll spirit,' Stash asserts, 'comes from Pan.'

The legend echoed the stories that Brian had studied about the blues – how it was the Devil's music; how in the dark nights of Mississippi musicians dreamt of the Devil, thought he was the one who inspired their best songs. As a forbidden god who played the pipes and revelled in his own fertility, Pan was a figure to identify with for a man who'd wandered far from home with a guitar and already spawned a number of children. Others saw the parallels, too: Marianne Faithfull, who understood Brian and empathized with him while all too conscious of his faults, described him later as 'a voluptuous, over-ripe god . . . gone to seed'. Yet the powers of Pan, while short of satanic, are none the less dark and potent. 'Pan is a very dangerous sort of power,' says Stash. 'The word "panic" comes from the name Pan. It's significant that Brian was attracted by the notion of Pan, and at the same time in awe. Awe is the right word.'

Brian's interests and obsessions would come to define the Rolling Stones for ever. His fascination with chaos, dark forces and lasciviousness would permeate the band's music and image; Mick and Keith would follow in his wake. Dancing with the devil would come at a high cost. In the process, though, they'd make great art.

The Stones juggernaut shuddered and picked up speed that summer of 1965 when Satisfaction became their first US number 1 – it hit the top of the charts on 10 July. Relationships and locations remained as fluid as ever, for the band and its founder. In June, after the close of the band's third US tour, Keith was due to move into his new flat, 5 Ambassador House in St John's Wood, but it was delayed. Mick headed for 13a Bryanston Mews, after a brief stay with the photographer David Bailey, while Keith, after a few days at the Hilton, moved in with Brian – a demonstration that, as ever, the power balance within the band continued to oscillate.

At some of the parties that summer, Keith could be seen laughing at Mick and Oldham, the two ambitious characters whom emerging heads were starting to mock openly as the dope and acid was being passed around. At other times the pendulum swung the other way, as on that secret trip to meet Allen Klein in August. Keith and Oldham had gone for a schmooze on Klein's yacht with Bobby Vinton, the *NME*'s Chris Hutchins and a bunch of friends. They were making their way upriver to Shea Stadium for the Beatles' landmark show. It was a momentous, thrilling occasion, and Hutchins was enjoying the party buzz when he joined Klein, Oldham and Keith on the bridge. 'I walked in, and they were discussing how they could get rid of Brian. I don't mean kill him . . . they were discussing how they could ease him out of the band.' Hutchins knew all about Oldham's contradictory moods, that 'manic grandiosity', but he was shocked to hear the subject being raised. It was 'mean', but most of all, he knew it would damage the band: 'He was such a major factor in the Stones. But I think he was a bit heavy for them. He was really serious about music, and about life.'

Brian was certainly always ready to seek out new experiences, but things were never straightforward. He'd do great, profound things in a flaky way, his first trip to Morocco that August being a good example.

Brian had kept in fairly close contact with Linda Lawrence. He'd told her she was 'too good for him' but had turned up for the birth of their son, Julian, on 23 July 1964. Linda had known about his relationship with Dawn Molloy, but even when Brian had moved out to Chester Street 'I was always hopeful we'd be making up'. So when Brian invited her to join him on a visit to Tangier, her heart leapt again, though she soon realized 'he was trying to help me expand my own life – and to move on'.

The pair stayed at the El Minzah in Tangier along with Robert Fraser, who had probably suggested the exotic destination. Brian's old bête noire Deborah Dixon, the woman he'd thought was a ghoul, was there too, as was Donald Cammell. There were some idyllic trips, and at one old palace Linda and Deborah did a photo shoot; this was where Brian probably first met the artist Brion Gysin, a friend of Bob Fraser's. The stay was marred by press intrusion and mixed messages, but Brian's intent was clear, says Linda: 'He had explained we weren't going to be together, but he wanted me to meet people who might be able to help me with my career. It was mainly a positive thing. Then he went off again, and Robert Fraser invited me to London.'

Linda turned up at one of Fraser's parties in London, and the gallery owner slipped LSD into her drink. Then came a trip to Paris with Cammell and Dixon; the pair bought her beautiful clothes and lingerie, and introduced her to Anita Pallenberg. Eventually, Linda began to feel 'uncomfortable – Donald was definitely trying to set up some sort of sexual scene'. Linda wasn't tempted by the idea, returned to London, and gave up on her hopes of Brian.

With the notable exception of Andrew Oldham, many people around the Stones liked Linda and saw her as a stabilizing influence. Certainly, where Linda resisted temptation, Brian jumped in. All the way.

The advent of Allen Klein brought not so much a change in the atmosphere around the Stones as an intensification of it. There'd always been the obsession with gangsterism, inspired mainly by Oldham, who saw thugs like Don Arden as a role model; yet Brian, and Keith too, were just as fascinated by unsavoury characters. Klein guaranteed airplay for the band in the States, 'but we didn't want to ask about how exactly it was done', says Gered Mankowitz, for insiders were certain Klein boasted Mafia connections. Brian, the Robert Johnson fan, was more aware than anyone of the Faustian implications of the deals that were being made. And he, more than anyone, revelled in the darkness that was gathering, in the embryonic Swinging London's combination of aristocratic decadence and gangster chic.

Robert Fraser – 'Groovy Bob' – was the embodiment of London's emerging scene, and would be Brian's companion for much of the next two years. Bob emerged from what was a comparatively nouveau riche family: his grandfather was Gordon Selfridge's butler, but his banker father Lionel was the archetypal self-made man who in 1945 became a Companion of the Order of St Michael and George and later funded Robert's education at Eton. It was at Eton that Robert became friends with Christopher Gibbs, who owned a hip antique shop, was one of the aristocracy's leading dandies, and would also become a Stones intimate over the course of 1965. Gibbs's reminiscences of Fraser have some obvious resonances with the life of Brian Jones. 'Robert was my friend from the age of thirteen, or something like that,' says Gibbs. 'He was an extraordinary, mercurial being, very sharp antennae for what was happening in music, film, painting, writing, anything creative. And then, quite efficiently, he dulled all those sensibilities and did himself in. He was a great experimenter, took all those drugs before anyone else thought of it. Then he got HIV before anyone else thought of it, and died, before anyone could really treat that terrible affliction.'

As well as collecting art, Groovy Bob collected people – by the end of 1964 he'd already become friends with Cammell, Dixon, Pallenberg, Hopper and Berman. Brian and Mick were two of the most treasured additions to his collection. The old aristocracy was teaming up with the new aristocracy. 'Bob, Chris, they were nurturing these guys,' says Michael Rainey, who became Brian's friend around the same time, 'so they could have them . . . so they could become part and parcel of some secret little cabal.' Rainey in turn came from celebrated stock: he was the son of the party-loving society figure Marion Wrottesley, was well known for his eye-catching yet elegant style, and in October 1966 became one half of the young aristocracy's hippest power couple when he married Jane Ormsby-Gore, contributing editor of *Vogue* and daughter of Lord Harlech. As the two sets cosied up, Rainey was a fly on the wall. 'The music was the equalizer,' he says. 'The pop aristocracy – the Beatles, the Stones – were beginning to mingle, not just with the aristocracy but with people outside their own class. It was like birds of paradise, where the two separate sides do these little dances and when they get into position they can sit and natter. And things were said in between the lines.'

Rainey loved Brian as a fellow dandy. He watched both Brian and Mick make their way into this new milieu with diametrically opposed motivations. Brian wanted to experiment, seek out new experiences; Mick seemed desperate to join the aristocracy. Rainey despised this dull and conventional ambition. He believed he hung around with Jane Ormsby-Gore hoping she'd elevate him in society. 'I think he wanted that leg-up, and my wife kind of liked collecting these young boys, as her followers – this was before we were married.'

In exactly the way he boasted of his fling with Pat Andrews, Mick loved to flaunt his conquests, real or imagined. This was all part of the misogyny around the Stones. Brian was certainly not innocent, but Mick's actions were more considered, designed to maintain his status as top dog. Soon his name and Jane's were being publicly linked – it's generally thought that Lady Jane referred to her – and Mick seemed to relish the effect it had on Rainey. Rainey detested his 'cockiness', but he also noticed how quickly Mick learned. 'Mick was being taught how to deal with people's emotions, or men's insecurities. And he [planned he] was going to be somewhere, in the higher echelons of society. Brian wasn't of that ilk, he didn't work like that.'

A little social climbing was to be expected; but Rainey believed Mick's was excessive. He remembers Mick describing a stately home he'd just visited. He adored it, he told Rainey. 'It's got the most wonderful Georgian chinoiserie wallpaper.'

'I remember thinking, Gosh, you have learned fast,' says Rainey.

As he watched all this jockeying for position, Rainey never heard Brian complain about being gradually frozen out. He suggests that this was 'because he could never quite put his finger on what was happening. Obviously Mick, Oldham, maybe Keith, were in a little cabal of their own. With him as the victim. There's a secret between the three of you, and he knows it – but only by osmosis.'

In retrospect, the signs were obvious for all to see when the group resumed work in September, with two dates in Ireland which were captured by director Peter Whitehead for the movie *Charlie Is My Darling*. A riveting document, it epitomizes Andrew Oldham's erratic brilliance. Oldham could spot talent in the raw, and in Whitehead he picked out a future giant in his field. 'Andrew was ruthless; and he was brilliant. He gave me total freedom, absolutely total freedom. I met him on the Monday, he knew about [Whitehead's movie] *Wholly Communion* . . . then it was, OK, we're rolling on Friday morning.'

Whitehead would make many widely respected films, but *Charlie Is My Darling* has a force and simplicity all of its own. It depicts a cataclysmic psychic energy being released, and it shows how each of the protagonists struggles to adapt to this momentous force. The sketch of Brian in particular is fascinating – intimate, poetic and laden with portents. Captured just as he was dreaming of manning the escape pod, today it evokes both his rise and terrible fall.

Whitehead had expected to document a fascinating phenomenon, but when the cameras rolled at Dublin's Adelphi Theatre on 3 September 1965, he was transported by the raw power and paganism of the spectacle. 'Once it started, bloody hell! I was interested in opera, Bartók, Miles Davis and others, so I was a little bit aware of music based on twelve-bar blues . . . but I'm certainly smart enough to know the *extraordinary* discipline and power. It was just astonishing, and I suddenly thought, Oh my God, I've got to take it seriously – and I did. Then there are two thousand kids going berserk and I could see why you couldn't resist it. I've said before, for me it really was a pagan festival, initiates identifying with their god.'

The portrait of Brian shows both his power and his weakness. Indisputably, Mick's is a towering presence, a cheeky, boyish sexuality. But Brian's blond, Aryan elegance is more than a foil – he defines the Stones as a band rather than a backing group. Throughout this period, sporting a Gibson Firebird or Vox Phantom – a futuristic, phallic adornment – he is a potent figure, a little devil, adept at goading the crowd into violence, unleashing panic. Brian is still, manifestly, holding some power; yet, as Whitehead observed, his desperation to demonstrate that power highlights his weakness. 'From the first moment, I recognized that Brian Jones, of them all, was really determined to give me a good impression, and make sure I never took my eyes off him. But I wasn't aware, nor was anyone else really, there was a very deep rift between himself and the other two.'

Whitehead remembers that the interview with Brian was 'very long, and fascinating. He was prepared to talk, I think because already I sensed he was the outsider.' Somewhat fey, Brian looks straight at the camera, and he could simply be talking about the short shelf-life that everyone expected of the Beat groups of the time when he tells Whitehead 'my future as a Rolling Stone is uncertain'. 'That can have two meanings,' says Whitehead, 'meaning the Rolling Stones might last six months or three months or what-ever. [But] he was already considering whether he should get out, and not be the guitarist in the corner.'

It's easy to sense a haunted quality, or premonition, in Brian's outlook. If Brian did feel isolated or vulnerable, his anxiety would have been exacerbated had he known, as Oldham would later reminisce, that when it came time for playback 'Peter and I were falling about [laughing], [re]playing bits to make sure Brian had indeed spewed out this nonsense'. Whitehead's recollections don't square with Oldham's: 'Brian was articulate. More articulate than Mick or Keith. He did have this . . . feminine side to him. He was more into gossip, yes, and could come over as being a bit wishy-washy. But ultimately, he didn't have the brutality and certainty of Mick Jagger.'

So in September 1965, the one-time leader of the Stones could feel the balance of power, the limelight, inexorably slipping away from him. Fatefully, just days after his encounter with Whitehead, Brian would make the ultimate double-or-quits bet and team up with Anita Pallenberg. They would become the sixties' hottest, most dangerous couple, celebrated for damaging each other.

The twenty-one-year-old actress, born in German-occupied Rome, was fluent in four languages and had already made connections with the Living Theatre and Andy Warhol's Factory. Apparently undeterred by her rejection in Paris, she walked up to Brian in the wake of the Stones' show in Munich on Tuesday, 14 September. In later years she would describe how she arrived after Brian had been picked on by the cabal, that he was desperate for solace. But he was also desperate for kicks. Even early on it was obvious that together the pair seemed to unleash some thrilling, uncontrollable energy. 'Anita was a stunning creature,' says Pete Townshend, 'I mean, literally stunning. It was quite hard to maintain one's gaze. One time in Paris I remember they were so sexually stimulated they could hardly leave the room before starting to shag. I thought Brian was living on a higher plane of decadence than anyone I would ever meet.'

As a couple, they simply intimidated people, and revelled in it. 'They frightened me,' says Gered Mankowitz. 'Anita exuded an extreme sexuality that I was frightened of. She was extremely exciting but she was dangerous. I was also very nervous around them, because there was a thing going around of spiking people's drinks, and Brian was supposed to do that.'

Together with Marianne Faithfull, who had first appeared on the scene in 1964 although only officially unveiled, as Mick's new consort, in October 1966, Anita Pallenberg redefined the Stones' reputation. Cynics reckon she latched on to Brian in the mistaken belief he was the leader of the Stones, then ditched him having realized her mistake. Not so, says Stash, the man who witnessed their first meeting in Paris: 'Anita and Brian were very different people – Anita got a lot out of Brian, and she admired him, for what he was capable of. And she grew him, the way women do grow one.'

As Peter Whitehead noted, Brian was already demanding – of love, attention and new experiences. In this respect, he and Anita were very alike. 'She was very much bent on things happening, and pushing, taking things to the edge,' says Stash. 'A very brilliant individual in her own right. A talented person. A wild person.'

With Anita on the scene, the centre of gravity of the Stones shifted again: Mick and Keith still had a lockdown on the song-writing, but Brian regained his primacy in terms of the group's image. As he dressed more extravagantly – multicoloured stripes, ruffles, velvet – Keith, with his cheeky face and chunky leather coats, looked at first like a jobbing apprentice, before later becoming transformed in Brian's image.

Anita completed Brian, and theirs was a potent alliance. They didn't seem to care, and they seemed totally to lack any sense of decorum or empathy for others. Marianne Faithfull – whose command of detail isn't necessarily comprehensive, but whose understanding of the emotional landscape is always accurate – was thrilled, and shocked, by their amoral behaviour. They seemed impossibly old and decadent, but also behaved like wilful children. Marianne remembers one night when Linda Lawrence, along with her father Alec, arrived at their flat, holding baby Julian, in an attempt to chase money Brian had promised them.

'We're in a bad way, we need some help! Please!'

Up at the windows, Brian and Anita simply cackled, enjoying the spectacle, and refused to come to the door. Linda was 'devastated. My dad was angry, but I was simply hurt and depressed. It would always remain one of my worst memories, for ever.'

In her wildness, in that touch of evil, Anita was the perfect partner for Brian. Just before meeting her, Brian had taken delivery of a black Rolls-Royce, registration DD666 – which, legend would have it, signified 'Devil's Disciple' followed by the number of the beast. It wasn't planned that way, says Stash. 'It just happened. I don't believe Brian was even aware [of the number], till it arrived.'

Brian's fantasies of leaving the Stones ebbed away. He would never raise the subject again. Anita gave him the confidence to compete with Mick and Keith; doubtless he also sensed that if he left the Stones, he might lose the glamour that attracted her to him.

The fourth US tour towards the end of the year ratcheted up the tension a few more notches. Again it would be Brian pushing everything to the edge. A few days into the tour he was hanging out with Bob Dylan, whom he seemed to prefer to be with rather than the members of his own band. On 9 November, he took part in what is often described as one of the great lost musical moments of the sixties. In fact, the headiness of the experience derived almost entirely from the shock of witnessing the Big Apple suddenly enveloped by darkness.

Brian had spent the afternoon in the Village with DJ Scott Ross, and the pair were being driven uptown in their limo when all of a sudden the lights went out all over the city.

'It's the end of the world!' Brian exclaimed, only half joking.

The chauffeur drove tentatively, block after block, every junction a near nightmare without traffic lights, for what seemed an endless amount of time, up to the Lincoln Center. Yet when they arrived at the hotel, their troubles had only just begun. 'The hotel was surrounded by young girls,' says Ross, 'and the garage doors wouldn't open. When they realized it was a limo, they recognized Brian in there, and we had to run for it. I had my hair pulled, so it was bleeding – they'd take your hair, your clothes, anything. So it was a long way up to our rooms.'

The pair had only just got to Brian's room, still in the pitch black, when there was a knock on the door. It was Bob Dylan, who reputedly greeted Brian with the line 'How's your paranoia meter now, Brian?', which is precisely the sort of brilliant one-liner Dylan was spooling out at the time. Scott Ross doesn't remember that exact line, but agrees 'that was exactly how it was – flip comments, sarcasm, cynicism, always that kind of commentary'.

Dylan joined Brian and Ross in Brian's room, his entourage trailing behind him, 'Robbie Robertson, and a lot of others; then we lit candles, sat on the floor in a large circle, and passed joints around'. Someone produced guitars, and Brian, Dylan and Robertson played late into the night. No one noticed, or knew, what Mick and Keith were up to on the same evening.

In mid-November, the band took a couple of days' break in Miami. Anita flew over to meet Brian – an event recorded in the world's press, which was starting to follow their romance. All the Stones were grateful for a break: already they'd become habitués of the American lifestyle, with its eager staff and twenty-four-hour action. Their hotel was on a beach with a dedicated area where guests could potter around in little motorboats – 'like dodgems, really', says Gered Mankowitz. Anita remained in her room while Brian was one of the first out, eager to try any cool little gadget. 'He comes down, jumps on [this] boat and just heads straight out to sea. Completely disregards everything. Runs out of petrol and is towed back in. He was beaming, absolutely beaming, as this boat was being towed back. I can see him now.'

It was one of those minor selfish, childish acts that requires lots of tedious grown-up tidying in its wake; the boat operator was offended and upset, and the hotel management announced that the entire tour party was banned from using the boats. It was a trivial but significant example of the way Brian often expected people to clear up after him, like a toddler. In such a manner did the childishness around the Stones escalate. In 1964 it was often Keith, Stu or Mick who indulged in petty behaviour, like leaving Brian behind on the way to a gig. Now Brian felt more empowered, he revelled in being difficult. Some people, notably Andrew Oldham and Gered Mankowitz, certainly reckoned that Anita's arrival on the scene seemed to give him even more licence to act in a wilful fashion. Those people who, unlike Phil May, hadn't seen Brian being picked on grew almost to despise him. 'It was simple attention-seeking behaviour,' says Mankowitz, who believes a barrier was crossed during that tour. 'It began to get to the point where it was difficult for him to surprise people with his behaviour.' Mankowitz cites one particular incident when the band's mini-motorcade was stuck in traffic in Chicago and Brian simply walked off and didn't reappear. 'No one knew what happened or where he went.'

Ian Stewart, Andrew Oldham and, intermittently, Mick and Keith shared Mankowitz's mounting contempt for Brian's behaviour as the tour progressed to a close on the West Coast in early December. Yet one insider, right at the heart of their creative process, had a very different take.

Brought up in a little town in Michigan, Jack Nitzsche was one of a small group of ambitious outsiders who made their mark on the Hollywood scene from the late fifties. By the early sixties he was on salary at Specialty, reporting to Sonny Bono, working with Little Richard and Larry Williams, writing out sheet music and overseeing compilations. Nitzsche's stock rose in tandem with Phil Spector's, and when Oldham became infatuated with the latter, adopting the same shades and haircut, he hired Nitzsche as an assistant, to hang out, arrange and produce on sessions. Although 'hired' is perhaps the wrong term: all Nitzsche ever got in the way of remuneration was a mention in the credits, and later a gold watch, in recognition of his contribution to million-selling hits like Satisfaction. He never complained; but when Oldham boasted of his new Roller with tinted windows, as Mick had bought his Aston Martin, Keith a Bentley Continental and Brian another Roller, Nitzsche's friends thought he was insane.

Brian was the Stone whom Nitzsche respected the most – although, as he mentioned frequently to his friends, Brian was just as much of an enigma as Mick and Keith. Nitzsche always felt himself excluded, never quite sure what any of them thought of him. Even so, bit by bit he began to understand how they operated. It wasn't pretty.

It was on the West Coast that the rivalry between Mick and Brian gained an extra, nastier edge – because Brian, as local kids like writers Ken and Harvey Kubernik testified, 'made a bigger impact locally'. Ken Kubernik reinforces an impression shared by Toni Basil and most of the young Hollywood in-crowd: '*Everybody* glommed on to Brian. He was the centrepiece of the Stones.' Jack Nitzsche was one of the few people who could track Mick and Brian's relationship in both Britain and in the US, and he reckoned that on the West Coast, with the obvious public adulation of Brian and the way that bands like the Byrds would base their style, their haircuts, on him, the atmosphere seemed noticeably different.

To make things worse, it was Brian who seemed to have his own little social group. Often it would be Nitzsche and Basil, or he'd wander off to stay with Wallace Berman or other members of the West Coast's hip crowd. 'Brian was really excited by the underground art scene,' says Basil, 'and this was a period when art and pop music were mixing. You had Dennis Hopper and Peter Fonda, who made the first film where they used popular music. People gathered together, artists from different disciplines, all excited to be out together.'

For nearly fifty years there's been revisionism from the likes of Andrew Oldham and Keith Richards that Brian was out of it for sessions during this period, slumped useless over a guitar, drooling under the influence of a cornucopia of pills. Yet those around him in LA don't remember him being conspicuously out of it – although it's possible he saved his binges for when he was hanging around Oldham and the other Stones, in a bid to blot out the hostility. For much of the time in LA it appears he was on top form.

By the new year he was avoiding the usual teenage-oriented

clubs on the Strip to avoid getting hassled, choosing instead less predictable destinations such as a tourist-oriented joint which hosted a hypnotist, Pat Collins. Collins was well into her act, impressing all the starry-eyed visitors, when she appealed for volunteers to be put deep into a trance. A queue formed. Brian turned to his companions, giggling, then joined the line. Collins marched slickly through her routine, hypnotizing her volunteers in twos and threes before getting them to perform the usual ludicrous humiliations, like imagining they were eating the most delicious pie they'd ever tasted. Then she came to the long-haired guitarist, spoke softly to him, lulled him into a trance. His chin dropped; his eyes slowly closed. Then he swivelled around to the audience, lifted his face and extended the middle fingers of both hands, as the crowd erupted into laughter.

Denny Bruce, later the drummer with the Mothers of Invention as well as a noted blues producer, shared a house with Jack Nitzsche, attended many of the RCA sessions for the Stones albums *Out Of Our Heads* and *Aftermath*, and often chatted with his friend about those sessions and how Mick in particular responded to Brian's popularity on the West Coast. 'Jack said he had the feeling when they got to the States that Mick had this jealousy, that a lot of the girls liked Brian rather than Mick. Which wasn't so much the case in England. Brian just had a look, a way of moving around, that really excited the audience.'

Mick's feud – or, more accurately, rivalry – with Brian was exacerbated by drugs. By the end of 1965 they were becoming de rigueur; but for Mick, who liked to observe, to control, they were at best pointless, at worst frightening. It was infuriating for Mick that what seemed to him to make Brian unreliable actually made Brian hip. And the fact that he was indisputably hip became inescapable as 1966 dawned. This was the key difference between Brian and the other Stones, for better or for worse. As Jeff Dexter, one of the key scenesters of Swinging London puts it, 'Brian inhaled, the others didn't. They were tourists. Does that make sense?'

Brian Jones's ascendance into an emerging new hierarchy had already been publicly demonstrated, on 5 December, the final date of the Stones tour, which also inspired the first public Acid Test, run by Ken Kesey and his Pranksters – the first time a San Francisco R&B band, the Warlocks, performed under their new name the Grateful Dead. In the following weeks, stories filtered out that Brian had turned up for this crucial event, briefly appearing on stage with Jerry Garcia, as if to give the emerging California counter-culture his blessing. It wasn't true. 'We did go to the Stones venue and pass out pamphlets,' says Prankster Ken Boss, 'but Brian showing up was just a myth.' The myth would circulate for years, though, cementing Brian's reputation as the Stone who was unafraid to venture into new psychic territory. As the music scene changed in 1966, Brian – very much like George Harrison in the Beatles – would become a new figurehead. But peace and love, as Jack Nitzsche observed, were in short supply in the Stones camp.

Out Of Our Heads, released in July 1965 in the States, was recorded in Chicago and LA, a scrappy affair based on a string of covers with a scattering of Nanker Phelge numbers. Split mainly between December 1965 and March 1966, the recordings that became *Aftermath* were a huge leap forward, and resulted from block bookings at RCA. 'That was kind of unheard of,' says Denny Bruce. 'The sessions would start late and go into the early morning, something no one else did.'

Today, we still think of Andrew Oldham as responsible for that classic run of early, hip, focused Stones recordings. Oldham did indeed have a particular genius – and for most of those classic sides its main achievement was the recruitment of Jack Nitzsche. For it was Nitzsche, says Bruce, who performed most of the duties George Martin took on with the Beatles. 'Often with the songs they would usually have no more than a riff or something. And thanks to Jack being a good arranger, he was the one who would sit at the piano and help structure the song. With a guitar band you get jamming and something's gonna come out of it. And it was Jack who would start holding them to a song structure.'

Where Oldham, the nominal producer, had come to hate Brian – 'the cunt who gives me trouble' – Jack, the man on the studio floor, had an entirely different attitude. 'He always loved Brian,' says Bruce. 'He used to say, "He's the real Rolling Stone. The one who's not just happy being in a blues band. The adventurer."' It was during the sustained sessions that gave birth to *Aftermath* that Nitzsche started to realize how badly Brian was treated. Like Phil May, Chris Hutchins and Dave Thompson before him, he was shocked by the brutality within the Stones.

'I didn't get to every session,' says Bruce, 'but Jack would tell me what was going on when he got back. And there was one session where Jack, the next day, said, "You know, Mick and Keith really can be nasty, man. Last night, Brian just wasn't allowed to contribute to a song they were working on. He had a harp part he thought he would work out. And they went, 'All right, go out in the studio.' They made him do it five or six times, where he had blood on both sides of his mouth from wailing so hard on the harp. But they hadn't even rolled the tape."'

Keith and Andrew Oldham's recollections of *Aftermath* would focus on Brian being zonked out, on Oldham disconnecting him, and on Brian being a victim of his own excess, being paranoid, says Keith, 'that someone was going to roll him out, which wasn't true'. Nitzsche's descriptions, shared after those long California nights, tell a different story, of Brian wanting to contribute but being cut out. 'According to Jack, [Brian] just sat there, dejected, slumped, no longer contributing,' says Bruce. 'So the signs were there, even then.'

Brian was, most people agree, a highly sensitive individual; this was his gift and his curse. 'Early on, when Andrew Oldham made fun of his family car, this Humber Snipe, he couldn't bear it, it made him feel really stupid,' Linda Lawrence recalls. 'But that sensitivity is what made him a great musician. You have to have that open sensitivity to be able to play like that.' By abandoning the prospect of leaving the band he'd formed, this sensitive man was exposing himself, as Nitzsche and other observers noted, to some vicious treatment. Yet, as happened so often in Brian Jones's messy life, from out of the struggle he brought forth music of quite extraordinary sweetness.

7

Paint It Black

TIME TO REFLECT, to hang out and to plan had been cruelly curtailed over the last few years, but as 1966 dawned, Brian returned from a short holiday with Anita to his Chelsea mews flat for his first proper stay there since he'd moved in the previous March.

Those were chilly weeks in London. Brian felt the cold keenly and kept his fan heater on full time in his flat, now a veritable Aladdin's cave of records, books and musical gear. But the creative atmosphere in London was warming up fast. This would become Brian's major distraction from the bitterness within the band, as he realized that he could set the agenda once more. And just as he'd persuaded his more conservative bandmates to hop on the blues train, so he'd drag them along in his wake through 1966.

Brian was the first Stone to move to Chelsea, a couple of years before Mick, early enough to define the area's new vibe, with its blossoming hip new clothes shops like Hung On You and Granny Takes a Trip. Brian as a character had always been afflicted by self-doubt – that terrible failure, as James Phelge pointed out, ever to be satisfied – but he was braver than his fellow Stones. With Anita Pallenberg by his side he got braver still. It was Brian who was linked to the movie crowd, to Warhol's Factory, to Bob Dylan, as the British Beatboom passed into history. Nigel Waymouth, the artist and designer who'd define the look of English psychedelia, had known Brian since the Marquee era, and noticed how he was starting to dominate the band's look: 'There was this peacock side to him. He was the pretty boy, he was young and wanted to show off. I don't know what his finances were like, but he always dressed beautifully – and was probably the most flamboyant of all of them.'

Michael Rainey, who had opened Hung On You just a couple of months before Waymouth's Granny Takes a Trip, was one of the first to spot that subtle change in the balance of power: 'I think that Keith was looking at Brian, with Anita on his arm, and realized he had a lot of self-confidence. That he was taking a lot of acid and whatever other drugs, with Anita, whereas Mick never really took anything. Marianne always said Mick was afraid of drugs. Mick wasn't the rebel.'

The fact that he still retained, or had even built up, some of that magical aura of hip inspired and irritated Mick Jagger and Andrew Oldham in equal measure. Just as irritating was the fact that it was Brian who probably got on best with their biggest rivals, like Dylan and the Beatles. Keith was shy; Mick was cautious; Brian would often drop in on Paul McCartney for a natter, 'mainly about music', says Tony Bramwell, who hung out with the pair. 'You'd chat about where you'd been – although none of us would ever know where we were, anywhere, apart from where you'd had a certain meal or played a certain hall. Mostly it was, Where did you get that jacket, those shoes?' It was Brian whom the Beatles invited down for the sessions that ended up as their emerging masterpiece *Revolver* – it's

Brian you can hear clinking the glasses in Yellow Submarine. 'The Beatles objected to most people coming in [to sessions], but Brian they liked around,' says Bramwell. He also recalls that when the Byrds first came over to the UK and the local scenesters were trying to find someone to make them feel at home, they chose Brian. 'I took them round to his little mews flat. He was the perfect host, chatting, whacking out a few joints, just a nice, sincere guy.'

By the spring of 1966, the London scene was splitting in two, between the old rockers who talked about birds and beer, and the emerging heads whose conversation took in conceptual art, cosmology, ley lines and altered states. Brian, usually with Anita, was at the centre of the latter group, spending more and more time with Bob Fraser – often with his photographer friend Michael Cooper – whose gallery and flat on Mount Street became a playground for both aristos and rock stars. Some of Bob's detractors reckoned he was just 'a star fucker' who'd hang out with anyone famous, but Bob's friend and biographer Harriet Vyner vehemently disagrees: 'I know many people suggest that Robert just wanted to hang out with Brian Jones and the rest of the Stones because they were famous. In fact, in those early days Robert was at least as glamorous as they were. Although part of the (still mysterious) establishment, Robert was an authority on cool and esoteric subjects.' In those early days, says Vyner, Fraser was probably closest to Brian, as 'the most culturally adventurous of the Stones at that time, especially with Anita by his side. But if Brian Jones had been an unknown but sexy blues geek, [Robert] would have been just as enthusiastic about him – Robert was drawn to wayward energy and talent rather than celebrity.'

The bravery with which Brian launched himself into a new scene, the thirst for knowledge, the fascination with arcane culture – all these qualities that had made him the founder Stone now made him a powerful force as the band moved into new, exotic territory. But some of his traits – his terrible insecurity, his un-happiness with his lot – were just as crippling in this new environment. In early February, he invited *Record Mirror* to his Elm Park Lane flat for an interview which was revealing – perhaps too revealing. He told the magazine, 'I'm not personally insecure – just unsure. If someone told me I could write and egged me on, I suppose I could do it. It's like jumping in at the deep end and not knowing which way you are coming up.' His statements were, of course, an indictment of the Stones' dysfunctional relationships. One deterrent in terms of Brian's writing was the hostility people like James Phelge and Jack Nitzsche had witnessed. But his insecurity and compulsion to nitpick were part of the problem, too.

Once again it was out in California, with a different set of com-panions, that Brian's self-doubt seemed to subside. After a whirlwind globetrotting session – from New York for *The Ed Sullivan Show* to debut the new single 19th Nervous Breakdown, out to LA, then off to a riotously successful debut tour of Australia and New Zealand early in March 1966 – Brian was back in Los Angeles, where he could hang out with Jack Nitzsche, Wallace Berman and other friends.

The couple of days' rest and recreation followed by sessions with engineer Dave Hassinger at RCA would turn out to be one of Brian's last lengthy stays in the city. Nitzsche, who'd known Brian for a couple of years now, would always be Brian's main supporter within the little recording crew, though his influence would wane as Andrew Oldham became distracted from the Stones, focusing on his own Immediate label. Yet right to the end, Nitzsche found Brian hard to fathom.

Nitzsche had by now spent years in Hollywood and had surely

developed a good knowledge of the entertainment business's more exotic erotic activities. But then there would be evenings when he'd talk with Brian until early in the morning, including a time when the group had discovered some high-quality pot which came, explains Nitzsche's housemate Denny Bruce, 'from a certain region in Mexico. It had this beautiful herbal taste. Then after a while, you realized you were really stoned.'

Brian looked immaculate that night in a maroon velvet suit and white silk shirt, until the point when he ventured into the kitchen, made a mustard and mayonnaise sandwich, and proceeded to munch on the bizarre assemblage, his eyes closed. Bruce started giggling helplessly as mustardy drool leaked out of the corners of the stoned Stone's mouth.

Once the sandwich had been dispatched, Brian wandered over to the couch and sat himself down alongside Nitzsche. Bruce looked on. Minutes stretched seemingly into hours as Brian remained locked in conversation with the West Coast arranger, whispering intently into his ear. Suddenly Nitzsche got up and walked over to Bruce.

'He just put his tongue in my ear!'

'So . . . what was he saying?' Bruce asked his housemate.

'I don't know, man, some kind of bullshit . . . but I think he really likes me!'

Nitzsche would discuss that night with his friend several times over the next couple of years but never could decide whether Brian was indulging his urge for experimentation or simply enjoyed unsettling him. Spookily, Nitzsche had the experience replicated with Mick, who spent another night whispering provocatively into his ear. The questions multiplied in Nitzsche's mind. Was Mick bisexual? Was Brian bisexual? Was this some power trip to put him off his guard? Were the come-ons simply a kind of initiation into the Stones' inner circle? Were Mick and Brian competing to seduce him, just like they did with women, to enhance their alpha male status? The answer to all of those questions was probably yes – but Nitzsche was never quite sure.

For all his fellow Stones' criticisms that Brian was transfixed by stardom, during his last few trips to LA Brian became more and more obsessed with evading the crowds and hanging out with the same tiny circle of people, like Nitzsche and Wallace Berman. In 1966, Berman noticed, Brian tended to avoid the Sunset Strip. 'People say he liked being famous,' says Berman's son, Tosh, 'but my dad noticed it really bugged him. He was definitely not comfortable in that environment. It became a huge burden.'

One night on the Strip, at the Trip or some other nightclub, Brian and Berman were deep in conversation about jazz or the Kabbala – two subjects on which Berman was particularly erudite – when Rodney Bingenheimer, the self-styled King of the Strip, known for his unabashed, unironic worship of celebrity, walked up and interrupted the pair. Subjected to Bingenheimer's trademark non-stop Hollywood hipster slang, Brian begged to be left alone, without success. Finally, he booted the influential DJ in the backside, and he and Berman ran out of the club, cackling.

Yet whenever there was a chance of picking up new information or new ideas, Brian was fearless, 'like a scout searching out new sources or new influences', says Berman. Keith would sometimes tag along on such expeditions, Tosh remembers, but would remain quiet; Brian was the one making connections. One typical example was Richard and Mimi Fariña, whom he met several times towards the end of 1965 – their explorations of stripped-down Appalachian music inspired Brian's purchase of a dulcimer. Then there was his relationship with the Byrds, who'd regarded him as an icon since the Stones first appeared on *The Ed Sullivan Show*. Founder member Gene Clark later revealed that the band's first major self-penned hit, Eight Miles High, was cooked up with Brian in Pittsburgh, when the pair bumped into each other in late November 1965. 'I wrote the melody and lyrics in a hotel, with Brian,' he explained. 'I thought he should have got a credit – but he didn't care.' All these experiences would permeate Brian's definitive contribution to the album that would become *Aftermath*.

Aftermath was the most fully formed, adventurous and sustained Stones album since the band's debut, defined by Mick Jagger and Keith Richards' songwriting – which for the first time was shaking off the Spector obsession of their manager – and Brian's transformative musical interventions, which lifted many of the songs from run-of-the-mill to inspirational.

Were Mick and Keith grateful? No.

For all the focus on the Jagger-Richards songwriting team, it was never a conventional partnership; it was really just a brand, for whatever the Stones put together. Often, the songs would be Keith's: he'd come up with an entire structure, including, as he points out, 'some of the lyrics. Like the idea, maybe something about I Can't Get No Satisfaction.' Later, as Mick's guitar technique improved, he too would complete songs almost unaided. But whatever the origins, credit would go to the Jagger-Richards brand. All of which was eminently reasonable, except when the inspiration for a song came from outside the partnership – as in the instance when, according to Jack Nitzsche, the band was working on a fairly hackneyed F#m, E, D chord sequence, similar to the Animals' Please Don't Let Me Be Misunderstood, Dylan's All Along The Watchtower and a thousand rather more forgettable tunes.

The session would have gone nowhere but for the fact that the Baja Marimba band, a ludicrous novelty Mexican outfit, had left their instruments – including a marimba – in one corner of the huge RCA studio. Brian went over, started experimenting, and after a few minutes came up with what Eddie Kramer, one of the Stones' key engineers at Olympic studios in west London, describes as 'genius. A riff that makes sense of what could have been a nonentity. Because he could think out of the box.'

Nitzsche was the one who saw the marimba part as key to the song, for he was the contributor who, unpaid, did for the Stones what George Martin did for the Beatles. And Under My Thumb, one of the best-known songs credited to Jagger-Richards, was accordingly transformed from forgettable to unforgettable in the hands of Nitzsche-Jones. It's worth pointing out that the backing track had its own subtle genius – Charlie's stomping, upbeat drums and one of Bill's most fluid, propulsive basslines. In a grandiose feat of revisionism, Keith memorably theorized that Mick's sexist, put-down lyrics maybe 'opened their minds to the idea that, We're women, we're strong', although in truth the appeal of the song comes from the tension between the sweet, upbeat ambience and the sneering put-down of upstart girls. It may have been obnoxious, but it was honest. Mick Jagger would inhabit a role in many of his best-known songs, but in this one, as Marianne Faithfull and others point out, he was essentially portraying his own attitude – and that of his bandmates, including Brian and Keith.

Aftermath demonstrated Brian's unique genius, that ability, as Kramer puts it, to think outside the box. Kramer, who'd be heavily involved in the band's next album, today states, 'Much as I adore Keith, I must preface everything by saying that I always considered Brian the most gifted of the Stones, musically speaking.' Keith would develop his own distinctive understanding of sound, layering acoustic guitars or processing instruments through cassette recorders, but Brian was the one individual who understood, says

Kramer, 'tone colour. His sense of tone colour was magnificent, that's how he'd think out of the box, to put a different tone colour on something to make it speak. That's exactly what he did with the marimba part.'

'Well, without the marimba part, it's not really a song, is it?' says Bill Wyman.

Nitzsche and Brian, on harpsichord and dulcimer respectively, added a similar touch to Lady Jane, a limpid ballad with a lyric widely considered to have been inspired by Jane Ormsby-Gore and a tune that was, once again, transformed by Brian's counter-melody. More fundamental still was his contribution to a song that started out with Bill messing around on the organ, doing a piss-take in tribute to ex-manager Eric Easton's earlier career as an organist on the chicken-in-a-basket circuit. Charlie joined in with stomping on-beat drums, while Brian fashioned a melody on the sitar. Mick added his vocals, tracking Brian's sitar line, and the Jagger-Richards song partnership notched up one of its greatest songs, Paint It, Black. According to Bill, 'funnily enough, it was never credited as a Nanker Phelge composition . . . I can't think why.'

Brian's influence within the Stones would never be stronger than within Paint It, Black, a song whose melody he wrote, according to Bill, a sound that would never have happened without him. All this in a period of which Keith speaks with resentment, because Brian wasn't playing guitar. In this resentment we can sense that it was not Brian who was conservative, as Oldham suggests; the band, after Brian's departure, were happy to keep the same groove for four decades. Eric Burdon is one of many who regard the song as the summit of the Stones' early achievements, but an avenue that the band would never fully explore: 'Paint It, Black, that song influenced me so much that I recorded it three times with three different bands. And as a musician, Brian was the one who was pushing for that direction.'

Brian's exploration of Eastern themes paralleled that of George Harrison, who'd added sitar to the Beatles' Norwegian Wood the previous October, and recorded Granny Smith (later retitled Love You To) at Abbey Road on 11 April. George's exploration of Indian music and philosophy, which culminated in a visit to Bombay that November, would have a significant cultural impact on the Western world, popularizing Buddhism and other philosophies. Brian's own take on the sitar was distinct: Paint It, Black, with its Eastern pentatonic scale rather than the straight European classical scale of Norwegian Wood, integrated the new sounds into a wider blues context, and anticipated an understanding that we've attained only recently, of how much modern blues-derived music has roots in North Africa.

'It's very relevant today,' says Burdon. 'Paint It, Black has an Eastern feel, the influence of Islam. And no matter how you feel about Islam – we have this perception that it's the enemy – the music is amazing, the art is fantastic, [and] if you can insert that into rock'n'roll, you've got something that's really special. That's what Ry Cooder would end up doing later, mixing other cultures, all of which are close to blues.'

Andrew Oldham and Keith Richards saw Brian's investigation of ethnic music as an affectation, a diversion – a distraction from playing guitar. He was 'pretentious', says Mick Jagger, the devotee of Georgian chinoiserie. Yet history has vindicated the opinions of the unreliable, maddening, pretentious founder of the Rolling Stones, the man who told Mick and Keith the blues would be huge, the man who committed the sin of being right.

Today, our knowledge of ethnic music has broadened to the point where it's incorporated within a wider tradition rather than regarded as exotic, spicy ear candy. We know how Arabic and Sudanese music informed the blues, as did Scottish music, that these cultures have borrowed from each other for centuries. Hence our new understanding of world music, on the basis that as well as being different, it is similar. Brian Jones was the first popular musician to spot this. 'I think he would have taken that music another stage further,' says Burdon. 'The last time I heard of him, I was driving around in the south of Spain, Seville, and I heard, "He's across the water in North Africa, recording musicians." But the rest of the band weren't happy about changing direction. Why would they be? Right around the world they were the second band only to the Beatles – fame, fortune, good times. Why would they change that for some freaky music?'

In the survivors' accounts, there's no one who extols the potential new directions suggested by Brian's ideas. Perhaps there simply wasn't the time to discuss it, in the crazed goldrush. Instead, memories centre on the lazy, irresponsible Pan side of Brian, like the night when he arrived at the studio during the *Aftermath* sessions semi-conscious under the influence of some unknown drug. In later years, Oldham would sketch out the episode in detail: Brian collapsed in a fetal position on the wooden floor at RCA, out cold, a mess of ill-assorted fabrics. The atmosphere was dark and heady, each musician occupying himself with his instrument, and an earth hum buzzed from Brian's Fender amp while Mick fumed, shooting significant looks at Oldham. Finally, the manager stepped over and flicked the toggle switch to off, obeying Mick's unspoken command. Oldham would later recollect this as a moment of heavy portent, the instant when he realized Brian was doomed. Yet, given Jack Nitzsche's memories of how Brian was being manipulated and humiliated during Stones sessions, the moment could hardly have come as much of a surprise.

What Oldham doesn't reveal is at what point he realized that he, too, was starting to outlive his usefulness. In the same way that Mick had learned from Brian in order to function without him, so he'd picked up on many of Oldham's techniques, from his camp conversational style to the upfront brutality with which he'd announce a decision. Oblivious of such issues, Oldham prepared for the next ostentatious step in his own career – the move of his Immediate label to their own swanky offices on New Oxford Street – and embarked on another round of self-promotion. At his old Ivor Court office, the mantra had been 'We're gonna make money'. In the new era, buoyed up by Klein's financial deals, the message was 'We've got money and we're gonna spend it'. Mick remained supportive of Oldham's bigger business empire, producing the expensive, rootsy and commercially disastrous *The Art of Chris Farlowe*, recorded later that year, but as he gathered more experience producing other artists he was also starting to wonder how much Oldham actually contributed to the Stones sessions.

Mick's careful calculations, the way he monitored the odds, were out of fashion in London's glorious spring and summer of 1966, when it seemed that, having paused for breath, popular music was leaping into a gloriously thrilling Technicolor unknown. Brian, with Anita Pallenberg alongside him, had shifted the axis, and over the next few months Keith would be drawn towards him. Maybe it was a genuine attempt to rebuild their friendship – that's Keith's take. Maybe it was simple commercial good sense, for without Brian the Stones would have looked square that summer. Brian became, to use artist Nigel Waymouth's words, 'the peacock' at the cutting edge of dressing and drugging, the two major innovations of 1966. And as psychedelia was crystallizing, the sexy but rather earnest and ambitious Mick Jagger was just a little out of place, as was his manager, according to the counter-culture crowd and heads like Jeff Dexter, the man who explained the inter-band rivalry with the words 'Brian inhaled'.

Dexter was spinning discs at a notable party in Chelsea as that wondrous year started to get going. The building was packed with key scenesters including Waymouth, producer Mark Miller Mundy and many more when there was a knock at the side window – Mick Jagger and Andrew Oldham, ready to make an impression on the beautiful people. A couple of the assembled throng opened the door, and as the pair walked in, skinny, cool and excited, the hub-bub lessened for a moment.

'Hey!' one of them, probably Oldham, announced. 'Guess what, we've got some joints!'

There was a moment's silence, before someone commented, 'Well smoke 'em then!'

'We were all pissing ourselves with laughter,' says Dexter. 'Like I said, tourists.'

Keith, in the meantime, gravitated towards Brian and Anita. His motives were complex, but principally, says Stash, the Stones' founder still had a hold over him. 'Brian would be able to pull up a flute, say this is a quarter-tone off – he had this amazing musical ability. Whatever is being said now, by the modern band, is all rubbish in the sense that Brian was actually looked up to.'

Keith's own long-term relationship with the model Linda Keith was on the rocks at the time. Keith had been relatively faithful, compared to Mick, Brian and Bill, but Linda had her own drugs problems, of which Keith wasn't especially tolerant, and the couple were drifting apart. Back in February, Keith had splashed out on a beautiful thatched cottage which dated back to the thirteenth century and was rumoured to have once hosted Anne Boleyn. Surrounded by a moat – in which, Keith proudly told visitors, he'd found Saxon arrowheads – and situated in the tiny village of West Wittering, not far from a beach that faced the Isle of Wight, Redlands was the ultimate period pad. Yet after the first few stays, driving there in his new Bentley Continental, Keith became something of an absentee owner, spending more and more time hanging out with Brian.

Michael Rainey remembers well this newly empowered Brian, who with Anita and Keith in tow formed the centre of gravity of the Stones. Anita pushed Brian into more outrageous outfits, says Rainey: 'The Arabian Pashas, the Nazi uniforms, I think that was all her idea.' Brian, the sensualist, the narcissist, took naturally to such extravagance. Mick, in contrast, saw clothing as a tool, something to be used in the business: 'he was only interested in dressing to project. Like, are the clothes gonna make my show even better?' Nigel Waymouth remembers Brian embodying a distinctly British vibe: 'It was an aesthetic movement, a Wildean, fin de siècle look about the way we dressed. It wasn't just psychedelic drugs, it was velvet and William Morris prints, and frilly shirts.'

Brian floated like a beacon through the London social scene during the band's snatched breaks. On 24 April, he and Anita flew to the Luggala Estate in Ireland to celebrate the twenty-first birthday of their friend Tara Browne, son of Lord and Lady Oranmore and one of the heirs to the Guinness empire. Tara was a likeable floppy-fringed regular on the London scene; he owned the shop Dandie Fashions, could often be seen driving down the King's Road in his psychedelically painted Buick 6, and shared regular acid sessions with Brian and Anita. The British social scene, with its centuries of tradition, was changing almost beyond recognition. Although Mick – still with Chrissie Shrimpton, despite documenting her increasing insecurity in songs like 19th Nervous Breakdown – was a key figure, Brian, with Anita on his arm, was a far more flamboyant symbol of the new, exotic pop aristocracy.

The old aristocracy had a sense of entitlement, of continuity. There was none of that here. This was a world of change – senses in overload, meters running into the red. A potent example of the insecurity, the volatility of the London scene came at the end of May with Bob Dylan's show at the Albert Hall, the culmination of a tour that saw irate acoustic fans shouting 'Judas!' at the skinny suited-and-shaded speedfreak. Brian turned up with his friend Stash to experience a whirlwind of angst and aggression. When the pair dropped in to see Dylan in his cramped suite at the Mayfair hotel, they were shocked by the sight of several people in his entourage openly shooting up. Another night, they attended a party at actor/director Christian Marquand's apartment and Dylan cornered the pair in the bathroom, saying, 'You know what I'd do if Woody Allen was here? Punch him in the face, knock his glasses off and tread on them.'

'Dylan was extremely aggressive,' says Stash, 'way, way out there. He would corner you, jab his finger into your chest, and he would go on and on with this amazing rap. Then he'd try and enlist you in a vendetta. He'd have these passing whims, like a hatred of Woody Allen or [writer] Terry Southern – "let's get him", all of it like a whirlwind.'

Dana Gillespie, Dylan's lover while he was in London, saw him off at the airport, then hosted a farewell party in the basement of her parents' house in Furlough Square. Brian and Anita turned up and, like many women, Dana was bowled over by this exotic creature. 'Anita was wearing a rugby shirt, black, with knee length boots. And that was it. She was beautiful, absolutely stunning.' After the party, Brian, Anita and Stash bundled into Dana's little Austin A35 and went on to antique dealer Christopher Gibbs's house on Cheyne Walk, where someone handed her a glass of punch and said, 'Drink this.' 'I think it was liquid mescaline – I was completely off my head.' Freaked out, Dana insisted on driving home, a terrifying experience under the influence of this hallucinogenic drug; the traffic lights throbbed in rainbow hues. 'I think they were trying to instigate a scene with Anita. But I was young, wasn't really prepared for it . . . God knows how I got home.'

This was Dylan's last public outing before his motorbike accident, which seemed to turn him into a completely different person. For years afterwards fans would speculate whether some of Dylan's songs referred to the Stone he spent the most time with. The figure of the dancing child, for whom time is on my side, was widely identified with Brian, as was the line 'something is happening . . . but you don't know what it is, do you, Mr Jones?' But Dana and Stash vehemently disagree. 'There are always those myths, but the Mr Jones line would never be about Brian, it's far too direct,' says Dana. 'It's a fantasy,' Stash concurs. 'Certainly Brian didn't even suggest there might have been a reference.' Yet there was no doubt that for a short time Dylan was obsessed with the Stones' founder. As Nico, one of several lovers common to both characters, later pointed out, '[Dylan] wanted to be Brian, not a folk singer.'

The Stones' fifth American tour opened on 24 June 1966 in Massachusetts. The influence of Allen Klein was starting to become all-pervasive – Oldham was frequently absent, but Klein's connections guaranteed constant airplay as the band played in unthinkably huge stadiums to crowds of ten to fifteen thousand screaming fans. The Stones' sound was in flux, inconsistent, thrilling: Brian's guitar-playing was still tight, picking out a wilder version of the jagged melody riff for The Last Time, but for the first time Keith's guitar was on a different, higher level throughout – heavier, but beautifully honed rhythm parts. This would be Brian's final tour of America. In his memoirs, Oldham reckoned, 'Brian was more often hospitalized and missed a number of live dates.' Records suggest he actually missed only one show (for that matter, for all his supposed unreliability, the best estimate is that Brian missed around twelve Stones shows in his life out of a total of around 930). What's undeniable, from surviving live tapes, is that Brian dominated the sound, from the urgent wail of Not Fade Away's harmonica through to the fragile luminosity of his dulcimer and sitar parts, which interlace perfectly with Keith's guitar. Instead, it's the songs where Brian is not integral which falter: Mother's Little Helper is a messy Kinks rip-off, and Satisfaction, a song which the band would take decades to master live, is a lumpen shuffle. At the apogee of their success so far, there was still a sense it could all fall apart in a year or two.

Beyond the intimidating presence of Dylan – who seemed to spool out songs within minutes – another potent new entry to the British music scene appeared within the first couple of days of the tour when Linda Keith, who'd recently disappeared to New York, told them about an amazing guitarist, Jimmy James, who was playing at the Café Wha? in the Village on 2 July. They went along and were impressed; so was Chas Chandler – former Animals bassist, and aspiring producer – who turned up at Linda's instigation a couple of nights later. Linda, it's said, gave Jimmy James one of Keith's Fender Strats, around the time Chandler encouraged him to come over to London and change his name. Brian would be one of Jimi Hendrix's key supporters in Britain; in turn, Hendrix would sometimes give Brian refuge in the dark days to come.

By the time the Stones convened for more recording sessions at RCA on 3 August, the band sounded tired. Maybe, as some said of the album spliced together there and later in London, the whole sound was tired. But maybe Brian Jones was running out of road, too.

Certainly his trip to Tangier that August was a little set-piece in his life, a demonstration of both his power and his helplessness. The city was the perfect location for the scene. Tangier had a uniquely twisted, depraved history, and boasted its own special brutality. 'The city had never tolerated broken men,' commented writer Ian Finlayson. 'Scenting the blood of a man at bay, it never hesitated to move in for the kill.' It was known for housing femmes fatales and vamps – literally: beautiful women like Lib Holman, who killed off two husbands, and the famed Vampire of Tangier, who kept phials full of the blood of rent boys. Its magic was potent: jaded English characters would venture there and somehow become trapped, never returning to their homeland. Among the Stones' inner circle, Robert Fraser was one key link to Morocco; the other was Christopher Gibbs. And in the background lurked the dessicated presence of Paul Bowles, the writer who had moved to the city in 1947 and remained at the centre of its cultural life, a spider sensing the vibrations across its web. Bowles wrote one great novel out of his Morocco experience, *The Sheltering Sky*, then holed up in the city, taking young Moroccan boys as lovers in that time-worn fashion of sexual colonialism; he later watched as his wife Jane, a more natural writer than he, went mad. Bowles's influence was still potent in 1966, but the vibe was changing as characters like William Burroughs and his friend Brion Gysin – the maverick artist, writer and inventor of the cut-up technique, as well as self-styled inventor of the magical but never quite functional Brain Machine – made their mark.

Brian loved the city, the way the pavements were crowded with people in native dress, their donkeys plodding alongside them, the streets full of shit and exotic sounds. For this trip, he and Anita were accompanied by Gibbs, who'd first visited Morocco around 1960. Fraser was always more indulgent of Brian, for the pair

201

shared a congenital unreliability, especially when it came to paying back loans. Gibbs, who'd remain friends with both Mick and Keith, had a much more nuanced view of Brian, who he reckons 'had just enough charm to get away with being an absolute nightmare. Just. Because he *was* a nightmare.'

Somehow, Brian's time in Tangier seemed to epitomize his key character traits – the most outgoing Stone and also the most unreliable. He was the Stone who had travelled the most, hitch-hiking across the south of England, sleeping on floors; yet by the time he hooked up with Gibbs and Anita at the El Minzah, he'd become addicted to the whole star trip, staying in luxurious hotels, leaving clothes strewn around and lapping up the attentions of complaisant Moroccans. All this informed Gibbs's view of him as 'the most selfish, the most spoilt, the most wilful, the most thoughtless, demanding, wheedling, maddening, sweet and charming person'.

The Moroccans Brian encountered shared the same mix of emotions. It was likely on this trip that he first met Mohamed Hamri, who was briefly the lover and later friend, pupil and assistant of Brion Gysin. Hamri came from a small village named Joujouka (often spelt Jajouka), up in the Ahl Serif mountains, where his uncle had been leader of a remarkable group of local musicians. In December 1954, Hamri and Gysin had launched their own restaurant, where celebrated visitors like Christopher Isherwood and Cecil Beaton would savour Moroccan food, listen to the exotic sounds of the Master Musicians of Joujouka, and ogle the young dancing boys. A few years after the venture broke up, Hamri launched a solo restaurant of the same name in Asilah, a few miles down the coast, where Brian became a regular visitor.

Hamri and Gysin would become friends with Brian, spinning stories of Joujouka filled with myth, magic and music. But Brian was also a pain, turning up to dine at the restaurant, then after praising the food extravagantly complaining he'd had problems changing his currency and would have to pay for the meal next time. The wealth, the presence of flunkies and the plentiful supplies of hash simply acted to amplify the selfish traits that had first surfaced in his teenage years. Most friends remember Anita challenging Brian, taking him to the edge, adding a dark glamour that allowed him to outshine Mick or Keith. But Gibbs, during that trip, saw the relationship in an entirely different light: 'There might have been a sensual buzz to it, and there was a sort of chemistry – but it was destructive. Because they were so different, in character and experience of life, of what turned them on and how they could cope.'

Brian and Anita holed up in the El Minzah, with Gibbs attending on them. The blond-haired lookalikes argued constantly, Brian hectoring Anita, who shot back fiery retorts, enraging Brian, who finally lashed out. 'I couldn't say whether he was lashing out in general, or trying to hit Anita – and I'm sure he couldn't say either,' says Gibbs. 'But he was in a rage, and [swung his arm], and instead of connecting with Anita, his fist connected with a metal window frame. And he broke his arm, which is not a good thing for a musician.'

In fact, it seems Brian broke a bone in his wrist. An ambulance whisked him from the El Minzah to the Clinique Californie where he was forced to stay for the best part of a week. Anita, unfazed by the drama, went off for adventures with Gibbs. During one of their first days of 'freedom' they chanced across Akhmed, a diminutive, energetic character who seemed to be looking over his shoulder enticingly. They followed him into his tiny shop off the Escalier Waller – steps leading down from the Minzah towards the fish market. Inside, the shop was empty but for a few items of jewellery and a large box covered by a blanket. It was filled with hashish.

With such pleasures on offer, Anita 'wasn't at all downcast. We did go and see Brian, every day,' Gibbs points out, surmising that remaining calm in the hospital, eating three meals a day and being attended to 'by a bossy Moroccan nanny with a hairbrush saying do what you're told, or wallop' was the best thing for him.

At first it was thought the injury to his wrist was potentially serious. After returning to London, Brian had follow-up visits with a Harley Street surgeon and recovered full use of his hand within a few weeks, in time for him to make a competent job of his guitar work for the band's short UK tour in September, sporting a velvet jacket and brandishing a brand-new Gibson Firebird.

By the autumn, Brian and Anita were officially installed in what would become one of London's most legendary rock star pads: 1 Courtfield Road, overlooking Gloucester Road tube station – 'a veritable witches' coven of decadent illuminati, rock princelings and hip aristos' as one of the key participants, Marianne Faithfull, describes it. Marianne was a crucial contributor to the decadence: in those first weeks she had sex with Brian (half-hearted and rather unsatisfactory, she says), then moved on to Keith, who turned her over to Mick with the words 'He's not that bad when you get to know him, you know.' Even today, after accusing Mick of some of the most Machiavellian and cynical behaviour in the history of popular music, she confirms that judgement: 'I don't really blame Mick, for anything. In a funny way, I understand.'

Brian and Anita played the part of renaissance decadents; Keith, who spent more and more time at Courtfield Road, became the funny, flinty character we know today over those months; Marianne brought sweetness and light to the heady mix. 'She was funny, and intelligent, and witty, and beautiful,' says Keith Altham. Yet Marianne was also sensitive, like Brian, and was destined to be damaged profoundly by what transpired over the next six months.

The psychodynamics were mind-bogglingly complex, considering what we know in retrospect. Some visitors reckoned Keith's infatuation with Anita was obvious, or speculate that Brian's distrust of Anita caused tantrums and violence. Stash Klossowski, one of the few outsiders who was close to all three, remembers a very different atmosphere: 'Keith didn't mention that time in his own book – he seems to have erased it from his memory. But Brian and Anita didn't slap each other around then. It wasn't Brian's style – it was easier just to disappear than to get in a fight. Personally I never witnessed that.' Today, it's impossible to disentangle Keith's true feelings – like many male musicians, he's not necessarily interested in what makes other people tick. One of his key descriptions of Brian is as an unpredictable 'bunch of guys', but as James Phelge points out, 'then he calls Mick a bunch of guys, too. I don't think he can really remember.'

Instead, it's left to Marianne Faithfull to deliver an account that actually sketches in other characters and tries to understand their motivations. She recalls being worried by the vibrations she was seeing. Marianne had, initially, set her sights on Keith but 'knew in my heart of hearts that Keith was in love with Anita'. She found Brian maddening, irritating, a self-indulgent Pan figure who was adrift, desperate to impose himself as he continued to be manoeuvred into irrelevance. Like Pan, Brian was being demonized, she reckons – by Mick, who would later pull the same trick on Andrew Oldham; and then, she adds, 'it started happening to me'. Above all, she remembers the long genesis of one of the Stones' greatest songs, which sprang from two of Brian's obsessions – Elizabethan lute music and Delta blues.

'It's a cross between Thomas Dowland's Air on the late Lord Sussex and a Skip James tune' – that's how, according to Marianne, Brian introduced a plaintive, haunting melody that he'd worked out on a recorder. Keith, like a dog with a bone, picked up on the melody. The pair laboured over the song for several weeks, with Brian also contributing piano to an intricate, almost baroque arrangement. 'Look,' says Eddie Kramer, who started his engineering work with the Stones that year and would soon work closely with Jimi Hendrix, 'I was amazed when he played those melodies, both by the way he thought to use it, and the way he played this thing – it was a descant, or the next size up, something you'd see in English schools. Mick and Keith, not to put them down, would never have thought of something like that.'

Mick later described Ruby Tuesday as a great song, even though he hadn't written any of it. Perhaps it doesn't matter that the Jones-Richards partnership was never credited – it's likely that Brian never asked. In all the sadness that pervades the era – Keith's loss of Linda Keith, the impending ejection of Andrew Oldham, the imminent breakdown of Brian – it's a moment of pure, sweet beauty. Whatever great ballads Mick and Keith would summon up after Brian's departure, only Wild Horses, a tribute to Marianne Faithfull, comes close.

Throughout popular music there has always been tension over songwriting, debate about at which point a crucial riff defines a song and should be reflected in the credits. Yet even notoriously hard-nosed operators like David Bowie would offer up a slice of the songwriting income when a riff, like Carlos Alomar's needling funk line on Fame, is the first, central building block of a song. But with the lock that Keith, Mick and of course Oldham had on the management, such generosity was never on offer for songs like Ruby Tuesday, Paint It, Black or Under My Thumb. Stan Blackbourne, the Stones' accountant from 1965, was one of many who thought this completely inequitable. 'I used to say to Brian, "What on earth are you doing? You write some of these songs and

you give the name over as if Mick Jagger has done it. Do you understand, you're giving 'em thousands of pounds!" All the time I used
to tell him, "You're writing a blank cheque!"'

Devoid of support within management, however, there was little
Brian could have done, even had he been assertive enough.

Marianne sees Brian's defining contribution to Ruby Tuesday as
a Herculean last effort to regain his place at the centre – a musical
gift to the band that might elicit some thanks and appreciation. 'He
desperately wanted someone to say, "Good work, Brian!"' she says.
'But of course, no one did.' The attempt brought Brian no credit, in
any sense of the word. That fiver, again.

And so 1966 dwindled to an end, a vivacious, colourful, mostly
joyful year which made the dark moments seem more unfair,
harder to deal with. On 17 December there came a cataclysm: the
impossibly gilded youth of Tara Browne was terminated when
the twenty-one-year-old jumped a red light and smashed his Lotus
Elan into a parked lorry. His girlfriend, Ossie Clark model Suki
Potier, survived. Brian, Anita and Keith were all deeply affected by
Tara's death. The trio spent much of Christmas at the Georges V
hotel in Paris, blotting out reality on downers.

Chrissie Shrimpton, Mick's long-term girlfriend, finished 1966
in a similarly miserable state. Mick had first appeared in public
with Marianne on 15 October, at the launch of counter-culture
journal *International Times*, or *IT* (whose founders included Barry
Miles and Graham Keen, Brian's chums from that square old place
Cheltenham). Chrissie discovered the relationship was over when
she read it in the papers. A couple of days later Chrissie was
hospitalized in a reported suicide attempt. British newspapers glee-
fully followed the breakdown of their relationship, alleging that
Mick had arranged for the removal of Chrissie's possessions from
their flat, and later returned her hospital bills unpaid. Mick and

Marianne announced their inauguration as a celebrity couple with a shopping session at Harrods and an interview with the *Mirror*'s Don Short. With Marianne – feisty, independent, fragile and impossibly glamorous – at his side, Mick would acquire a new potency.

As for Brian, as ever there was a compulsion to find fault. Even in the flat of his dreams, with a renewed friendship with Keith and a celebrated love affair with Anita Pallenberg, still he often pondered and became morose. Towards the end of the year Peter Whitehead turned up to film the Stones again, ostensibly to make a promo film for the upcoming single Let's Spend The Night Together. Whereas Stash and, to some extent, Marianne remember Brian making a meaningful contribution in the studio, Whitehead's camera captured a profound transformation. Brian was barely functional. 'He was a total embarrassment, to himself or to anybody else. You couldn't talk to him; it was like he was paralytically drunk. Yup, he was a wallflower – and by that time you know, he's gonna have to get a grip or he's had it.'

Throughout his interaction with the Stones, neither Brian nor anyone else had ever mentioned to Whitehead that Brian was the founder of the band, or mapped out their first influences. 'That makes it even sadder,' he adds. 'He would have felt exploited – and raped, basically. Somewhere he was broken along the line. But no one thought about it. Especially the speed at which things were happening – so much information in every direction. There was no room for weakness of any kind.'

The sense of storm clouds gathering started to spread, of course, blown by a desire to sell newspapers. The generation gap that had opened up in Brian's teens continued to crack ever wider. Some parts of the media welcomed this youth rebellion, the growth of expression and new ideas. But the same people who'd issued dark warnings about the Beats in 1960 were just as intent on exposing the homegrown threat, as British rock music grew up. The stormtroopers of the establishment in 1966 are familiar to us today: strident newspapers, eager to horrify their readers and sell more copies, ready to expose corruption with an open cheque-book, acting in collusion with an unaccountable and demonstrably corrupt police force. 'We didn't know it yet, but people were paying attention to us,' says Donovan, who would be the first victim of a new alliance.

Donovan Leitch was something of a figurehead of the Bohemian movement; he'd already namechecked London's hash-smoking youth in Sunny Goodge Street, a song of blissed-out reportage that depicted the city's switched-on scene, just in case anyone had failed to notice. And in January 1966, the documentary *A Boy Called Donovan* constituted the proverbial red rag to the establishment's bull.

The film, directed by Charles Squires, was intended to document Donovan's vagabond past (incidentally, it featured Brian's old girl-friend Linda Lawrence, whom the singer would pursue over the following years). Squire requested a beatnik party as the centre-piece of the film so Donovan, with Dave 'Gypsy' Mills, a companion since the singer first hit the road in January 1963, assembled a group of acquaintances from their old haunts. Donovan arrived late to the party, to see his friends 'in the throes of this crazy party, all out of it, openly rolling joints, smoking, dancing. I said to Charles, "What have you done?" And he said, "Well, it's a bohemian party, so I brought twenty gallons of wine!"' At one point the local police showed up; with their old-school deportment and handlebar moustaches, they looked like extras. But they weren't, and their presence over the next few months would become less comedic and more sinister. That summer,

Donovan's Sunshine Superman became a hit in the US, its title incorporating the current slang term for LSD, with a B-side that happened to be called The Trip.

Up to that point it's arguable that the mass media and even the police had regarded musical performers as cheery, useful characters. Once the Stones, the Beatles and Donovan started to break outside that showbiz box with mocking social comment and talk of expanding consciousness, they began to constitute a threat. Some of Donovan's descriptions of what followed sound like the reminiscences of a conspiracy freak – but for the fact that it's all there, on the record.

Donovan's old friend and running-mate Gypsy Dave was the first to notice the signs. He and Donovan shared a flat in Earls Court, and during a time when Donovan was away around the summer of 1966, Gyp found a policeman attempting to break in through a rear window. 'He threw him out,' says Donovan, 'but this was the first example. And from now on, it's going to get organized.' There were other portents: suspicious officials in the USA, and then evidence that their flat was being watched from a building opposite. Later, after a move to a new flat in Edgware Road, an old girlfriend attempted to track down Gyp, contacting the police to find out his whereabouts, and was drawn into the saga.

It was indeed getting organized, and the man responsible was Norman Pilcher.

Detective Sergeant Norman Clement Pilcher, aka Semolina Pilchard, aka Groupie Pilcher, was rising fast that year. A family man from Kent, he was popular with his colleagues thanks to his ready wit – 'leave it to yer old dad' – his hard-working attitude and his sizeable network of informants. In his mid thirties, Pilcher was comparatively young for his rank, and he gathered a youthful team around him who were impressed by his souped-up Ford Cortina, his gun licence, his modish gangster chic outfits – and his hunger for publicity. It was with Donovan, whose flat was a regular hangout for the Beatles, the Animals and others, that he would start to make his name.

At 1.30 a.m. on 11 June 1966, there was a knock on the door. Gyp ran down the stairs to investigate and saw his old girlfriend through the window. He opened the door, 'then the girl stands aside and in come nine burly policemen with Pilcher', Donovan recalls. 'And they smash the place up. I'm jumping naked on the back of policemen's necks, they're smashing up beautiful things in the room, it's terrible. They've been down the pub of course, and we were roughed up.' The squad had also broken into the flat below, rented by Donovan's agent, Ashley, and girlfriend Anita. Up in his flat, Gyp's old girlfriend cowered in the corner. 'And this is how they use people, this poor girl who was dragged into it.' Finally, Ashley told Donovan that 'they found two ounces of Lebanese in my place, and they found two ounces in yours'. 'You know,' says Donovan today, 'we couldn't even find that stuff to buy in London. The little bit of hash we did have, we'd already smoked.'

With this first raid, Pilcher established his modus operandi. There would be accusations of planting evidence ('he had good connections', says Donovan, for he had access to good-quality drugs to plant), dragging in innocent parties either through bribery or blackmail, and close collaboration with the tabloids, who were instantly tipped off about Donovan's bust. Then, once the pair were taken to the local police station, Pilcher demonstrated, for the first but not the last time, the most surreal part of the process. 'Sorry about this, we're only doing our job,' he told Donovan. 'Can I have an autograph?'

Semolina Pilchard would gather quite a few more rock star signatures in the coming months.

211

8

Butterflies and Wheels

BACK IN THE 1920s and 1930s, Brian Jones knew, making music was a life-or-death proposition: a blues singer who hit the road with a guitar in the Southern states took his life into his hands. This was part of the music's force, an intrinsic part of the legend of blues singers like Robert Johnson, who'd died of strychnine poisoning, aged 27, crouched on his hands and knees, coughing like a dog. Brian, the first Stone to delve deep into the blues, was more aware than most of the forces that threatened the music's first pioneers. Fatefully, he had little clue that he was about to face a similar assault from forces who found his lifestyle an affront to their values.

Posterity would ascribe the undoing of Brian Jones to a woman; yet the hammer blow, it turns out, came from a very different source. In a cruel twist, the corrupt, cynical attack of the establishment which was the making of Mick Jagger and Keith Richards proved to be the breaking of Brian Jones – the real butterfly broken on the wheel.

*

The year 1967 began beautifully. Back in September 1966, Anita Pallenberg had started work on her first big movie, *Mord und Totschlag*, directed by the twenty-eight-year-old wunderkind Volker Schlöndorff, his follow-up to *The Tin Drum*. The film was based on a true story, of a woman who'd killed her friend more or less accidentally; rather than go to the police she hires two men to dispose of the body. 'The picture was about the total absence of old values,' says Schlöndorff; 'an unresolved crime story, no redemption, no morals.' Anita played the main role, and Brian had joined her for the filming. The media firestorm around the couple was so intense that Schlöndorff lent them his little flat in Munich as a hideout. (Brian and Anita became embroiled in a mini-scandal soon after their stay in Munich, when Brian dressed up in an SS uniform for a playful but ill-advised shoot for *Stern*, all of which helped secure their status as the definitive bad-boy-and-girl couple.)

The shooting was well in progress when Brian asked if he could do the soundtrack. Schlöndorff's reaction was, 'I'd love to – but I can't pay you.' Brian's response was, 'Well, I'll do it for free.' Largely as a result, Schlöndorff spent quite a lot of time with Brian at the end of 1966 and the beginning of 1967 and considered him 'amazing. He was a Shelley-style character, a dandy. He could be spoiled and nasty, but at the same time he was creativity incarnate, and had great intuition.' Schlöndorff was struck particularly by Brian's sensitivity; he seemed to sense mood, and instinctively understand what was necessary for a film. 'He also had quite an education, and quite a horizon, so I really thought, this is the best music I could ever get for a movie.'

Once the main movie edit was completed, in January 1967, Brian joined Schlöndorff for a spotting session, working out the main themes and timings. He was full of ideas. 'He'd say, "Yeah, there could be country music here, a Highland style here, we'll have Nicky Hopkins playing here,"' says Schlöndorff. 'So we establish a list, take the timings, and we get a spotting list, with all the timings for the scenes and short descriptions.'

Schlöndorff was delighted with his coup. When he arrived in London in February, he met Brian at Courtfield Road. Brian started playing him various themes on the sitar – 'and that was when I realized nothing was actually ready'.

Once Schlöndorff actually got Brian into the studio, however, the work went well. Engineer Glyn Johns remembers Brian being 'together, and hard-working'. Drummer Kenney Jones agrees: 'We started around eleven in the morning. He was alert and was wonderful to deal with.' Jones recalls that Brian had a real knack for working with musicians, a distinctive emotional insight. 'He was guiding me – I had to improvise a drum solo part. This was for a chase, around a playground I think, and I had to use a kind of emotional technique to fill in the blanks and get the excitement going.'

For those who claim Brian couldn't write, this score is the counter-evidence. One particular theme, a sweet, stately recorder melody that resurfaces several times, is as good a testimony of his potential as you could wish to find. But Brian was also infuriating: he procrastinated; he delayed committing to ideas. This was his main problem, for as Schlöndorff points out, 'in creativity, you have to be ruthless'. Then there was that old bugbear, his sheer unreliability. 'Most of the time it was just a nightmare to get Brian to the studio. First of all he would only work at nights. I would show up at five or six to pick him up, but to get to the studio and get him going . . . he had no discipline whatsoever.'

Worst of all, there was Brian's insecurity. He'd always been like this, oversensitive, but the damage his fellow Stones had inflicted on his ego over the previous few years meant that Brian's neediness was becoming pathological. 'He was driven by this narcissistic need, to be recognized, to be loved, for attention. And Anita was stronger than he was at that moment. She could control things, by giving attention, or withholding it, or by treating him in a very condescending way. Then he'd get nasty, in the sense that he's the one who's got the money or whatever, so he'd punish her that way. And I'm certain he'd treat her physically badly, too. So he already was, in some ways, an unhappy and pathetic figure.'

As an experienced director used to working with high-maintenance people, Schlöndorff still had a wonderful time working with Brian. Asked if he could have been a soundtrack composer, he agrees without reservation. Likewise, Kenney Jones is certain that, with a songwriting partner, Brian could have gone on to write pop songs. But to function as a rock star, he needed a certain hardness. Over the years, that essential carapace, such as it was, had become weaker rather than stronger. 'I tried to help him,' says Schlöndorff. 'I understood that doing something on his own was very important for him – more important for him than for me.'

Inside the safe womb of the recording studio Brian continued more or less to keep things together. In the wider world, though, events were spinning out of control. On 23 January the Stones had their first substantive disagreement with Andrew Oldham over his insistence that they board the revolving stage at the close of *Sunday Night at the London Palladium*, the old-fashioned variety show on which Oldham had booked them to mime three songs. There'd been differences of opinion before, for instance over the definitive take of their last Oldham mini-epic Have You Seen Your Mother, Baby. This was the first time Mick said no to his mentor. In

Oldham's view, the Stones' rejection of this little showbiz convention at the Palladium contributed to what happened next. It's a rather ridiculous notion, given Oldham's own relish for manufactured outrage. In fact, the wheels were already rolling.

The *News of the World*, the now-defunct British tabloid newspaper well known for its disapproval and comprehensive coverage of all kinds of sex and sleaze, fired the opening salvo of the inter-generational war on Sunday, 29 January under the headline 'Pop Stars: The Truth That Will Shock You'. The story focused on Donovan. In what would become trademark style, the tabloid worked closely with Norman Pilcher. The detective had handed on details of the woman, Suzanne, who had helped them gain entry to Donovan's flat. Her sensationalized interview formed the core of the story. 'Again,' says Donovan, 'this is how they used people.'

For several years now the British press and the new generation of British musicians had been engaged in a cosy compact: pop stars helped sell newspapers. Yet by the beginning of 1967, the schism between traditional entertainers and the emerging rock aristocracy had become glaringly obvious. This generation gap, once disparate and diffuse, was now clearly delineated; both the music and the Technicolor clothes distinctly announced a break with the sober Britain of the austerity years, the buttoned-up nation overseen by righteous Victorian statesmen. The *News of the World* picked up on a growing hostility to these druggy, foppish upstarts and used it to drive news-stand sales, under threat following a string of scoops obtained by their great rival tabloid the *People*.

The following Sunday, 5 February, the *News of the World* followed up their Donovan story with a far more satisfying scalp: Mick Jagger, who in an undercover interview boasted about his history of drug-taking. Except, of course, it wasn't Mick Jagger. The Rolling Stone the undercover reporter had spoken to was Brian

Jones, at one of his regular haunts, Blaise's, which at 121 Queen's Gate was only a few blocks away from Courtfield Road. Some sources suggest the 'interview' was several months old; more likely it took place in January, when Anita was away filming *Mord und Totschlag*. The eager reporter had found the perfect dupe. Brian, as ever, was happy to expound on his status as a drugs pioneer. 'I don't go much on LSD,' he informed them, 'now the cats have taken it up. It'll just get a dirty name. I remember the first time I took it – it was on tour with Bo Diddley.' Brian was actually talking about marijuana. The misquote was almost certainly deliberate, for the mention of LSD, illegal since the Dangerous Drugs Act of June 1965, fitted the newspaper's agenda much better. The identification of Brian as Mick was possibly accidental, but insiders like Marianne Faithfull believe that too was cynical and deliberate: as the figurehead of the Stones, Mick's celebrity would help sell more papers.

The stage was now set for a showdown between the straight world and the alternative world. Mick's horror at reading the article, on his return from a trip to San Remo and Cannes with Marianne, was intensified by the fact that he had hardly experimented with LSD. In future years his status as a near martyr in the struggle for decriminalization of drugs would be accompanied by the professed belief that drugs were 'a bad idea'. Similarly, the *News of the World* would later deny that they in any way represented the forces of the establishment. According to managing editor Robert Warren, the confrontation was 'never as important as people make out'. Still, with allies of convenience or not, the battle was on.

Andrew Oldham was as horrified by the *News of the World* report as Mick: the furore had profound implications for the Stones' immigration status in America, and after a conference between Klein, Oldham and Jagger, Mick announced, via a TV interview with Eamonn Andrews, that he would be suing the newspaper for libel. He had a clear alibi, and the newspaper soon became aware that its shoddy reporting had opened it up to the potential of heavy damages. That week, the *News of the World* assigned two of their most aggressive reporters, Trevor Kempson and Mike Gabbert, to the case, hoping for a lead that would incriminate the Stones and ward off the possibility of an expensive libel settlement.

A familiar pattern began to emerge involving mysterious vans parked outside band members' houses, and clicking sounds and echoes on phone lines. As Mick, Keith and Brian would soon discover, just because you're paranoid doesn't mean they aren't after you. Despite Warren's assertions that the police and the *News of the World* were not acting in collusion, the press and police remained in close contact until on the evening of Saturday, 11 February the phone rang on the news desk. 'It was enormously fortunate,' recalls Warren, 'that it happened to be an informant.'

The police raid at Redlands at 8 p.m. on Sunday, 12 February, prompted by a phone call from the *News of the World*, was a defining event of the decade. Brian and Anita, fatefully, were absent. Brian was planning to come down for what was intended as a blissful, unifying band weekend but was struggling to complete the *Mord und Totschlag* soundtrack and finished too late for the drive down to West Wittering. The weekend ended up bonding Mick and Keith in a far deeper way than anyone could have comprehended, while Brian's absence would have consequences that were just as significant.

The stay had been planned, probably at the suggestion of Robert Fraser, as a kind of cross between a religious festival and a scuzzy party. The central design was for Mick to have his first proper acid trip, helped by Californian 'acid evangelist' David Schneiderman, who travelled around with a mysterious suitcase full of drugs and paperwork. Hanger-on Nicky Kramer and Keith's chauffeur, a Belgian named Patrick, were the only outsiders in a party that also included Fraser and his servant/lover Mohammed Jajaj, Fraser's friend Michael Cooper (who shot the cover for *Sgt Pepper* in March and was becoming virtually a house photographer for the Stones), and Christopher Gibbs.

Schneiderman administered acid to Mick, Keith, Marianne and the others just before noon on the Sunday morning. Mick and Marianne, who had never tried acid before, felt sick at first. Then the drug kicked in. Marianne thought the experience opened Mick up, removed some of his defences, his artifice. Just as profoundly, it bonded Mick and Keith, who'd become estranged over the last year. Acid made them see each other in a more sympathetic light. From that point on, says Marianne, 'they became the Glimmer Twins'.

The trippers frolicked around West Wittering that Sunday afternoon, wandering around the garden then driving down to the beach, where Cooper's photos document the disparate little group. They returned as the sun went down and had just settled in the living room when a visitor arrived: Tony Bramwell, soon followed by George Harrison and wife Pattie, who'd driven down in George's Mini.

Bramwell didn't find the gathering that beatific. 'I'd gone down because I had a girlfriend in Selsey, round the corner. But when I got there, there was just a lot of shit people that I really didn't like. Robert Fraser always got up my nose. So I wasn't there for more than ten minutes before I left for Selsey.' George and Pattie didn't stay long either. 'I think George actually sussed the same as me,' says Bramwell. 'The Beatles mixed with nice people!'

As Marianne relaxed in the bath, savouring the acid afterglow, the forces of the opposition waited in the narrow lane leading up to Redlands. Events had moved fast since the *News of the World* had phoned Scotland Yard late on Saturday evening. According to Steve Abrams of the *International Times*, the Yard declined to act on the tip, believing that busting Mick Jagger for possession of pot would be the best possible advert for the drug. So the information was passed to Detective Stan Cudmore of the local police in West Sussex. Cudmore, with Chief Inspector Gordon Dineley, assembled a team of eighteen officers, including Rosemary Slade and Evelyn Fuller for the purpose of performing intimate body searches on women – namely Marianne. The informant was apparently well briefed on exactly who was at the cottage.

When Keith saw a face staring in through the window at Redlands, he assumed it was just a fan getting too close, as they so often did. A few moments later, after loud hammering at the door, he opened up to be faced with a warrant and police officers spilling into the house.

Detective Evelyn Fuller, the woman Keith had seen at the window, searched through Marianne and Mick's room, taking careful note of the pink ostrich feathers on their bed, Marianne's white bra and Edwardian blouse, and also several books on witchcraft, including *Games to Play*. Fuller was joined by another detective who searched a green velvet jacket and found four pills. They were Stenamina seasickness tablets that Marianne had bought in San Remo. Mick, the gallant, said they were his. Marianne's presence – she was naked but for a large fur rug with which she'd covered herself after her bath – shocked the assembled detectives, who took her unperturbed grande dame demeanour as conclusive proof of the consumption of evil substances. This shock was not a development they would keep to themselves.

As the cops continued to search, they finally came to Bob Fraser, who tried to intimidate them with his upper-class haughtiness, then turned over eight tablets. Schneiderman too handed over various substances. Cooper managed to evade a search, but several of Keith's items were removed, and the guitarist was informed about a key clause of the new Dangerous Drugs Act, passed the previous June: 'Should the results of our laboratory tests show that dangerous drugs have been used at the premises and are not related to any individual, you will be held responsible.'

'I see,' Keith replied, perceptively. 'They pin it all on me.'

That night, Brian phoned Keith to say he'd finished his work on *Mord und Totschlag* and was coming down. 'Don't bother,' Keith told him. 'We've been busted.'

In the first days after the raid, no one within the Stones quite appreciated the magnitude of the drama that was about to unfold. But at least one person was, in addition to problem-solving, thinking about the bigger picture. Where others saw a crisis, Allen Klein saw a perfect opportunity.

When the main players convened for a meeting later in February, Klein took charge – the tough guy who would see off the villains. Andrew Oldham, in contrast, could hardly conceal his fear. 'We were told that, after the Stones, the police were gonna go for the suits,' says his Immediate partner Tony Calder. 'And I never saw a man pack his bag so quickly. He was terrified.' Klein seemed to understand Oldham's paranoia and instructed his young, volatile business partner that the only way to avoid further busts, and press intrusion, was to lie low. Gered Mankowitz was by now Oldham's main confidant in the organization. They discussed what was going down, and the instructions Klein had given Oldham: 'Don't hang out with them. Don't communicate with them. And whatever you do, don't talk to the press.' It seems Klein's advice made Oldham more paranoid, not less. He felt he was 'in very dangerous territory', says Mankowitz. 'We were told to keep a very low profile and given the impression that we were on very thin ice.'

Klein's words of wisdom meant that Oldham would remain largely absent over the following months. The embattled Stones saw this as cowardice, Oldham deserting his post as the battle intensified; his disappearance became a key factor in his estrangement from the band. This left Klein in sole charge and ultimately ensured he took control of the Stones' Impact Productions catalogue. 'He was always playing a double game,' says Mankowitz. 'Clearly Klein was the most horrible and manipulative person. I can see that now, but could not then.' Oldham's position had become all the more vulnerable because in September 1966, after relinquishing business management to Klein, he'd handed over press duties to old-hand PR Les Perrin.

Oldham was not the only immediate victim of the Redlands bust. From this point, says Marianne, Mick's irritation with Brian reached a new intensity and transmitted itself to Keith. The pair reckoned the whole business had started with Brian shooting his mouth off in Blaise's. The fact that Keith had chosen to stage a drugs party, inviting outsiders into the group's midst when they believed they were under surveillance, didn't seem to figure in their analysis. Christopher Gibbs comments, 'You know about the bust. That was to a degree brought upon themselves by themselves. Obnoxious behaviour at one time or another. It was all in the stars. So there's no point looking for villains.'

It was cold in England that February. The weekend of the 11th when they'd scampered down to the beach was an aberrant spell of clear blue skies in a cold, grey month. Desperate for an escape from both the clouds and rain, which had rolled in again, and the grim atmosphere, Keith, Brian and Anita were the key enthusiasts for a flit to Morocco. It provided the perfect opportunity to stretch out in the Blue Lena – Keith's Bentley Continental, a beautiful, sleek, powerful beast kitted out with sumptuous leather seats and a state-of-the-art hi-fi system complete with eight-track cartridge player. Despite owning the car for a year, Keith still hadn't passed his driving test. In the wake of the bust he'd had suspicions about Patrick, his chauffeur, so for this trip he decided to use the services of Tom Keylock, who'd first driven for the band in late 1965 and proved his worth during the band's last UK tour at the end of 1966.

Born in 1926, Keylock was a tough guy – 'half protecting angel, half Mafioso', as Volker Schlöndorff describes him. He was ex-military, had served in Palestine, and reputedly fought with the Royal Parachute Regiment at El Alamein. Like Reg, Oldham's old driver, Keylock satisfied the band's fascination with hard-man types, with connections to the underworld. As Sam Cutler, later the Stones' road manager, points out, 'the Stones have always loved gangsters and had these shitheads working with them'. Keylock was resourceful and calm in a crisis, but over the years many people came to share Cutler's impression that he was 'a shifty bastard'. Shifty or not, Keylock would be the most objective observer of what transpired over the next fortnight – two weeks that would finally sunder the trio of individuals who had united just five years before.

The travellers assembled in Paris, leaving Keylock to bring Blue Lena over on the ferry: Deborah Dixon, Anita's old friend – for once without her consort Donald Cammell – Brian and Anita, plus Keith. Their intention was to speed through France and Spain, take the ferry out to Tangier, then follow the trail west to Marrakesh where they'd later meet up with Mick and Marianne.

The shenanigans started while they were still in Paris. History would have it that the trip was spoiled by Brian's paranoia and testiness. Doubtless that was a factor, but Anita's natural tendency to take things to the edge was just as important. In an interview about the trip, Keylock remembered her playing mind-games from the moment they were asked to settle the bill at the Georges V hotel. Keylock handed the receptionist Keith's Diners Club card, only to be told by the manager, 'Sorry, monsieur, we don't accept Diners Club.' Keylock asked around for money; none of them, Anita included, had any cash. Keylock continued blustering while Brian and Keith, who still seemed thick as thieves, chucked their bags into the Bentley. At one point he handed over a cheque on which he'd forged Keith's signature, only for the manager to spot the ruse. 'This is no good! I call the police!' Finally, Keylock placated the manager with another cheque, signed by Keith under the manager's nose, before they all jumped in the car, Keylock hit the accelerator, and they sped south. Only later, says Keylock, did he discover Anita had 'rolls of francs on her that could choke an ox. She didn't need no bread.' It was escapades like this that made him conclude, 'I didn't get on with Anita too much. She used to do brains in.'

A few people, friends of Brian's, hate Anita, blaming her for what would happen over the next eighteen months. Stash, Brian's closest friend over the period, and the man who'd helped introduce her to Brian, sees it differently. Brian loved Anita because she took things close to the edge. That was her magic. 'She believed one shouldn't settle into some mock bourgeois domesticity. Anita was always for keeping things rough. And for them to be ready to answer some difficult questions.' Brian's relationship with Anita was volatile and full of confrontations, insecurity and needling because that's how they both wanted it. Keith kept Anita on a tight leash, a regular rock'n'roll old lady; Brian fought with Anita, and gave her more freedom. As Stash points out, 'Anita could go further with Brian than she could with Keith.'

In different accounts, Keith has suggested various motives for staying so close to Brian and Anita around this time. Some of his motivation was simple friendship, shards of which remained from their early guitar-weaving days. Yet even removing Anita from the equation, Keith's attitude towards Brian was an unfathomably complex mix of admiration and resentment. Brian was brave yet lazy, inspirational yet soul-sapping. Worst of all, he was simply better at some things – and he still seemed, in a profound way, to be the soul of the band. After all the work Keith had put in, he had not escaped Brian's shadow. 'Look how Keith remained squeamish about talking,' says Stash. 'Very shy, and all that. So Brian had [become] a kind of front man for the band.'

The atmosphere was heavy, loaded with more than just the smoke from the cigs and the spliffs, as Keylock drove the four of them south, the back of the car festooned with blankets and multi-coloured cushions, Keith keeping the eight-track player constantly fed with music. Keith says Brian moaned all the way to Toulouse, that there were bad vibrations; Keylock remembers Brian being in high spirits, looking forward to his birthday on 28 February, ready to celebrate it in style. Brian was also smoking cigarettes like a chimney in the back of the Bentley. It was this, maintains Keylock, that contributed to coughing fits and chest problems that by the time they reached Toulouse left him gasping for air. 'He never stopped whining about how ill he felt,' says Keith. 'He was a hypochondriac.' Yet when Keylock took Brian to the Centre Hospitalier d'Albi in Tarn he was admitted immediately with suspected pneumonia. Once again, Keith reckons Brian was suspicious and didn't want the others to leave; Keylock says he was 'heroic' and told them to proceed without him, that he'd catch up later. 'It was Keith who said, "Let's split,"' says Keylock. '"Are we gonna leave him here?" "Yeah, fuck him." So I phoned the office to tell them [and] away we went with Keith and Anita [plus Deborah Dixon], over the Pyrenees down to Malaga, where we got on the ferry to the El Minzah.'

When Brian arrived at the hospital, nurse Marie Gillet looked at the pale figure with the blond fringe and silk suit and thought she was dealing with a girl. She gave the patient Cédilanid, a drug normally used to treat an irregular heartbeat, and left him to rest. Over the next week she kept a close eye on the patient in Room 13. Brian spent his time playing guitar, and celebrated his twenty-fifth birthday, one day after his arrival, with a milky coffee. The telegrams he sent to Anita, care of the office or the El Minzah in Tangier, were loving, saying he was looking forward to recuperating in the sun. Over that week, sitting in the hospital office, he wrote countless times to her. 'There was vast correspondence,' says Stash, 'lots of letters. Which are all very mysterious now, never mentioned.' Nurse Gillet thought him a model patient: 'Shy, and kind.'

Meanwhile, as the Blue Lena cruised into Barcelona, even Deborah Dixon, a woman who was well used to Donald Cammell's sexual intrigues, found the atmosphere too heady to bear, and disappeared back to Paris. It was in the back of the Blue Lena, somewhere on a dusty road during the drive through Franco's backward rural Spain, that Anita and Keith became lovers – Keith says it started with a blow job between Barcelona and Valencia. Shy as ever, he'd waited for Anita to make the first move. Tom Keylock knew that something heavy, irretrievable, was kicking off. 'Did I know about it? Yeah, but what could I do about it? Nothing to do with me.'

The trip to Malaga was picaresque: Keith and Anita bonding in the back of the car, a romantic dinner in Valencia, followed by hassles with the police after the restaurant refused to accept the

Diners Club card. Then when the pair returned to their hotel they found a telegram waiting for them from Brian, asking Anita to come and get him. Anita and Keith took their time: around four days later she returned to collect Brian, flying with him to London where, after a series of medical tests, he was pronounced fit to travel. Marianne Faithfull, on a weekend break from rehearsals for Chekhov's *Three Sisters*, was engaged as a travel companion, and the odd trio duly flew to Tangier via Gibraltar on Saturday, 10 March.

Brian was pale, washed out, and for once dressed formally: black and grey suit, white shirt and tie. Marianne thought he was having a mental breakdown and a drugs breakdown all in one – so they decided to drop acid on the flight to Gibraltar. It was there that Marianne noted one of the most beautifully bizarre and unlikely incidents of Brian's life. Still high on acid, he decided they should get a cab out to the Rock to see the Barbary apes, pampered creatures on a small nature reserve overseen by the British military garrison. His plan was to play them a tape of his *Mord und Totschlag* soundtrack. The three of them approached the animals with respect, bowing to them before Brian pressed the play button on his portable recorder. The beasts seemed positively alarmed by the impressionistic sounds and scampered away, screaming. Brian, says Marianne, became hysterical and started sobbing. At that point she realized there was some new element to Brian and Anita's relationship.

'Don't you think Brian looks so pale?' Anita kept asking Marianne. 'Not very alive?'

Brion Gysin, one of Tangier's most celebrated residents, was the one who announced, 'The Rolling Stones are here, the Stones are here!' Hearing that the band was in town, he'd run round to his friend Paul Bowles to spread the news. Bowles had never heard of the band, but not much was happening in the city so he dropped in to see the group, crashed out in Gysin's apartment, remembering that they were 'very much rolling (in money) . . . and very stoned'.

It was all a little too much for Bowles, who was there only briefly. The same applied to Christopher Gibbs, who missed out on the drama. Mick and Robert Fraser arrived later, while Marianne returned to London for more rehearsals.

Gysin, himself a visionary who'd spin complex tales and conspiracy theories, make crucial innovations in literature and loved living on the edge, respected Brian as a musician but considered him a 'selfish child'. When the troupe moved on, out of the crammed streets of Tangier into the wider open spaces of Marrakesh three hundred miles further west, Gysin joined them, disturbed and fascinated by their excesses. He would later initiate Brian into some of the most potent music of his life; and during this trip he would be an unwitting player in his fall.

Brian's final humiliation would take place in the Es Saadi resort, a luxurious holiday complex comprising a tall modern hotel with huge pool surrounded by half a dozen villas styled in various gothic or fantasy themes. High terracotta walls and black iron railings sheltered occupants from the noise and incessant hassle of the frenetic ancient city. Cacti, fragrant oleander bushes and Grand Jose palm trees clustered around the route to Brian's villa, a stuccoed, apparently old building a few hundred yards from the hotel. The resort offered a womb-like serenity and security. But there were dead pigeons caught in the palm trees and Arabic metalwork.

A second observer of the ensuing action came from a rather different milieu. Society photographer, set designer and acid-tongued diarist Cecil Beaton – or 'Fair Cecily' as his friend Diana Vreeland loved to call him – was a veteran visitor to Es Saadi. Beaton was a close friend of Queen Elizabeth the Queen Mother, a connoisseur of aristocratic glamour with imposingly high standards: he once observed of the Queen that, although possessing nice manners, she would 'make an extremely good hospital nurse or nanny'. Beaton was drawn to this novel yet strangely decadent aristocracy. His diary provides a beautifully rendered, exquisitely detailed portrait of the exotic party. 'It was a strange group,' he wrote, 'three Stones, Brian Jones and his girlfriend Anita Pallenberg, dirty white face, dirty blackened eyes, dirty canary-yellow wisps of hair, barbaric jewellery. The drummer [sic] Keith, an eighteenth-century suit, long black velvet coat and the tightest pants.' Beaton was fascinated by Mick, analysing his looks as an eminent art historian would appraise a sensational Rubens or Titian canvas. Mick was 'very gentle, with perfect manners', Beaton wrote. 'His small, albino-fringed eyes notice everything. His skin is chicken-breast white and of a fine quality. He has an inborn elegance.'

Beaton joined the group for a drive into town for an evening meal, taking note of the rugs, pop art cushions and sex magazines in the back of the Blue Lena. They all returned to the hotel around 3 a.m. The following morning, Beaton again calmly appraised Mick as he arrived at the swimming pool, noting that in the strong light his face looked 'a white, podgy, shapeless mess; eyes very small'.

Then Brian arrived at the pool, 'in white pants with a huge black square applied at the back. It was very smart in spite of the fact that the seams are giving way. But with such marvellously flat, tight, compact figures as they have, with no buttocks or stomach, almost anything looks good on them.'

By now, Gysin was well aware of the tensions around the band. 'The action starts almost at once. Brian and I drop acid. Anita sulks and drops sleepers. [She] goes off to sleep in the suite she shared with Brian. Keith has plugged in and sends great throbbing sounds winging after her and on out into the moonlight over the desert. Robert [Fraser] puts on a great old Elmore James record out of his collection. So, as the acid comes up on me, Brian receded into Big Picture. Looks like a tiny celluloid Kewpie doll, banked all around by a choir of identical little girl dolls looking just like him, chanting his hymns. Tom [Keylock] the sinister chauffeur shows up, rolling his eyes, hovering over Brian, whispering in his ear like a procurer.' Gysin claims to have attempted to walk between Keith and Anita but was prevented from doing so by their locked gaze, which had become so intense it made a physical barrier. Gysin saw an acid vision of a glass link joining the two of them, revolving and throbbing, 'as bad as a laser beam. I don't like the look of that so I check out of the hotel immediately.'

Gysin's part in the story isn't over, however. The next day everyone went off to explore, heading out for the desert, except Brian, who remained in his villa, depressed and ill. When they returned, Brian had recruited two Berber hookers and tried to entice Anita into a foursome. It was the kind of sex game he and Anita had revelled in many times before. This, however, was one time too many. 'It wouldn't have been unlike her to get involved,' says Stash. 'If you're interested in somebody else, things you would have enjoyed together, you're no longer able to. It's pain and awkwardness until you split up.' Sensing that Anita's defection was imminent, Brian was forcing a confrontation, inviting rejection.

In future years, the story was spread that Brian attacked Anita violently when she refused to participate in the sex game; more recently, Keith revised his claim, saying Brian had attempted to attack Anita but that she had actually broken a couple of Brian's ribs and a finger, and that they feared his retaliation. In any case, says Stash, 'Violence of any kind is reprehensible. But you have a man weakened by pneumonia, dazed, the desperation of a man who feels things are slipping out of control.'

Keylock suggests a simpler dynamic: 'Why did he do it with those whores? He was off 'is 'ead, innee?'

Gysin saw the women, tattooed Berbers with breasts like blue basketwork. 'Expensive ladies,' he wrote. 'Cost Brian a packet – the whole packet. Anita and the Stones. His life as a musician. Eventually, his life.'

Disgusted, frightened, or simply in love with someone else, Anita ran to Keith, who worked out a plan. Mick shouted for the bills while Keylock asked Gysin to distract Brian. The writer took him to the city's celebrated Jemaa el-Fnaa, an ancient gathering place full of snake-charmers, hucksters, dancing monkeys and musicians beating out hypnotic rhythms. Always a poor negotiator, too keen to show his interest, Brian paid an inordinate amount of money for a hookah which the vendor insisted was a rare antique, adorned with ancient teeth and bones. When he returned to the Es Saadi, his friends were gone.

Gysin described the events he witnessed as 'mythological'. They were certainly much mythologized. One of the myths, much favoured by Brian's father – a man who barely knew his son – was that Anita's disappearance killed him. However painful her abandonment was, this was not the case. Brian knew Anita was a force of nature – her leaving him wasn't the shock. It was the traitorous actions of Mick and Keith that devastated him. This was a pair of multimillionaires who'd whinge about a fiver for the next fifty years yet barely mention how they'd abandoned their bandmate penniless in an alien country. The loss of Anita was terrible; the betrayal by his fellow Stones was infinitely worse.

'Brian loved Mick and Keith,' says Linda Lawrence. 'He really did. He considered them brothers. This was like having your own family reject you.'

'He phoned me. He couldn't believe what had happened,' says Stash. 'What had occurred . . . they didn't confront him, Keith never stood up to Brian and said, "You motherfucker." He didn't say a word. He just decided to leave. That was what Brian was the most shocked by – the way he was simply abandoned. No money. Just stuck in a hotel, on his own.'

Brian Jones could be petulant, impulsive, wilful, irresponsible, selfish and indeed sometimes acted like 'an arsehole', as road manager Sam Cutler remembers. Keith and Mick's leaving of him in Morocco was the embodiment of their own, distinctive nastiness. From now on, people like Cutler, Marianne and Nitzsche tend to repeat the same description of how it worked: totally, utterly cold.

Gysin remembered Brian collapsing in shock at the realization that his friends had left him, with no information about where they'd gone. Still, his memory that Brian spent two days sedated in unconsciousness must be an exaggeration: after spending a night with Donald Cammell in Paris, Brian was back in London on the 18th.

Today, in a Twitter age when private squabbles quickly become public property, Brian's silence over being abandoned by his band-mates would be a remarkable example of omertà. In the decades since, we've all read thousands of words by the Rolling Stones on Brian's unreliability, his treatment of Anita, those fateful five pounds, the twelve gigs he missed out of over 930. In the spring of 1967, Brian made no public complaints about his bandmates, nor in private, either.

'I never heard him slag off the [other] Stones,' says Mim Scala, who became friends with Brian and his later girlfriend, Suki Potier, in the aftermath of Morocco. 'He might have gone on to Suki about it, but I never heard him say anything about Mick or Keith. Not once.'

'It was quite astounding,' says Stash. 'Brian would get massive volumes of correspondence sent to him, from fans who complained about Mick. But Brian knew the value of Mick. And he knew the value of Keith.'

'There was this sort of bravado,' says Michael Rainey. 'I'm all right, you know. He never complained to me about anything.'

In fact, while the conventional portrait of Brian in the wake of Anita's departure was of a broken man, his ego, his conviction that he and Anita were still a golden couple, was still somehow intact, as Stash confirms. 'He asked me, "What do you think? Do you reckon I have a chance to get Anita back?" I thought he did.'

But as the spring rolled on, the psychodrama within the band became overshadowed by external threats. In the wake of the Redlands raid, the *News of the World* had announced a major drugs bust but not the identity of the suspects. That all changed on 18 March when the *Daily Mirror* named Mick and Keith, jumping the gun on formal charges, which reached the Stones' solicitor, Timothy Hardacre, on the 20th. The news came as a shock because the Stones, according to one of their dealers, Spanish Tony, had dispatched him to bribe the police (although Keylock would later maintain the story was fantasy).

Meanwhile, there was continuing paranoia about the identity of the informant. Hanger-on Nicky Kramer was beaten up by a friend of the Stones in an attempt to make him confess, an incident described by Christopher Gibbs as 'very unpleasant, awful. I'm sure [Nicky] had nothing to do with spilling any beans.' David

Schneiderman, the most likely suspect, disappeared to California. Keith still suspected Patrick, his chauffeur at the time. More recently, some have pointed the finger at Tom Keylock, whose brother was a police officer. The *News of the World* continued to be well informed, revealing that George Harrison had been at Redlands that evening – seemingly incontrovertible evidence supporting the otherwise paranoiac theory that the police wanted to bust the Stones rather than one of the Beatles, who were more beloved by families and the establishment.

Against such a background of backstabbing, suspected duplicity and violence, the Stones' short European tour, which they'd announced in happier times back in February, should have been a disaster. Brian, still hoping to get Anita back, pulled himself together yet again, telling people he'd been taking guitar lessons to get back his edge – but called Stash, begging him for moral support. In fact, the European shows, chaotic and under-rehearsed as they were, capture the band at a beautiful peak; Keith's guitar playing is tougher, more muscular – a portent of what he'd be playing in 1969 – while Brian's instrumental work was 'beautiful', says Stash. 'The press were asking, "What is that instrument?" They meant the dulcimer . . . people were flabbergasted, in great admiration of Brian's musical abilities.'

Beyond the new toughness and density of the sound, though, one change was inescapable. Right up to 1966, Brian had been the main foil to Mick. Now, further back on the stage, paler, he was overshadowed by Keith, who seemed to have taken on some of Brian's dark glamour. The Glimmer Twins, bonded by acid visions and betrayal in Morocco, were further forged amid riots in Vienna and Zurich and police intimidation in Warsaw.

When the band returned from tour, Brian looked for solace with Linda Keith, the woman who had inspired Keith's lyrics for Ruby

Tuesday; both were damaged and increasingly isolated, but Brian was far from broken. Still he did not acknowledge that the power in the Stones had now passed irrevocably to Keith; still he reckoned there was a chance of regaining Anita. Early in May he enlisted Stash, once again, as moral support for the premiere of *Mord und Totschlag* in Cannes. 'Brian was OK,' Stash recalls. 'He did cling to me, said you have to come to Cannes. And Volker Schlöndorff was calling me too, saying you have to make it.'

The festival was a bittersweet experience. Brian's score for the film – sophisticated, experimental yet often accessible – was widely praised. Both Schlöndorff and Stash remember one moment when Brian was introduced as composer of the soundtrack and walked down the stairs alongside Anita, beaming as the cameras flashed, finally given the attention he craved. But his fantasies of a reconciliation with Anita remained unfulfilled.

Keith stayed in the background. He was careful, acting all relaxed and friendly with both Brian and Stash, but remained in his room when it was time for dinner – a dinner on which Brian had placed all his hopes. 'I'd said it was a possibility to get her back,' says Stash. 'Volker was delighted, the premiere went off beautifully, and we all had an extremely fun evening. You can see it from the pictures. But Anita had made up her mind. So after a nice evening, they mutually agreed to let it slide. But windows open, and windows close – it wasn't a case of total despair.' Stash adds that the whole evening was 'extremely cordial'. But as Schlöndorff points out, 'nothing can ever be cordial in such amorous fights'.

As the summer of 1967 approached, Brian was battered but hardly broken. His life was only marginally more chaotic than those of the rest of the organization. Andrew Oldham, paranoid and seemingly manic-depressive, would himself descend into near madness over this period, and volunteered for electro-convulsive therapy to exorcize his demons.

George Chkiantz, soon to become one of the key engineers at Olympic studios, is one of the few of his studio brethren to have kind words for Andrew Oldham, who he reckons had a keen eye for detail and a talent for picking out a good mix or take. But by May 1967 he too shared Mick and Keith's consensus that 'Andrew was going for a certain sort of style. And that style was starting to move on, so he became more and more irrelevant.'

Oldham's preoccupation with Immediate was a crucial factor in his estrangement from Mick in particular. Oldham had used Mick to establish the credibility of his label, and around the beginning of 1967, Mick asked for a word with his manager and mentor.

'Andrew,' he told him, quietly but assertively, 'you know I've done a lot for Immediate. I think it's fair you give me a piece of the action.'

Oldham was incredulous: 'You're fucking joking?'

Soon both men were shouting, with Mick repeating, 'I only want a third of it!'

This was Oldham's moment of hubris. His conviction that he was more important than his protégé would lead to his losing the Stones, and his label too. 'It was a big argument,' says Tony Calder. 'Andrew wouldn't give a piece of Immediate to Mick – and it was the biggest mistake he ever made. Andrew didn't ask me at the time, he only told me later, and I was so fucking angry. I'd have given Mick a third. That's when we started to fall out big-time.'

Some time around April, Mick and Keith had discussed their intention to jettison Oldham with Allen Klein – and discovered, says Chkiantz, a problem. 'They'd got Allen Klein in, among other things to make them all unbreakable contracts. And he'd written up Andrew's and, guess what, it was unbreakable.' Hence, with

Klein mediating, Mick and Keith arranged that Oldham, who was in any case keen to stay safely Stateside, would keep away from the studio. Yet there was another aspect of the contract that became an open secret at Olympic. 'Because of the contract, Andrew would still get the producer's royalty,' explains Chkiantz. 'But then they discovered he was responsible for the recording costs. So therefore *Satanic Majesties* took for fuckin' ever!'

Recording for this new album had started in February with Oldham, and continued without him from early May. The sessions were often a meandering, unfocused mess. In this context it was Brian who as much as anyone pulled the music together. In particular, along with session pianist Nicky Hopkins, who'd joined the Stones camp after working on *Mord und Totschlag*, Brian transformed the future single We Love You into a half-decent song. 'The part Brian added on the Mellotron was absolutely brilliant,' comments Chkiantz. The Mellotron was a primitive sampler, also used on the opening of the Beatles' Strawberry Fields, and the example at Olympic was particularly tricky to operate. 'It's only if you tried playing that instrument that you'd realize how difficult it is, what coordination you need to get anything resembling a rhythm,' adds Chkiantz. 'The capstan motor wasn't powerful enough, so the more keys you pressed, the more it slowed down. Playing it took a special kind of genius.'

Indeed, that summer Mick would comment that the upcoming album was largely electronic, and was based on Brian's experiments. Wags might argue that this was simply a way of evading responsibility for what would justifiably be regarded as the Stones' worst album to date. Still, even in his fragile state, Brian continued to hold a measure of power.

Certainly when Sonja Kristina, later known as the singer of Curved Air but at the time an up-and-coming folk singer, encountered Brian – during the first post-Oldham Olympic sessions, most likely early in May – she regarded him as the psychic centre of the Stones. Brian had turned up at his new regular haunt, the Speakeasy, where he could often be seen chatting with Jimi Hendrix. On this night he had arrived dressed beautifully in an array of Moroccan silks and multicoloured fabrics, but after some accident with a spilled drink he'd borrowed a shirt and waistcoat from a waiter – yet still he looked an imposing, psychedelic presence. Sonja, who'd just turned eighteen, arrived at the club with her friend Romi and sat next to the star. 'He seemed very gentle. Spaced out, in a very nice, fluffy kind of way. He was on his own, apart from a driver.'

Back when Sonja had first seen the Stones close up, at *Ready Steady Go!*'s Mod Ball in 1964, she had regarded Brian as the premier Stone, a pioneer of R&B. Three years later she felt no reason to change her mind: he remained for her at the cutting edge of the new look and the new turn-ons of the London scene. The trio chatted about music, as well as more esoteric subjects, before Brian suggested they go back to his place for a smoke.

In the car, that gentle attitude changed – he was 'antsy, kneeling on the seats saying stuff to the driver, telling us how he couldn't drive any more' – until finally the party arrived at Courtfield Road. Once in the flat, Sonja and Romi marvelled at the pale shagpile carpet, the telephone in the toilet, the colourful rugs and the collection of exotic instruments. Out of the car, Brian was happy again, taking phone calls and at one point listening to a mix of that day's recording at Olympic down the phone. The trio talked late into the evening about spiritual matters, visions they'd all had, the occult, and in particular about the god Pan. Brian told them he'd heard stories from Brion Gysin of how a group of musicians from a tiny place in Morocco called Joujouka performed a ceremony which summoned up the god. 'He was talking about the Pipes of Pan . . . then my friend Romi, who was very psychic, started having visions. Of Brian being this god Pan.'

They convened to Brian's bedroom for a night that was sensual rather than sexual, fondling each other, popping amyl nitrates, talking endlessly and softly. Eventually Brian passed out and the girls tucked him up, carefully. In the morning he greeted them again, quietly, wispily, once again vulnerable. Then he put on his Afghan coat and floppy hat and went out to face a new day. Embattled as he was, he still seemed a potent figure. 'He had insight,' says Sonja. 'He was undoubtedly a unique person. It would seem from Romi's reaction that he was a very special person indeed.'

All the Stones felt embattled on 10 May. After the failure of their efforts to fend off the police, Mick, Keith and Robert Fraser finally appeared at Chichester Crown Court. They faced a trio of layman magistrates chaired by Basil Shipman, a well-known figure in local circles. Mick faced charges of amphetamine possession for the Italian pills, Keith for allowing Redlands to be used for the smoking of cannabis, and Fraser a more serious charge of heroin and amphetamine possession. Schneiderman was charged in his absence, but his identity was concealed. Thus began a classic confrontation between the establishment – or, more specifically, the small-town squirearchy – and the upstart youth, an encounter of tangible brutality that would stretch Mick in particular to the limit.

Today, we think of the Stones drugs bust as the moment when the establishment was faced down and conquered. The confront-ation would mark out Mick Jagger and Keith Richards as icons of insurrection. But as Stash Klossowski points out, 'What turned out to be the making of Keith Richards would be the breaking of Brian

Jones.' Stones accountant Stan Blackbourne insists that 'the police definitely wanted Brian – he was public enemy number one for them' – and he attempted to shield him from some of the attacks. It's likely that both the *News of the World* and the police had been told by their informant that Brian would be present at Redlands, so now they were determined to nail him. As his bandmates listened to the charges at the little town court, and the Stones' barrister, Geoffrey Leach, questioned the police, the establishment turned up for a second go with a neatly planned flank attack.

The day after returning from their film premiere at Cannes, Brian and Stash recuperated at Courtfield Road, trying to work out what was happening with Mick and Keith and waiting for the afternoon papers for updates from Chichester. The phone rang incessantly and the pair answered all the calls, many of them from journalists they knew well. The questions were mostly the same. 'They were asking, "Have you been busted?"' says Stash. 'We were thinking, Have we been asleep and haven't heard anything? And remember, we were waiting for news from Chichester and all the while the press have been tipped off, in a major way, that a bust was going down – before it had even happened!'

Brian and Stash checked that there were no drugs around the flat. 'There's nothing here that I know of,' Brian reassured his friend, but they were still hurriedly looking around for any paraphernalia left by visitors when the doorbell rang. Stash ran down, and was relieved to see Mohammed Jajaj, Robert Fraser's servant, who'd come to help clean up. The pair spoke briefly in French, Mohammed reassuring Stash that he hadn't seen anyone around; then a group of strangers suddenly appeared, pushed Mohammed out of the way and rushed into the flat.

Stash and Brian were still trying to work out if the intruders were press or police when a couple of them pushed their way into

Together, Brian Jones and Anita Pallenberg unleashed a thrilling, dark energy, 'living on a higher plane of decadence than anyone I would ever meet', says Pete Townshend.

Above: Rehearsing for *Ready Steady Go!*, May 1966. Newly empowered, Brian redefined the band's musical agenda with sitar, marimbas or recorder. 'I always considered Brian the most gifted of the Stones, musically speaking . . . he could think out of the box,' says engineer Eddie Kramer.

Below: August 1966. Brian, the 'reach-out Stone', is the first to investigate Morocco, here with Donald Cammell (obscured), Robert Fraser (in shades), Deborah Dixon and Linda Lawrence, at the El Minzah, Tangier. The trip was partly engineered to help Linda 'move on', she recalls. Her calming influence was missed.

The fateful trip to Morocco, March 1967. With friend Akhmed on the Escalier Waller (**above**); Brian the piper (**left**); and (**below**), Michael Cooper's famous snapshot of Brian at the Es Saadi hotel, as he senses Anita's imminent defection. Some claimed her departure destroyed Brian; not so, says his friend Stash Klossowski. It was the betrayal by his fellow Stones that was devastating. 'They didn't confront him . . . he was simply abandoned.'

Above: Monterey, June 1967, and a sideways glance from manager Andrew Oldham, himself soon to be surplus to requirements. In the wake of his friends' betrayal, and his own drugs bust, Brian was upbeat. It wouldn't last.

Above: Brian with Stash (to his right) after their bust by Norman Pilcher, 10 May 1967. 'We thought it was ridiculous, and would all be cleared up,' says Stash.

Above: Brian with Anita and director Volker Schlöndorff in Cannes, unveiling Brian's soundtrack at the premiere of *Mord und Totschlag*. The ex-lovers' meeting was 'cordial', says one friend, but there was to be no reunion.

Left: 3 August 1967: Brian with Suki Potier, Ossie Clark model and ex-girlfriend of Tara Browne. Ladylike and well mannered, she was incapable of helping Brian, now isolated from his fellow Stones and 'public enemy number one'.

Right: At the High Court for his appeal against a drugs conviction, 12 December 1967. His legally advised isolation had by now resulted in 'absolute despondency'.

Below: Through 1968 and 1969, Brian invariably sought refuge 'from the pressure of being a Rolling Stone'. Here he finds peace in Sri Lanka, *circa* January 1968.

Above: Retreat to Redlands. In the summer of 1968, Brian recaptured the old blues magic – until his second drugs bust (**left**), on 21 May, after at least seven police raids. 'Brian was killed by the establishment,' says Stash.

Below: Joujouka, in the Ahl Serif mountains, Morocco – a magical place where Brian was happy, and where he planned his own musical escape route, with Cleo Sylvestre (**below right**). 'If only I'd pursued it,' she says today.

Above: Fadeout: Brian's last public appearance with the Stones, the disastrous *Rock and Roll Circus*, December 1968. 'They were determined not to let him drag them down,' says Pete Townshend.

Above: Brian's father Lewis, mother Louisa, and sister Barbara, with Suki Potier at his funeral.

Left: Anna Wohlin with Frank Thorogood, the builder she later accused of murdering Brian, even though in the aftermath of his death, says a friend, she thought 'it was definitely a drowning'.

Left: Brian's driver, Tom Keylock, at Brian's beloved Cotchford Farm. Keylock's apparent fabrication of a deathbed confession by Frank Thorogood would inspire theories that he himself was responsible. The real story is not so simple.

The piper who loved Pan, Sri Lanka, January 1968. Demonized by his old bandmates, victimized by the establishment, he nonetheless 'changed the face of rock'n'roll'.

Brian's bedroom and looked under the mattress – 'And out popped – I can still see it – a purple Moroccan-looking wallet which had this iffy-looking grass in it. My first reaction was, Who among the many girls we'd had round had left that behind? But in fact it was obviously planted by people who knew what they were doing. Because they wouldn't have found it that fast otherwise.'

As the police swarmed around, varying emotions engulfed both Brian and Stash. They weren't so much scared as confused, and occasionally they laughed at the bizarre scene unfolding around them which seemed 'totally insane – just incredible'. Then one officer, who they discovered later was the infamous Norman Pilcher, brandished a small phial he claimed to have found. Amid the buzz of voices and shouting, Stash heard the word 'cocaine', but as he and Brian rushed over to take a look, Pilcher smiled at them and said, 'Well, I'm not going to charge you with this, am I? For one thousandth of a gram?'

Pilcher's combination of aggression and unctuousness accentuated the roller coaster of emotions, for of course the next morning the newspaper headlines screamed that cocaine had been found in Brian's flat. 'Bullshit,' says Stash. 'And so it went on.'

The realization that this was all a high-profile set-up meant to intimidate and break an upstart musician began to dawn when the pair stepped out of the flat on their way to Chelsea police station and saw a TV news crew, all set up and waiting for them. By the time they'd been bailed out and arrived at Allen Klein's suite at the Hilton, the footage had been edited and was being shown on the *Six O'Clock News*.

Brian stayed at the Hilton that night. Although Nicholas Fitzgerald, a self-styled friend of Brian, later claimed he was depressed and on tranquillizers, Stash, who was with Brian at the hotel, contends that he survived that first encounter intact, that he was more shocked and annoyed than despairing at the ludicrousness of the charges. 'You can see in the photos from that day it was all hilarious – we are laughing and smiling,' says Stash.

That old rebelliousness, the total disrespect for authority that had characterized the teenage Brian, survived his first victimization by the establishment. But his lack of physical stamina, first noticed by Brian's friends back in his teens, would ultimately undermine that defiance. Although Brian and Stash laughed the first day, 'we weren't smiling when the police gave a completely erroneous account of what went on', says Stash, who's still outraged at the treatment he and Brian received. 'And we didn't smile when we had to appear again on bail.' Stash found himself stretched to the very limit over the next couple of years. For Brian, that initial bust caused a cascade of consequences that were catastrophic.

Some of Brian's friends blamed Allen Klein and his fellow Stones for what would happen next. Stash, for one, stands up for Klein: 'He got us out and bailed within a couple of hours.' But it seems that Klein also advised Brian, during his stay at the Hilton, to avoid Courtfield Road and keep the police guessing as to his whereabouts. This would have a marked effect on Brian's stability. More serious was the advice of Brian's lawyers. 'The lawyers bear a great deal of responsibility for what happened,' says Stash, 'because these establishment people looked at us like a bunch of idiots – my own lawyer, David Napley, was very disapproving. They all had this patronizing, dreadful view we were all mentally ill children. And they told us, you have to stay away, one from the other. And Brian, you have to stay away from the rest of the Rolling Stones. Now, some of us drew closer together under adversity. But Brian . . . he became totally estranged.'

9

The Kindness of Strangers

BRIAN KNEW HOW to deal with bigots and rednecks. Back in 1965, when walking the streets of Greenwich Village with Nedra Talley of the Ronettes, the dandy arm-in-arm with the black woman would regularly attract shouts of 'Hey, who do you think you are, faggot?' He'd laugh, give them the finger, and keep walking, unconcerned.

But those rednecks weren't organized like the police and tabloid newspapers, who seemed especially to hate Brian Jones. The forces of the establishment were a motley crew. The *News of the World*, in 1967 as in 2011, sold millions of copies with its unique concoction of moral outrage and near pornographic intrusion into private lives. Detective Sergeant Norman Pilcher craved fame and recognition. Backing them up were a bunch of minor dyspeptic personalities, self-styled worthies, suburban officials and legal types. This was a species celebrated – or, more often, derided – in Britain for hundreds of years, right back to the days when they were the butt of William Hogarth's scabrous popular etchings. Yet, while mocked, this group kept a tight rein on power – and Brian Jones was their ideal victim.

Caroline Coon was co-founder of Release, an organization formed to protect youths who'd often simply disappear after being picked up for drugs offences. Release was on the front line of the fight against a zealous and often corrupt police force, and the organization shared Stones accountant Stan Blackbourne's belief that, for the establishment, Brian Jones was Public Enemy Number One. 'Every time the establishment saw a picture of Brian Jones, they saw a political statement. He was remarkably honest about what he was, and to that extent he was very vulnerable. Because he was blurring gender, with long hair, those clothes, his love of exotic cultures, his rejection of orthodox religion. Wearing those clothes, that was a political as well as a fashion statement.'

Over a period of around twelve months, the police attempted to bust Brian on at least seven documented occasions. The establishment, ill formed and ill assorted as it was, retained a special, visceral hatred for him because, as Jeff Dexter puts it, 'he was a dandy – and dandies were always frowned upon by certain members of the straight society'. There was a price on Brian's head; breaking him would make people money. 'He was so beautiful, so glamorous, therefore he was commercial,' says Coon, 'in the sense that he would sell newspapers. Which meant that whatever cop could get him was going to get a lot of kudos. That's why Groupie Pilcher in particular wanted to get him, for the fame.'

In the immediate aftermath of the raid on Brian's flat, Allen Klein 'for once, was absolutely brilliant', says Stash. The management at the Hilton, where Klein retained a suite, viewed the prospect of hosting a notorious rock star and accompanying Polish-French bohemian jetsetter with extreme distaste. Klein simply intimidated them into letting the pair stay for the next couple of days, both of them 'still laughing', says Stash, at the ludicrous charade. The day after his bust, Brian demonstrated his defiance with a shopping trip to Chelsea Antique Market; yet later that day the mood darkened when the police attempted another bust, pulling over his Roller and searching him and Stash as they were heading for the West End.

The irony of a man purchasing boxes full of clothes when he had no fixed abode would only dawn a couple of weeks later, on 2 June, when the pair appeared at West London Magistrates Court and elected for a jury trial. Up to this time, Brian had been upbeat. But when he realized he was being charged with the new, catch-all offence of allowing his house to be used for the smoking of cannabis – an offence that carried a maximum jail term of ten years – his resolution wavered. 'We were shocked by how these cops would lie – we thought the straight world was essentially straight,' says Stash, who was charged with possession of cannabis. 'To see Scotland Yard lying through their teeth was very frightening, I can tell you. It was suddenly a really ice-cold shower.'

For all his faults, Allen Klein had had good intentions when he advised Brian to keep changing his location and stay away from Stash and the other Stones. He issued the same advice to Mick and Keith – but they simply ignored it. In the wake of 2 June, Klein's advice and the suggestions of Brian's own lawyers ensured that Brian became totally isolated. 'After a few days of being together at the Hilton, this connection I had with Brian just tapered off,' says Stash. 'Because he had been told, like a schoolboy, you don't hang out with him.' Mick, Marianne, Keith, Anita and Michael Cooper would all cling to each other as threats, both external and internal, escalated. Mick, Keith and Robert Fraser's case, which had opened on 10 May, was transferred to a bigger court, to be heard by the Chichester Quarter Sessions at the end of June; Brian and Stash's case, in turn, would be heard at the London Inner Sessions in the autumn. In these ominous circumstances, it wasn't surprising that the cracks in the organization would open up.

Andrew Oldham, still convinced he was integral to the band's future and in constant touch with Klein, followed his mentor's instructions to lie low. 'Allen totally played Andrew, played to his weaknesses,' says Oldham's business partner Tony Calder. 'It was horrible.' Oldham only realized he was history in the course of a conversation in the control booth at Olympic, most likely around 12 June. Oldham had asked his favoured photographer, Gered Mankowitz, along for the discussion; Mick had brought Michael Cooper. 'Mick told Andrew, in front of me, that Michael Cooper was going to shoot the next sleeve,' says Mankowitz. 'And this showed Andrew had been removed, as being the controller of the image. So I knew I was finished – and that Andrew was finished. It was totally cold. I remember feeling for him terribly, it was agony.'

Although Oldham would later comment on the split with impressive sang-froid, the legal situation plus the schism with the band contributed to a near nervous breakdown. 'He was absolutely fuckin' terrified of the police,' says Calder. 'Then he was under a Dr Mac at a nursing home in Highgate, where it was all nuns, and they gave him electric shock treatment. He asked me to sign the form, I wouldn't do it ... but he went ahead with the electric shock therapy anyway.'

Once the split was formalized, around August, Klein took over all financial control, while Jo Bergman, who'd previously worked as an assistant to Marianne Faithfull, ran the London office. Yet even by the summer it was obvious the situation was a mess. According to Stan Blackbourne, Klein was largely absent when it came to fighting legal battles; Blackbourne and the Stones' PR Leslie Perrin ended up doing the work. 'At the Stones' trial Klein came in full of bluster but the job had already been done by us over here,' says Blackbourne. 'He only came over to get his own publicity.'

With Mick and Keith grappling with their own troubles, it's unlikely they gave much thought to Brian. Instead, it was left to the band's so-called rivals to give the isolated guitarist public support. Paul McCartney called Stash to offer legal help – 'He was telling me, "It's ridiculous, absurd, you have to challenge them"' – and took the estranged rock'n'roll aristo under his wing. He called Brian and asked him down to a Beatles session at Abbey Road on 8 June.

Paul liked Brian: 'He had a good old sense of humour; I remember laughing and giggling a lot with him.' He also noticed that he would 'shake a little bit', and with gentle concern speculated that he liked drugs a little more than was good for him. That day the Beatles were working on a bizarre experimental piece with the briefest of lyrics – 'you know my name – look up the number' – which John Lennon had, according to legend, lifted from a phone directory. They had been messing with the basic structure for two days when Brian arrived at Abbey Road, and though Paul expected him to play guitar, Brian had brought his old alto saxophone. In a four-hour session, the band recorded piano, drums, guitars, bass and vibraphone, while Brian added a sequence of off-beat ska-parody rhythm fills, played with perfect precision, plus a short, cheesy sax solo which closes the definitive edit of the song, the perfect finishing touch to the Goons-style silly voices and nightclub crooning. It was the only time a Rolling Stone contributed to a Beatles backing track. The song would not be issued until March 1970, by which time both the Beatles and Brian Jones had passed into history.

A few days after the Abbey Road session, Brian fled London for perhaps the ultimate episode of escapism, flying to San Francisco for the Monterey Festival, an almost unthinkably pioneering musical event. The first modern rock'n'roll festival, it was organized by a committee including Papa John Phillips, Lou Adler and Derek Taylor. Brian flew over to introduce Jimi Hendrix, still an obscure figure in the USA, catching the same flight as Eric Burdon, who unveiled his new, psychedelic Animals at the festival. 'We both dropped acid, and then went through customs together,' says Burdon. 'That was quite exciting.'

Brian had arranged to meet his old femme fatale Nico, who was herself estranged from the Velvets and looking to attract publicity in her own right. 'She was a tough piece of work,' says Guy Webster, who photographed her at Monterey and elsewhere. 'She walked around with Brian like a celebrated concubine at court – she was difficult, but we got on well. They were both high, and enjoying themselves.' Ever assertive and confrontational – 'and a little predatory', as Stash puts it – Nico spent much of their time together mocking Brian's clothes, his constant questions about whether a particular scarf went with a particular jacket: 'I made fun of him, but he said I was quite the same – and why should a girl spend more time than a man? I said I spent some time with simple things . . . [but he] looked like he had thrown it on. This provoked him, which I liked to do, frankly.' Nico thought Brian looked spotty – he needed a mother. But at the festival, Brian was almost constantly beatific; there were no snakes crawling on the floor there. 'He was very happy,' says Keith Altham, who travelled over as Hendrix's PR, 'walking around in lace frills and finery, a long flowing robe like he was Queen Boudicca of the pop festival. Considerably out of it, making dreamy little comments . . . he was good at dreamy little comments.'

Sometimes, the more worldly types like Altham thought this was all trendy druggy nonsense as Brian assured him, 'It's all changing, man, tell them about it back home.' Then Altham mentioned something about free love. With Nico on his arm, Brian looked at him from under his long blond fringe and replied, 'It's not free, Keith. And it's not love.' Altham took in the sight of Brian, with his Germanic lookalike lover towering over him, and thought to himself, 'Well, you've not lost *all* your marbles, then!'

Brian's speech introducing Jimi Hendrix, who would go on to deliver a jaw-dropping performance, was a big deal. Many British musicians – Eric Clapton, for example – were envious of Hendrix, but not Paul McCartney, who helped get him on the bill, and not Brian. 'They were kindred spirits,' says engineer Eddie Kramer. 'Brian in the studio was a creative genius – he wasn't afraid of anything. And that's exactly what Chas Chandler said when we were recording Jimi in the very beginning: "The rules are, there are no rules." And Jimi was like Brian – he would try anything.'

Unfortunately, but not surprisingly, Brian's willingness to try anything also extended to the festival's newest psychedelics, which included both STP and DMT – 'horrible, horrible drugs' as one connoisseur, Ron Asheton of Detroit's Stooges, described them. Combined with his new rootless lifestyle, poor diet and constant ill health – Eddie Kramer remembers his problems with asthma becoming more obvious from 1967 onwards – drug abuse and bad advice would soon, in his friends' view, contribute to the loss of the old Brian. Stash insists the isolation imposed on Brian following the bust forced a profound change: 'He simply fell into bad company. One guy I would single out, an American, introduced Brian to Mandrax. That was a disaster.'

Mandrax (known as Quaalude in the USA) was a legal sedative, similar in effect to barbiturates, which blotted out reality and helped Brian sleep. Over this period, sleep was what he craved: there are countless stories of his asking strangers to stay with him, to talk to him until he drifted away. But Mandrax relaxes muscles, hampers coordination, often turned Brian into a mumbling mess, and wouldn't take long simply to obliterate most of his musical abilities – that insight that had so often enabled him to transform Jagger-Richards songs from good to sensational. The deterioration was frighteningly fast and was already obvious by the end of June.

'It was horrible when Brian started taking downers,' Stash continues. 'I was at Robert Fraser's apartment one day, at 23 Mount Street, we were discussing what was happening, and Brian came to see me there. And he entered through the doorway and, attempting to cross the room, he hit every piece of furniture, bouncing from one to another like a ping-pong ball. It was a dreadful sight. He was a completely changed person.'

'He did have some shite friends, all these arseholes, right after the Monterey period,' agrees Tony Bramwell. 'Awful people. I think they fucked him up, more than the Anita thing.'

Previously, those people in the Stones circle who didn't like Brian at least had respect for him; he was a pain, attention-seeking and often telling ill-thought-out lies, but they knew, even grudgingly, he was a musical visionary. Now he was becoming a figure of pathos. 'He was a strange, fucked-up figure who I didn't get on with,' says Tony Calder. 'Yet if you set him a musical challenge, he would do it. But [in late 1967] he was a total victim. He'd put his arm around you, saying, "Would you like my coat?" Trying to buy friends. He was so desperate to find friends. He had nothing.'

By 27 June, Mick, Keith and Robert Fraser were deeply embroiled in their own troubles as the main trial opened at Chichester Sessions. Mick and Keith's barrister, Michael Havers, was a legal heavyweight who later rose to become chairman of the Conservative Party; but at Chichester the trio were faced with

Judge Leslie Kenneth Block, an ex-military man turned gentleman farmer and member of the Garrick and the MCC known locally as a 'hanging judge'. Fraser pleaded guilty to possession of heroin tablets, and was remanded in custody. Mick's defence for possession of Marianne's seasickness tablets was based on the fact that his doctor knew, and approved of, their use, and of course they were legal in Italy where they'd been purchased. Block minced no words in briefing the jury. 'You may think I am wasting my time in summing up,' he intoned, '[but] I direct you that there is no defence to this charge.' Thus instructed, the jury took fewer than six minutes to declare Mick Jagger guilty. As Mick reeled in shock, Block refused to grant bail – meaning both Mick and Fraser would spend that night behind bars. To emphasize the intimidating Victorian brutality underlying the case, the pair were manacled to each other when they were brought back to the Chichester court the next morning to hear Keith's trial and await sentencing. A photo of the pair in handcuffs, transformed into art by Richard Hamilton and entitled *Swingeing London*, would become a defining image of the era.

The case against Keith was based on Schneiderman's possession of cannabis and relied heavily on innuendo around Marianne's naked presence – which the British media lapped up eagerly, as newsrooms full of jaded journos drooled over fantasies of drug-fuelled orgies. Fertile imaginations soon concocted their own versions of what had happened at Redlands, which meant that Marianne became another, less celebrated victim of the bust.

Keith's trial was a similar ludicrous formality to that of Mick's, with one saving grace. Faced with a supercilious, sneering barrister who asked if Marianne's presence, cloaked in a large rug, was 'normal', he replied, 'We are not old men. We are not worried about petty morals.' Keith's defiance marked the point at which a shy, gawky kid with prominent ears became a bona fide rebel. His stance was more than justified, given that the prosecution's case against him was based on a generalized smear. Marianne's lack of inhibition, the prosecution suggested, could only be explained by drugs. The group was being prosecuted for a lifestyle choice, not a crime. Meanwhile, the defence for Keith revolved around the allegation that the affair was a set-up, that Schneiderman was a plant.

Mick, in contrast to the more sanguine Keith, was near breaking point as events unfolded. Judge Block was relishing his task, and as the jury pronounced Keith guilty, he ignored submissions from Havers that the newly created offence of which Keith had been convicted was intended to target organized drug-taking establishments operating for profit. Block handed down sentences of three months for Mick, six months for Fraser, and a year for Keith. That night, Fraser and Keith became prisoners 7854 and 7855 at the notorious Wormwood Scrubs and were issued with the standard prison fatigues and underwear; Mick, more isolated, was confined to Brixton Prison, a near broken man whom Marianne saw whimpering almost at the point of nervous breakdown.

In later years, the allegation that the police demanded a bribe, which was paid but promptly disappeared, was made repeatedly by Keith Richards and others. It's impossible to substantiate the claim. Some insiders such as Tom Keylock suggest that the supposed bribe money was actually pocketed by Spanish Tony, one of Keith's dealers. The *News of the World* would later admit to paying an informer, who would therefore have had a financial interest in ensuring the Stones were convicted. In today's legal landscape, this would be regarded as prejudicial. In 1967, the newspaper simply brazened it out.

The *News of the World*'s initiative would have grim results. Keith

Richards said that Fraser's imprisonment was 'probably the same as being inducted in the Army'. It's hard to conclude this is anything other than the callousness of the survivor: Fraser's gallery was placed in receivership while he remained in prison and his family would prove far less supportive when he attempted to resuscitate the business four months later. Friends – including Keith and Anita, Richard Hamilton, Paul McCartney and others – rallied round, but Fraser would close his gallery in the summer of 1969.

There was temporary respite on 30 June, when Havers presented an appeal at the High Court, arguing that the sentences handed down to Mick Jagger and Keith Richards were a judgement on their notoriety rather than their crimes. Judge William Kenneth Diplock granted bail, for the mammoth figure of £5,000 for both Mick and Keith; Stan Blackbourne and Les Perrin each provided personal sureties for £1,000. But Mick and Keith's release on bail was but one bright spot in an otherwise grim atmosphere. The band was short of money, short of a producer, and Brian's paranoia meter was on overload.

He had a new companion as his tailspin continued. In the aftermath of Tara Browne's death he'd been a vital, consoling presence for Tara's girlfriend, Ossie Clark model Suki Potier, who might have survived the crash but was severely traumatized. The pair had met the day before Brian's bust (Stash had designs on Suki, but called her over to their Paris hotel, deciding Brian's need was the greater). With her fine features and long blonde bob, Suki bore a strong resemblance to Brian – which meant she looked like Anita, too. Stash considered her 'an adequate replacement [for Anita]. But she was a jinxed person.' Mim Scala, another mutual friend, confirms, 'She was unlucky. But if you put it another way, she did survive the crash that killed Tara. Suki was a class act, a very beautiful girl who really loved Brian – she used to hang in there, and really cared about him.' Anita had been a powerful presence who would slap Brian back – although, of course, friends like Zouzou contend that Anita would initiate many of the dramas and violent spats that characterized their relationship. For all her resemblance to Anita, Suki possessed none of her predecessor's fieriness or indomitability. 'She was very much more ladylike than Anita,' says Scala. 'I think she was a debutante. She was certainly very well mannered. There was nothing of the street kid about her, she was simply very pretty and very quiet.'

Friends agreed that Suki was never a strong enough presence to arrest Brian's decline. But the question has to be asked – who would have been? For the assaults on and intimidation of Brian Jones, the dandy of the Stones, were more sustained and relentless than those that faced Mick and Keith.

A few days after the bust, Stash had been welcomed by Paul McCartney, who was evangelistic about showing solidarity with the establishment's intended victims and invited him to stay in his three-storey Regency town house on Cavendish Avenue. Brian visited Stash several times there, from mid May onwards. It was, incredibly, a mere five years since Brian had left Cheltenham as a young man with more focus and dedication than any of his peers, intent on assembling a gang to play his beloved R&B. Now, for the first time, he felt completely alone. The result was a profound despair. Over the course of Brian's visits to Cavendish Avenue, Stash was staggered by the transformation in his attitude. He'd simply given up. 'Instead of saying, "Fight the good fight!" which Paul McCartney was advocating, Brian was taking a totally defeatist line: "Oh, they're too strong for us." He was in a terrible state, preaching a tale of pessimism and woe. His sensitive nature got the worst of him, because there is that drawback, when extreme sensitivity makes you wimp out instead of toughing it out.'

Brian's ever-strengthening conviction that he was simply a victim and that his situation was hopeless was part of a vicious feedback cycle, for that self-pity inspired ever more wilful, childish behaviour, which estranged him further from his friends. McCartney happened to be away during Brian's final visit to Cavendish Avenue; a large tub of the then legal and extremely fashionable pharmaceutical cocaine had been left on the mantelpiece. 'It was out in the open, and Brian helped himself to it,' says Stash. 'All of it. I'm in charge of Paul's house, and I'm saying, "Paul will be really upset if it's gone," and Brian says, "Don't worry, I'll replace it."' McCartney heard from friends that there had been some kind of party and called Stash to ask what had been happening. 'And of course I say, "Don't worry, there's been no party, only Brian, and he's going to replace [the cocaine]. If he doesn't, I'm responsible." But of course, Brian never replaced it.'

Throughout June, Brian continued to descend into the abyss, and Suki was dragged down along with him, says Stash. 'Suki started out as well as anybody can be, very fresh and lovely. But Brian was like a kind of disease, he wilted Suki terribly. That's the sad aspect of this depression, the absolute despondency he sank into.' Stash managed to leave the country early in July, by which time the fight and optimism Brian had managed to sustain in the wake of his abandonment by Anita had completely vanished. Not only did he feel the Drugs Squad had him licked, he acted as if he was no longer part of the band he'd founded. 'He would speak to me as if he was not in the band any more,' Stash recalls. 'As if the band and he were separate entities. He'd talk about "them", not "us". He was the only one who totally caved in, where Mick and Keith toughed it out. Brian very soon after . . . fell apart.'

If Brian buckled where Mick and Keith merely bent, there was good reason. Stan Blackbourne's contention that of all the Stones it was Brian who was 'Public Enemy Number One' for the police was borne out by renewed harassment that continued even as Mick and Keith were making their appeal. On the run from Courtfield Road, Brian and Suki had temporarily holed up in the Royal Garden Hotel. For two or three nights around 2 July the couple were neighbours with the Monkees, who were in town for three shows at the Empire Pool, and who demonstrated their solidarity with the embattled Stones by wearing black armbands for the occasion.

Writers have commented on Brian's 'paranoia' over this period, yet even during this brief, secret hideout the police were stalking him. Les Perrin, like his friend Stan Blackbourne, had a background in the forces and had built up contacts within the police, who started to tip him off about upcoming raids. 'Leslie was a good guy who let me know when a police raid was gonna take place on a flat,' says Blackbourne. 'We could never reveal to anyone what was going on.'

Around 2 July, Perrin's phone rang with news of an impending bust at the Royal Garden; he and Blackbourne managed to make it to Brian's room before Pilcher and the Drugs Squad arrived, where they found Brian and Suki semi-comatose, attempting to blot out their troubles with tranquillizers. 'I put Brian over my shoulder, Leslie put Suki over his, [and] we went down by consent of the nervous manager through the service exit. Hundreds of screaming kids out front shouting out for the Monkees. We threw rugs over the back of the Rolls over Brian and Suki, with me and Leslie sitting on top.'

In the aftermath of the getaway, Perrin and Blackbourne decided Brian desperately needed professional help, and delivered him to a health farm in Hampshire, where Perrin knew the chief doctor. When Brian regained full consciousness he insisted on leaving immediately, though Blackbourne managed to talk him round.

'OK, I'll stay on one condition,' Brian told the Stones accountant. 'That you stay with me, and don't go home for all the time I have to be here. If you won't stay, I'll make a nuisance of myself.'

Later that evening, Blackbourne discovered his role was simply to stay with Brian until the guitarist fell asleep. Brian wouldn't even contemplate Blackbourne bedding down in the room next door – he begged the accountant to stay with him until he dropped off. This would become a recurring theme over subsequent months: the only way he could sleep was with someone watching at his side.

Brian's dire condition was hardly noticed around the Stones' circle; instead, the focus was on Mick and Keith's upcoming appeal, scheduled for 31 July. On Saturday, 1 July, *The Times*' William Rees-Mogg had penned an editorial based on Alexander Pope's poem *Epistle to Dr Arbuthnot*. The piece didn't mention Keith Richards or Robert Fraser; Rees-Mogg focused solely on the case of Mick Jagger, who had been jailed and photographed in handcuffs for possessing tablets that were completely legal in the country where he had purchased them. Rees-Mogg's argument was calm, logical and powerful, suggesting that the traditional values which the Stones were thought to challenge necessarily included those of 'tolerance and equity'. This *Times* editorial became a landmark, a potent polemic against the lynchmob mentality of many British newspapers, and was widely regarded as a key factor in the success of Mick and Keith's appeal. Pope's line 'Who breaks a butterfly on a wheel?' was powerful and appropriate and would become forever associated with Mick, who met Rees-Mogg the same day he received his conditional discharge, 31 July. But the image was far more applicable to the Stones' pioneering creator, still pursued by the police, and Mick's girlfriend, Marianne Faithfull, both of whose troubles were only just beginning.

Mick and Keith's case had indeed proved harrowing, but, as

Marianne says today, the trial represented a definitive moment 'for the Stones. But for me, it was a disaster.' A rumour that Mick had been engaged in cunnilingus with Marianne, eating a Mars bar out of her vagina, when the police raided Redlands had been circulating since the end of June, and was first referenced in print in *Private Eye* on 7 July. No one knows whether the tale emanated from the police or from Fleet Street, but it would prove as powerful an image as Rees-Mogg's butterfly, an inspired misogynist confection that would haunt Marianne for the rest of her life. 'It was awful, and it was a lie,' she says. 'I even wonder today, did my mother hear that story? And if she did, did she believe it? If she did it's terrible, and it's really frightening.'

Marianne was in a state of incomprehension and shock as the rumours continued to spread. Meanwhile, Brian checked out of the home in Hampshire only to sign himself into the Priory Hospital in Roehampton a couple of days later. (In this sad respect, as in many happier ones, Brian was again a fashion leader, for many rock stars, including Eric Clapton and Pete Doherty, would stay at the private clinic in his wake.) Although the reports are mainly second-hand, one anonymous doctor later described him as an especially needy patient: 'I think [Brian] wanted to treat me as one of his fans or his followers or his girlfriend or his chauffeur . . . you cannot ring [your doctor] at three a.m. [on] six, seven or nine mornings and say, "I've decided I must go to so and so, get up and come along." All the money in the world doesn't pay for this.'

Subsequent psychological reports focused on many of Brian's personality traits, notably his anxiety. The intriguing suggestion, one theorized by several of his ex-partners, is that Brian might have been suffering from a bipolar condition, one that was barely understood at the time, namely hypomania. A true diagnosis would rely on a full history of the individual, but many descriptions of Brian suggest a similar condition. Even in his more despondent moments there seem to have been episodes of manic or grandiose behaviour – if 'grandiose' is an adequate word to describe an incident Stan Blackbourne remembers from this period: 'Brian came in one day and he was dressed like the Archbishop of Canterbury. I said, "Good afternoon, Your Grace." He said, "Oh, you recognize me? How beautiful. Isn't it marvellous?" He'd been to Bermans, the costume people in Leicester Square. So he says, "Stan, thank you for all you've done, I want to take you out for tea, I won't take no for answer." I said, "Brian, you can't walk down the street dressed as the Archbishop of Canterbury." He said, "Oh, it's perfectly all right."'

Although Brian exhibited classic manic and depressive symptoms, for a meaningful diagnosis to be made the influence of drugs and lifestyle has to be eliminated. Given his heroic drug intake, it's impossible to arrive at a definitive conclusion. Stash, the man who spent most time with him in the first half of 1967, points out, 'This bipolar thing is a modern concept. When I first heard the term I thought it must be some extraordinary advantage, not an oddity to be remedied. Surely we all have some bizarre imbalance, otherwise we'd all be accountants.'

Whether or not there was a medical cause for Brian's mood swings, we'll never know. Of all the varying personality traits that Brian possessed, Stash suggests it was his sensitivity that was the most dominant. We hear this in his music. But it was also 'his undoing', Stash adds. 'He was incredibly vulnerable. You can see why he is accused of being cruel: cruelty is rage, a frustration that comes of deep, deep sadness and despair. It was very hard for Brian; this action of Anita's was very hard indeed. He was mean to her, but he was only ever mean in frustration at the fact that he was losing.'

Brian continued to be the most consistent and imaginative

contributor to the album the band was attempting to complete, *Her Satanic Majesties Request*, pulling together songs like 2000 Light Years From Home, but he fled the country for much of the summer, to Marbella, and later to Libya. One of the many times Keith Altham dropped in on Olympic to see what was happening, Brian showed him a string of brochures of far-off places in Africa and the Far East and told Altham of his fantasies of 'getting away somewhere, where I can get my head together'. Altham wasn't convinced: he suspected Brian was as likely to 'go to Tangier or somewhere, where he could get his head *un*together'.

When that summer Mick and Keith oversaw the cover design for *Flowers* – a messy grab-bag of assorted tracks for American release only – they rejigged it, a paltry effort featuring cut-out shots of each band member's head atop a flower stem. According to Bill Wyman, the pair decided to remove the leaves from Brian's stem: '[It was] their idea of a joke. Truth is, I never got it.'

In the years since, others have wondered why the promotional film of We Love You showed a clip of Brian so obviously out of it, at a time when he had a drugs charge hanging over him. Maybe it was an accident. Maybe that, too, was their idea of a joke.

As Jack Nitzsche points out, 'They could be real nasty.'

It would be hard to overstate the hostility and drudgery around the Stones as the rest of the world enjoyed the summer of love. Stan Blackbourne wouldn't hold out for too much longer. For one thing, he hated Allen Klein, whom he suspected of financial manipulation using Stones money. 'Klein was a bit of a nasty individual. I was finding out various things – he was using money earned from royalties or tours abroad to buy companies and sell them at a profit. I'm not saying that he never put the money back, but it was quite unethical.'

Business meetings at the Hilton became increasingly hostile, as the accountant challenged Klein: 'Why do we always have great difficulty in receiving money from America, when it's urgently needed? It seems to take ages before it arrives in our account.' Klein asked Blackbourne to discuss the matter in private, taking him up to his penthouse suite. 'That suite has quite a big balcony on top, it's the highest point of the building. He said, "If I have any more trouble, you'll go over the end." I kept calm and said, "Do you think that would be a good idea? There are so many witnesses – this isn't America, this is England."'

Blackbourne held out until the end of 1967, but around him he saw the Stones so embattled, with financial hassles adding to other stresses, that he often thought they were all on the point of giving up. All the Stones had money problems but Brian's seemed to be the worst as his legal fees mounted and he flitted from hotel to hotel; he was forced to borrow while he waited for the payments promised by Klein to materialize. Bill Wyman detailed one period when Brian accepted $300 from a Major Dawson in Marbella, who'd lent him the money to pay his hotel bill; Brian sent Klein telex after telex for money to repay the debt, while Keith received £20,000 to build a brick wall around Redlands. With desperately few allies, Brian was becoming mostly reliant on Blackbourne and Les Perrin, who with his background in the RAF continued to be a cool head in the near constant crises.

Later in the year it was Blackbourne who heard news of another raid and raced down to the house where Brian was staying. 'There were several guys, girls, completely naked, laid out all over the place, stoned up to their eyebrows. Brian didn't know where he was, he hadn't got a clue what was happening.' Blackbourne and his driver turfed out the hangers-on, opened the windows, and the driver took Brian to a safe refuge. 'There were one or two places we could take him. So I was there when the police arrived, looking at some papers nonchalantly, and when they came in they said, "Is Mr Brian Jones here?" "No." "When was he here?" "I dunno." Nothing was found. The rest of the boys didn't know about these things.' Perhaps in revenge, the police staged a raid on Blackbourne's office on Regent Street, complete with a search warrant.

Even with Mick and Keith's successful appeals, the general intimidation didn't let up. 'Groupie Pilcher was more the run-of-the-mill copper,' says Caroline Coon, co-founder of Release, which assisted the Stones. 'But some of the others used to go around like something out of the Mafia. One of them had Savile Row tailored suits and dark glasses. They really revelled in their power, would walk in [and] sit down in your office like they owned the world.' There were allegations that Pilcher engaged in similar intimidation tactics, turning up at Brian's new semi-permanent abode, a mansion block flat at 17 Chesham Street, claiming he needed to question him about a murder case.

Brian remained on the run for most of the autumn, from the police and seemingly from his own band. When the Stones flew over to New York on 13 September he smiled happily for the cameras, and although questioned closely by immigration officials, he seemed fairly chipper. But at a business meeting with Allen Klein the next day to discuss a formal announcement of their separation from Andrew Oldham, it was more obvious than ever that this was now Mick and Keith's show. The band assembled in all their rented finery for the Michael Cooper shoot but the expensive 3D cover didn't conceal the lack of inspiration for the *Satanic Majesties* album, which was released on 8 December. Keith Altham was one of many reviewers who liked the Stones but was shocked by the poor quality of the album. He reviewed it for the *NME* in the only way possible, by stringing together a nonsensical stream of 'absolute cobblers' to mock the album's vacuous hipness. A couple of days after the review appeared, Altham was walking down Wigmore Street at two in the morning when Marianne pulled up in a chauffeur-driven Rolls, jumped out and hugged him enthusiastically. 'What a wonderful review, darling! The funniest thing I've ever read.' As Marianne got back in the car and sped off down the street, Altham reflected how the fragile, gorgeous woman was the only person around Mick and Keith's camp to show any genuine sensitivity – or any real sense of humour, for that matter.

Maybe there was little to laugh about. After managing to persuade the prosecution to release his passport, Stash had spent most of the autumn in Rome. He returned to London at the end of October, ready for his and Brian's trial at the Inner London Sessions on the 30th. Brian, as for so much of this year, had fled London, in this instance for Spain, and the pair only met up to discuss their case the day before their court appearance.

Stash was shocked at what he heard: 'Brian told me he was pleading guilty. I told him it was the wrong thing. I pleaded with him, begged him. I wasn't concerned it was damaging my case, I was concerned that it wasn't right he should plead guilty – he simply shouldn't admit any guilt.' Brian's lawyers had advised him that, in a similar manner to Keith's case, it was likely that he had no real defence against the charge of allowing his house to be used for the purposes of smoking cannabis. There was logic to the argument, for any defence that the substances were planted, or that Brian's case did not conform to the intention of the law, was hugely risky. But the option Brian and his advisers chose – to plead guilty, and present his damaged mental state as mitigation – represented an act of surrender to the forces of oppression.

Brian had started out as the bravest Stone, the one who'd staked everything on the band when the others staked so little. This was his most flagrant act of weakness. 'It poisoned the well with Keith,' says Stash. 'The plan, this establishment conspiracy of the mediocrities, was to destroy the [band], to cut off the head in one stroke.' Brian pleading guilty made the other Stones more vulnerable, it would give Brian and the band serious problems with US immigration, and it also tarnished Stash by association. 'My lawyers said, "They don't have a case," and told me we were going to ask for costs. And the whole process of Brian pleading guilty weakened my case, too.'

It was with these arguments resounding in their heads that Brian and Stash arrived at the Inner London Sessions. Dressed soberly in a pin-striped suit, white silk shirt and blue polka dot tie, Brian possessed a certain swagger, but it was fragile. The forces that faced him were ominously similar to those at the Chichester court. Chairman Reginald Ethelbert Seaton was sixty-eight, claimed membership of the Scottish gentry and numbered archbishops among his nearly noble lineage. He was flanked by three more magistrates. Impassively, they listened as the prosecution announced that they had dropped the charges against Stanislas Klossowski de Rola, that they would not proceed with the charge of possession of cocaine. Brian then entered a plea of guilty to the cannabis possession, as well as allowing his premises to be used for the smoking of cannabis resin.

Whereas Mick and Keith had had Marianne and others in the dock alongside them, Brian had little support beyond a small gaggle of fans and a group of protesters led by Steve Abrams, a contributor to *IT* and more recently founder of SOMA, a pressure group to campaign against cannabis laws. Caroline Coon was also there with her boyfriend, DJ and Release activist Jeff Dexter, Chris Jagger (Mick's younger brother) and some others from the London counter-culture scene.

Brian's barrister, James Comyn QC, stood to present his case for mitigation. Brian was a brilliant man brought low by addiction, he told the bench. His client had 'never taken hard drugs. As for cannabis, he will cut it out completely. It has never helped him solve any problems. In fact, it has created problems. He says that no one should take an example from him.' Comyn detailed Brian's achievements as a musician and composer, adding – abasing his client still further – that Brian hoped his fate would act as a deterrent to his fans. The QC closed his case by arguing against an exemplary sentence: 'He has never been in prison – and it is my urgent plea that it is not now necessary for him to go to prison. People in the public eye are sometimes inflicted with a higher penalty, which sometimes can be harsh and even cruel.' This was a high-risk strategy, plainly alluding to the sentences handed down to Mick and Keith, which had been overturned on appeal.

Comyn then called Dr Leonard Henry, one of Brian's psychiatrists, to testify to his client's fragile mental state. Henry stated that a prison sentence 'would completely destroy his mental health. He could go into a psychotic depression as he could not possibly stand the stigma of a prison sentence, and he might well attempt to injure himself.'

Brian then took the stand. Comyn coaxed him through a set of questions designed to show his fragility – and his contrition. Brian agreed he had been lax in allowing others to smoke cannabis in his flat, then agreed to Comyn's suggestion that he would now forswear use of the drug. 'This is my precise intention,' he stated. 'They have only brought me trouble and disrupted my career and I hope this will be an example for anybody who is tempted to try them.'

After Brian concluded his testimony, there was a ninety-minute recess while Seaton and his panel considered their verdict. When Seaton returned, all the words he had heard were mere tears in the rain. 'I would be failing in my duty,' he informed Brian, 'if I failed to pass a sentence of imprisonment. These offences to which you have pleaded guilty are very serious. You occupy a position by which you have a large following of youth and it therefore behoves you to set an example. You have broken down on that.' As friends in the gallery gasped in shock, Seaton handed down a term of nine months for allowing premises to be used for the smoking of cannabis and three months for possession, the two to run concurrently. To compound the brutality of the sentence – more than Robert Fraser had received for possessing heroin – Seaton responded to the request for bail with an emphatic 'No!'

Brian 'didn't move very much' as he heard his sentence, Caroline Coon remembers. 'But it was obviously a horrible shock. You can see someone physically diminished by the process.' Stash was 'appalled by Brian's contrite look and distraught defeated expression. Poor Brian was in shock – having accepted to plead guilty he was definitely not prepared for what was coming.'

Brian was led down to the cells, ready for his transfer to Wormwood Scrubs. His meek submission to authority had been for nothing. Stash and especially Keith Richards were disappointed, even exasperated, by his guilty plea, the way he'd abased himself. But Coon, who'd witnessed many such fights in the wake of the 1965 Dangerous Drugs Act, points out this acquiescence was exactly what the system was designed to produce: 'I got a sense of this from all the other young men being arrested. It completely undermines your strength, your sense of yourself when people in uniforms, the state apparatus, can wipe you off the face of the earth. Unless you've had it happen to yourself, you can't imagine how vile it is, or the traumatic stress it's going to induce.' As for the criticism that pleading mitigation was an act of weakness, Coon insists, 'A lot of more powerful men than Brian Jones had to follow advice to put up whatever mitigation he could. These were the judges who used to hang you, or send you to Australia; there was nothing you could do about a hanging judge. I don't think he lost any dignity whatsoever using whatever means he could to keep himself out of prison.'

Coon had earlier seen Mick Jagger frightened and shaken in the Release office, trying to wrestle with the implications of his case. Now the flank assault on Brian Jones, even after sage voices like William Rees-Mogg's had exposed the hypocrisy of exemplary sentencing, evoked special outrage, which culminated in a spontaneous demonstration of sympathy with the brutalized dandy. 'Brian was much more vulnerable,' says Jeff Dexter, 'that's why we demonstrated. It was not right that a boy of that condition should be thrown in jail.' That evening a group of supporters including Abrams, Coon, Dexter, Chris Jagger, Susan Ziegler (Hoppy Hopkins' girlfriend) and four others marched down the King's Road, handing out fake joints and shouting 'Free Brian Jones!' It was a rainy, quiet night, and they protested unhindered for some time before the police arrived, insisted they needed a licence for their demonstration, and ultimately arrested the entire group. Dexter was slammed into a Black Maria hard enough to dent it, and was then charged with malicious damage of police property.

The following evening Brian was released from Wormwood Scrubs on bail subject to his appeal. He was a diminished figure – which was presumably the outcome Reginald Ethelbert Seaton had sought. The appeal was scheduled for 12 December, and in the weeks before it was heard, Mick and Keith's own hanging judge, Leslie Block, happened to be the after-dinner speaker at a gathering of Horsham farmers. Block kept his metaphors nice and simple, to suit agrarian types, for he spoke about farmers' problems with stones: 'I may say they are of no use to man or beast unless they are otherwise dealt with – by being ground very small, or to be cut down in size.' To guffaws from his audience, he went on to say that he and his fellow magistrates had done their best to cut these stones down to size, 'but alas, the Court of Criminal Appeal let them roll free!' Block's words were a blatant reference to an issue that was sub judice, as Brian's appeal was yet to be heard – but the judge was, of course, never censured.

As Brian waited for his appeal to be heard, the police, according to reports, stopped and searched his car once again as his current chauffeur, Brian Pastalanga, was driving him down London Embankment. Pastalanga stopped Brian as he attempted to jump in the Thames. A few weeks later Brian's appeal was lodged, based on a series of psychiatric reports that detailed his feelings of in-adequacy and the possible imminence of a complete mental breakdown. The dangerous dandy unmasked himself as an inadequate, and in return for this prostration before the authorities was fined £1,000 and given three years' probation.

The light is clear and white and the snow crunches underfoot as Marianne Faithfull walks from the sleek modern restaurant of her concrete-and-glass Austrian hotel to the bar area where she can light up. Last week she went to Vienna, to find out about her family's wartime history for an upcoming TV documentary. Tonight she will sing in a production of Kurt Weill's *The Seven Deadly Sins*, a work Marianne especially identifies with because she reckons she's committed most of them.

Marianne is a survivor of the onslaught that broke Brian. But this magnificent woman, whose mother and grandfather fought the Nazis and lived to tell the tale, felt herself utterly destroyed by the confrontation which cemented Mick and Keith's reputation.

'I felt crushed by the Redlands bust. My self-esteem went down so low, I think I would have killed myself. And I got the feeling people *really* wanted me to kill myself. Oh it was hard.' Only in recent years has there come any reconciliation with those dreadful days, aided by the closure of the *News of the World*, the newspaper that kicked off the whole nasty affair. 'I did feel good when it shut down. I danced on their grave. I've known that evil people come to no good.'

Yet it wasn't just the media and the establishment that nearly broke Marianne. Like Brian, she is a fascinating person, imperious ('I can't share a salad, I was an only child') yet with a sensitivity no one else within the Stones coterie could even imagine. When Marianne heard that Brian had died, she identified with his plight so much that she swallowed a bottle of barbiturates.

Why did she do it?

'Because I realized, when I saw all that happening to Brian, what they would do to me. I'd gone through the whole thing, watching it. And it was a terrible experience. The bit where they would pretend to be recording Brian and not have him plugged in. It was really terrible.'

Of all the Stones insiders, it's the women who stand up for Brian Jones. Her friend Anita Pallenberg has mentioned the feud against Brian, and Marianne uses the same terminology. Brian persuaded Mick and Keith to start up the Stones and in return was the victim of a 'vendetta', says Marianne. 'For being right.'

Marianne is fair, and adds, 'I did understand why they behaved like that – and Brian was asking for it. I do understand why they loathed him. [But] I saw him as another person with low self-esteem who needed to be helped. Not to be destroyed and humiliated and ground underfoot. Because that's what was going on.'

10

Bou Jeloud

B RIAN MAY HAVE been free from the threat of prison, but the escape had come at a heavy cost. The others had drawn together in their troubles; Brian was split apart from them. Hence throughout 1968 Brian and Suki were in retreat, from the police, from their own demons, from the deathly cold within the Stones. Brian could never quite get back in, as if he'd committed some unpardonable sin. As one person in the tangled, dangerous web of relationships put it, 'Whatever went down, went down heavy.'

By the beginning of 1968, Brian and Suki had found temporary refuge on the fabulous Berkshire estate of Sir William Piggott-Brown, the heir to a banking fortune who also happened to be a champion amateur jockey and owned one of the finest stables of racing horses in the south. Like so many bluebloods, Sir William latched on to the new rock aristocracy, investing in an agency, Scala Brown Associates, acquiring a slice of Island Records and swapping his Mr Vincent suits for kaftans and frilly shirts. Sir William's estate, at Aston Upthorpe, boasted acres of green fields for his thoroughbreds to gallop across, and dozens of perfectly preserved cottages where hipsters could crash out. Island's key rock act, Traffic, were residents for much of the year. Jimi Hendrix, Brian, Suki and others were frequent visitors for parties, which normally ended with dozens of beautiful people lying wrecked around the pool while George the butler made his way among them, neatly suited, trundling a wheelbarrow into which he'd load the detritus: empty bottles, crystal glasses, knickers, bras, amyl nitrate poppers. Although Traffic wrote the best part of an album in their little cottage on the estate, that was an exception to the rule. 'It wasn't creative, it was decadent,' says Mim Scala, founder of the agency that bore his name, and who would later initiate the Stones' contact with the French film director Jean-Luc Godard. 'It was great for all of us; a little madness took place. There were lots of girls, lots of bits and pieces, then it would be back to work in London on the Monday.'

Scala would become one of Brian's key companions over the next year, as much as anyone was key. Aside from Suki, he didn't seem to have any regular friends beyond hangers-on who'd ply him with Quaaludes or scrounge drinks when he was at the Speakeasy, the Revolution or Blaise's. Tom Keylock returned as his regular driver after Brian Pastalanga was sacked during an argument over a stolen camera; but Stan Blackbourne, the Stones accountant who had become his main supporter in the office, left for a quiet Klein-free life at Kassner, a music publisher. Many of Brian's confidants simply slipped away; Jimi Hendrix, who'd met up with Brian regularly throughout 1967, was one of the few who remained. The pair relaxed in each other's company, free from business hassles, talking and playing. 'It was lovely hearing them,' says Scala, who hung out with them at Aston Upthorpe and at his own flat. 'They were two of a kind, and they were happy.'

Although the Stones and the Jimi Hendrix Experience had overlapped during sessions at Olympic, there was surprisingly little interaction between the two. The Stones and their followers, even regular blokey ones like Ian Stewart, were 'surprisingly aloof', says Roger Mayer, who worked at Olympic and designed guitar processors for Hendrix. It was only Brian who seemed to get on with Jimi – 'maybe because they were both quiet types, really', says Mayer.

It's not known if they jammed together in 1967, but they hung out together more often over the first half of 1968, playing on acoustic or occasionally electric guitars, with Brian mostly playing slide. Sadly, their one studio session together, on 21 January, is a historic recording that is best left in the vaults according to Eddie Kramer, Jimi's main studio engineer. Jimi was in the early stages of working out All Along The Watchtower, with Dave Mason guesting on acoustic. Noel Redding had got bored and headed for the pub while the pair of them, plus Mitch Mitchell, persevered. The arrangement of the Dylan song proved tricky. Jimi shouted at Mason a couple of times as they worked it out, and the number of unsuccessful takes mounted. On something like take 21 a new instrument is heard: 'a piano. It's out of tune and it's absolutely horrible,' says Kramer, 'and it's poor old Brian, who had stumbled into the studio, drunk out of his mind.' Jimi was delighted to have his old friend turn up for the session, whether or not he was compos mentis. But as Brian continued to plonk away, Jimi started to look imploringly at Kramer, wondering how they could get him to stop without hurting his feelings. Finally Brian's head slumped over, and he fell asleep at the piano. The trio finished the definitive version of All Along The Watchtower, a complete rearrangement which Dylan would later adopt for his own performances, while the founder Stone snoozed away in the corner of the studio.

As the Stones planned for their next album, Brian initially seemed present only in name. Mick and Keith recruited new producer Jimmy Miller without consulting him, although the template they mapped out – cranked-up, compressed blues – was ironically close to the sound Brian had championed in the early days. With Brian broken, his self-confidence almost totally eroded, Mick was often quite kind: he arranged a meeting with Miller, who told Brian there was no pressure, he was welcome to contribute whenever he felt like it. Keith, meanwhile, was working on a dramatically new sound, finally abandoning the Chuck Berry riffs that had inspired him since his teens. Keith's new style was based around the Open D and Open E tunings, a style that had been Brian's trademark when he advertised for musicians back in 1962, only Keith used them without a slide.

Free from the influence of Andrew Oldham, Keith's creativity blossomed, as he laid acoustic guitar on top of acoustic guitar, processing the sound through odd objects like a cheap cassette recorder for a monstrous, lo-fi sound. Brian, too, was finally free of Oldham, the man who'd turned his guitar down in the mix ever since I Wanna Be Your Man, and stopped him doing interviews. But in the interim, Keith had learned all Brian's tricks. Brian had held on, made meaningful contributions to *Satanic Majesties*; with Mick and Keith back in control, that era was at an end.

Although Mick and Keith felt battered and betrayed by their own drugs bust, they would come to embrace the image that had been thrust on them of being counter-culture heroes. With Brian it was another matter: speak to any of their friends and there's a general consensus that he 'brought it on himself'. As Keith Altham, a close friend of Stu's, puts it, 'Part of it was his own fault, because he'd given information to the *News of the World* guys.' Even incidents outside Brian's control seemed to conspire against him.

On 16 March, after a session in which the band had laid down the beginning of several songs including Jumpin' Jack Flash, Brian returned home to Chesham Street to find the front door smashed in. In yet another drama, Linda Keith had ended a recently rekindled relationship with Brian with a drug overdose. Somehow the police had received a tip-off, broken in and carried Linda off to hospital. Yet again, Brian hogged newspaper headlines for the wrong reasons.

In a generally grim year, there were flashes of the old Brian, the explorer, the one who searched out exotic music. Around 20 March, this search brought him back to a location that embodied his youthful dreams – but it evoked more recent nightmares, too.

For several months, perhaps since the time Brion Gysin had taken him to the Jemaa el-Fnaa back in that fateful March of 1967, he'd been finding out about the music he'd heard there. The first of the Stones to trace blues back to Robert Johnson and Charley Patton, he'd since delved deeper still, into the African roots of the music, back to one of its likeliest sources: Gnawa music, an ancient form based around the hypnotic, unrelenting beat of the tbel drum, call-and-response chants like the earliest American work songs, and a musical scale that, with its flattened fifths and thirds, echoed that of American blues. The music had become something of an obsession, one he'd enthused about to friends like Mim Scala; so when Paul Getty Jr, who'd recently completed remodelling an ancient house – palace, really – in Marrakesh, invited him to stay, he leapt at the chance.

Brian enlisted Glyn Johns, once again, for the project. The plan was grandiose, brilliant even. His intention was to capture the rhythmic trance music of Gnawa, he told the engineer; then he'd take the tapes to New York and overdub R&B musicians, something taut and funky like the Cold Sweat style of James Brown. It was a visionary concept, anticipating the work of people like Peter Gabriel, even 1990s sampling culture.

Brian and Johns flew directly from London and were soon ensconced in unthinkable luxury in Getty's palace. The oil heir was at the high point of his drop-out phase, wearing kaftans (a little gawkily), and his wife Talitha was at the peak of her radiance, effortlessly stylish in expensively ethnic costume. The house had been remodelled by Bill Willis but retained its ancient textures, one luxuriously tiled space leading seamlessly on to another, many of them opening up into internal courtyards or arcades, all of them lit by candlelight at night. In the midst of this beauty and privilege, Brian refused to leave the palace. Instead, he proceeded to get absolutely stoned. 'I tried to get him out of the house,' says Johns, 'and I just couldn't manage it. He got out of it the minute he arrived, and remained that way more or less until we left.'

Brian had outlined the plan, what music to listen out for, so eventually Johns ventured out to the Jemaa el-Fnaa on his own, to be faced with a mind-bending kaleidoscope of sights, sounds and smells. He recorded several bands, handing over wads of dirhams – every bandleader seemed to know enough English to say 'make pay' the moment they saw a tape recorder. There were Berber groups playing the Amazigh folk style with bowed one-string violins, solo musicians, and a group of Gnawa singers: a chief who'd lead his group of singers in a call and response, the rhythm beaten out by exotic Moroccan castanets and the tbel.

Johns managed to cut a deal for the key Gnawa group to come back to the Getty house. There they played this sacred music, handed down from father to son, in front of Brian (by then recovered, transfixed by the power of the music), Talitha (who would be dead just a couple of years later) and Paul Getty Jr (who would become a virtual recluse after his wife's death). Brian would never proceed with his plan to work on the tapes; the story went around that they were faulty, that the level was wrong, although Johns maintains they came out fine. Today, we can speculate that it was the memory of the last time he'd visited the Jemaa el-Fnaa, when he'd listened to the music as Anita and his band of brothers disappeared, that prevented Brian from engaging with the project. We can speculate that it was his now un-conquerable insecurity that made him envision yet another scheme and not complete it. At the time, Johns simply concluded that this was another case of Brian talking big and not delivering. Yet there would be a more immediate, brutal reason for the idea being abandoned.

Back in London around April, Brian moved into yet another new home, at Royal Avenue House just off the King's Road, as the band cranked into action once again. Although he'd hardly had time to move his collection into the new third-floor mansion flat, Brian had started playing guitar again. Carrying excess weight thanks to the drink and downers, he was none the less the epitome of decadence in the promo film for Jumpin' Jack Flash, directed by Michael Lindsay-Hogg. Sporting bug-eye alien specs, silver lipstick and an ice-blue Telecaster, Brian dominated the visuals, alongside Mick, setting out a template for the Stones' fiendishly beautiful late sixties pomp. A few days later, on Sunday, 12 May, the band took to the stage in a surprise performance at the *NME* Poll Winners show.

The Stones unleashed Jumpin' Jack Flash to an ecstatic audience, and followed up with Satisfaction. The consensus was that this was the band at a new peak, Keith cranking out the main riff of Jumpin' Jack Flash on his black Les Paul Custom while Brian played the little trebly flourishes on a Gibson ES330. 'It sounded massive, they absolutely saved the show,' says Adam Kinn, who saw their set. The appearance was taped, broadcast briefly on TV, and then disappeared into the vaults. It would become one of the most requested live Stones tapes of all time, for this would be the last live show Brian Jones ever played with Mick, Keith, Bill and Charlie.

In the days after the performance it was obvious Brian had regained at least some of his powers, some of the confidence he'd lost in the months since Pilcher and his team had fitted him up. He chatted easily with John Peel and Johnny Moran in interviews for BBC Radio 1. In sessions at Olympic just after the *NME* show this troubled man managed to pull some perfect, eternal moments of beauty out of the ether.

The album that became *Beggars Banquet* was envisioned as a 'back to the roots' project. It's important to note that by this they actually meant 'back to Brian's roots'. It was Brian who first searched out the early music of Robert Johnson, Charley Patton and Son House, Brian who persuaded his fellow Stones of its potency, and Brian who showed Dick Taylor and Keith how to play in Open D, Open E and Open G tunings. In 1967 the Kokomo label had issued a new collection of Johnson recordings which inspired the Stones' cover of Love In Vain; Brian is thought to have played slide guitar on an early recording of the song, which presumably remains in the Abkco vaults. The song, and Johnson's dark magic, would become an integral part of the Stones' esoteric power. Yet, strangely, Mick, in the words of one respected expert on this music who met him recently, seems 'to have little sense of where [early American] music comes from. It surprised me. I don't think he had any curiosity or knowledge about it, whatsoever. He is obviously a bright guy – but there was no interest.' For a while, Mick tapped into Brian, Keith and Marianne's obsessions, it seems. But only when there was a record to make.

Some time between 13 and 20 May, Brian sat down in a circle

with Keith and Mick at Olympic and together they recorded No Expectations – one of the simplest, most transcendent songs of the Stones' career. His slide guitar part was subtle, totally without bombast or overemphasis, each little glissando anticipating the chord change by a beat, the perfect embodiment of the journey he'd embarked on in 1961. Brian would contribute several important parts to *Beggars Banquet*: this would be the last, best memorial to a sensitive soul.

Even while the Stones were recording, the Drugs Squad continued to stalk Brian. On the evening of the 20th, the band celebrated the conclusion of the first set of sessions by watching a preview of Stanley Kubrick's *2001: A Space Odyssey*, after which Brian returned to his flat in Royal Avenue House. At 7.20 a.m., Detective Sergeant Robin Constable – a figure who, like Pilcher, was well known to Release and other organizations – entered the block through a refuse hatch and led a team of police up to Brian's flat. As they swarmed into his room, Brian, who was already on the phone to Les Perrin, called out, 'You know the scene, man. Why do I always get bugged?' Their search apparently turned up a ball of wool sitting on a bureau in Brian's bedroom which the police unwrapped to reveal a lump of cannabis resin weighing 144 grains. 'Oh no,' Brian was reported to have exclaimed, 'this cannot happen again, just when we're getting on our feet! Why do you have to pick on me?'

The routine was sordidly familiar: the media had already been alerted and had prepared their headlines before the raid happened, and the police seemed to have a suspiciously prescient sense that the ball of wool contained drugs (although mentioned by name, Constable, unlike Pilcher, was never convicted of planting evidence and allegations against him were never proven). There was one crucial difference: Brian had been upbeat in the immediate aftermath of the previous raid; this time he was inconsolable.

Once again he was taken to Chelsea police station and charged, with the inevitable press in attendance; later he was brought to Marlborough Street Court, then released on bail. Press reports suggested Brian was whisked straight off to the Priory; Ron Schneider, Allen Klein's nephew and a man who'd enjoyed many cheery conversations with Brian back in the happy days on the West Coast, says Brian stayed at the Hilton before going to Roehampton. 'In that last drug bust he was very upset,' Schneider recalls. 'I remember him being totally drained.'

Desperate to find a new refuge, Brian begged Schneider to find him a room at the hotel; such was Brian's reputation, Schneider had to book under his own name, then accompany him to his room. Panicking, shaky, reduced to a child-like dependence, Brian insisted Schneider remain by his bed until he fell asleep. As the troubled guitarist finally dozed off, Schneider watched over him for a while before slipping out of the room. When they met the next day for a meeting with their barristers, Brian was so grateful for the companionship he walked up to Schneider, hugged him and kissed him on the top of his head.

Schneider felt sorry for Brian – but mostly, he says today, he saw him as the author of his own misfortune, thanks to his reliance on a cocktail of drugs. He saw no nastiness from Brian, whose isolation was, he insists, self-inflicted: 'he did have support, everybody did care for him, all of us tried to help. It was just one of those things.'

Perhaps Brian was beyond saving. Linda Lawrence, then in the throes of a star-crossed romance with Donovan, had returned from California and turned up to see Brian in the Priory. She'd made a shirt for Donovan's upcoming Albert Hall show as a kind of love offering, using a beautiful gold silk fabric from Liberty, with a matching smaller version for Julian, who was now nearly four. Brian's companion, probably Suki Potier, remained in his room while Brian came out to see his son, marvelling over his shirt, hugging him gently. As Brian sat there, on a chair in the hallway, asking Linda how she was and whether she was going back to America, Linda felt a remnant of that old warm feeling. 'But the spark, the light, the energy, was gone.'

Ron Schneider was in the Stones office, so he's a genuine witness, and he thought Brian's fellow band members were supportive of him as he gradually lost his way. Doubtless at times they were. Others tell a different story.

Mim Scala was one of the new sixties generation who turned their passions into a career. He'd become friends with Brian in 1967, and followed a typical new aristocracy routine: hanging out at parties, dropping whatever drugs were fashionable, and putting people together with people – which meant that by the beginning of 1968 his movie agency, Scala Brown Associates, boasted an impressive roster, including Christopher Plummer and Richard Harris. During a weekend in Paris he was drinking in Chez Castel when he recognized Jean-Luc Godard, and was soon enthusing to the *nouvelle vague* director about the London scene. A few weeks later the phone rang – it was Godard's producer, asking Scala if it would be possible for the French director to make a movie with the Beatles or the Stones. Scala made a few calls and soon had an agreement in principle from both bands. The Beatles had already made a good movie; the Stones were therefore the more attractive proposition. Godard arranged to start shooting in June.

By the time Godard's cameras were rolling, Brian was a fugitive ghost who seemed homeless, often kipping down for the night on a pile of cushions in Scala's office. Later in the year he'd take refuge at Redlands, of all places, but around June 'He spent a lot of time just driving,' says Scala. 'I don't know where else he used to go. He'd come to stay in the office and a few times at my flat. Then he'd disappear for a few days, and you never knew where he went.' Tom Keylock still seemed to be his main driver, a slightly sinister figure. In the aftermath of the second bust, Brian had teamed up with Suki again, but often he was on his own, in a condition that was 'very sad – diabolical', says Scala. 'He'd turn up, he'd have a bunch of crumped-up velvet clothes in the boot of the car, come in, crash out, eat something, fall asleep, be there all day. Then we'd go eat something down at Baghdad House, hang out for a bit. Then he'd be gone and I wouldn't see him again for a week, two weeks. Then like a bad penny he'd show up again. I never called him – he would just show.'

This was Brian at a new low, one from which he'd never truly emerge. Unlike Ron Schneider, Scala's impression was that there was simply no one watching the falling Stone's back: 'No, I don't think he was getting any support.' He adds that it's possible the tiny organization was doing its best but that Brian 'might have been paranoid that they weren't really helping'. Scala stops short of blaming Mick and Keith, whom he watched push the band forward, creating a song as Godard's cameras rolled. 'They were driving this band. Keith never stopped playing guitar, always had one in his hands. And Brian wasn't pulling his weight.'

Brian's isolation was such that he seemed not even to trust the Stones' regular lawyers. 'He probably didn't know what kind of instructions they were all acting under,' Scala says. 'He asked us to help him, hence we got in touch with Harbottle and Lewis.' Ultimately, the Stones office would find Brian a good barrister – he was represented by Michael Havers, defence counsel for Mick and Keith at the Redlands trial – but it was Scala who ended up taking

Brian to Mr Vincent in Savile Row to get a suit made for his court appearance, at Marlborough Street on 11 June. This time, Brian decided to fight the charge and maintain that the cannabis was a plant. He therefore elected for a trial by jury, scheduled for September.

Schneider says Brian got equal treatment. Others reckon that some were more equal than others. The drugs organization Release was in constant touch with the Stones throughout this period, and leading activist Jeff Dexter, who'd marched to protest against Brian's first arrest, observes, 'It was kind of weird – the Stones office themselves weren't that sympathetic to the whole plight of Brian. There was a sort of gap between them and Brian already.' The office was shell-shocked, under pressure, working at its limit. None the less, says Dexter, there was obviously 'a certain division'.

Chaos continued to engulf Brian. Jean-Luc Godard's film, *One Plus One*, was an inspired mess, simultaneously pretentious and an amazing document of its time. It presented Brian, just a week or so after his bust, as a sad, lost figure, barely comprehending as Mick, who has now become competent on the guitar, shows him the basic chord sequence for the song that will become Sympathy For The Devil, and Brian struggles to keep up. The song, based around Russian novelist Mikhail Bulgakov's *The Master and Margarita* (which Marianne Faithfull had lent him), would be one of Mick's finest compositions. Mick had taken Brian's tricks, Brian's obsessions, Brian's chaos, and turned it all into great art.

Brian's state was every bit as pathetic as the movie footage suggested. 'Physically he was starting to look dodgy,' says Scala. 'Blotchy, pasty, and his hands were getting blotchy with swollen fingers. I'd done weekend acid but wasn't whacked on a daily basis, like he was. His diet was pork pies with HP sauce and drugs. I don't know what he was taking: uppers, downers. He simply couldn't sleep most of the time.'

Brian never actually spoke of his victimized state. Keith and Mick's accounts would have you believe he whined incessantly, but few others remember that; he kept his silence about his troubles. Instead, his resentment of his persecution by the police, and his isolation, was focused on Suki. 'I was around from *Beggars Banquet*,' says Sam Cutler, later the band's tour manager, 'and Brian was acting like an arsehole of the first order. He loved picking fights with his girlfriends.' Mim Scala confirms, 'It was horrible. I used to cringe about what was going on. Suki would hang in there, really cared about him – and he was really awful to her. I remember one night coming out of the Speakeasy, Brian gets in the car and gets the driver to take off – so there's Brian going "Drive, drive, drive!" and this beautiful girl chasing him down the street. That kind of thing happened a lot, he just didn't care.'

The pair took their troubles with them wherever they went. On 4 July, Brian ventured back to Tangier, once again staying at the El Minzah, along with Christopher Gibbs. Gibbs had a fondness for Brian as a musician, the way he communicated with anyone, any-where, even some street musician with an old drum or hand-made pipe – which he'd always manage to get a beautiful sound out of – bonding with the owner across a cultural divide. But this trip exhausted Gibbs's patience. One night at the hotel, after yet another argument, Suki attempted to slash her wrists with a broken mirror. The long-suffering staff called an ambulance, yet again; then, when it arrived, Brian tried to palm Suki off on Gibbs, to get him to go in the ambulance. 'He was really trying to pass the buck, as was his wont. I wasn't interested: "No, get in there, mate, this is your baby."' Gibbs never warmed to Suki. It wasn't a universal view, but his assessment of them as a couple has the ring of truth: 'They were a disaster area. You know, as you go through life you know the people you can basically rely on. And there are some people who aren't reliable and they were never going to be, either of them.'

Over the time Suki and Brian were enmeshing themselves in a self-created chaos, Mick Jagger was planning how to tackle his role in another movie, initially titled *The Performance*, scripted by Donald Cammell. He discussed the part with Marianne, a far more experienced actor, who realized he had no idea how to go about it. She saw the character as dark and powerful, a pre-Raphaelite Hamlet who was also a little bit pathetic. The model, naturally, would be Brian. As rehearsals commenced, Marianne suggested an extra element, something stronger. So they added Keith into the mix. The result was the character Turner who, in a set dressed by Christopher Gibbs, speaking words written by Donald Cammell, with music directed by Jack Nitzsche, and involved in a threesome with Anita Pallenberg, was the perfect composite of the Stones' entire existence. While Marianne denies there was anything directly diabolical about Mick, she realized belatedly that by tapping into the essence of Brian Jones and Keith Richards, Mick would prove irresistible to Anita, the woman who had loved them both. Thus, even after Brian's ejection from the band, Mick would ensure that the coital oneupmanship continued.

When Nitzsche spent time with Mick at the end of 1968 after being called to work on the movie, he noticed the change – as if, having assembled Turner from the elements around him, Mick had decided to inhabit this character for life. Mick had been calculated before, careful at times, but now he was a different person. 'It wasn't loose and friendly any more,' Nitzsche would comment later, describing how Mick now had 'this aloof look – where he looks down on everybody'.

*

While Mick burrowed into Brian's and later Keith's psyches, Brian was embarking on the last great musical journey of his life – a journey that embodied many of his obsessions since reading Paul Oliver's *Blues Fell This Morning* back in 1961.

Brian's trips to Morocco had charted his life: his moving on from Linda, his impossibly tempestuous relationship with Anita, that terrible moment when Mick and Keith, the only brothers he'd ever had, left him in Marrakesh. During those visits he'd spent more and more time with Mohamed Hamri (running up bills at his 1001 Nights restaurant) and Brion Gysin, who considered Brian something of a dilettante (takes one to know one) but bonded with him over music, namely the mysterious, powerful Pipes of Pan from Joujouka.

Gysin had first heard the Master Musicians of Joujouka at a moussem – a celebration at the tombs of local saints – in Sidi Kacem. There were many strange, evocative strains of music that day, but Gysin was most taken with a group dressed in rough woollen djellabas and pointed leather slippers who had once, it was said, been musicians by appointment to the Sultan. 'That's my music,' Gysin told himself. 'I just want to hear that music for the rest of my life.' These were the Master Musicians of Joujouka, and Hamri would be both Gysin's and ultimately Brian Jones's entrée to their exotic, spartan realm.

Hamri was one of the many fascinating, multilayered cultural crossover types who seemed to gravitate towards the Stones, Brian in particular. He had been at the centre of his own Tangier feud, a love triangle between him, Brion Gysin and Paul Bowles, a notorious tightwad who once lent Hamri a suit that wasn't returned and resented its loss for decades. Gysin was far more relaxed, taught Hamri to paint, and admired his independence – the Moroccan had made a living as a pastry chef and smuggler, ferrying sweets and chickens between the French and Spanish zones in his country. Hamri's uncle was the leader of the Master Musicians of Joujouka – hence as a child, Hamri had danced Bou Jeloud, the powerful goat-man, a ritual of which it was said, 'If you put the goat-skins on, you never take the goat-skins off.'

It was Hamri who took Gysin to the source of the music – perhaps the first outsider to witness it. Brian would be another initiate. Once a year, the Joujouka musicians united to enact an ancient ceremony that Gysin was convinced was the equivalent of the Roman Lupercalia, or Rites of Pan. 'The point was to contact Pan, the goat god, who was sexuality itself,' he later told writer Terry Wilson. He found the music utterly seductive. 'You know your music when you hear it,' he would say. 'You fall into line and dance – until you pay the Piper.'

Gysin is often described as a friend of Brian's. He wasn't really: he considered him 'a spoilt boy' who'd do stupid things. He told Gysin he'd wrecked the Gettys' phone in Marrakesh, and kept badgering him about what he thought, whether the Gettys were offended, as if Gysin had any idea. But Gysin thought that Brian 'really could play guitar', and knew that Brian understood the music. For this reason they bonded over the Pipes of Pan.

The music was a glimpse into an ancient world, perhaps the very beginnings of the sound that had always entranced Brian. Yet the manifestation of the god Pan was something just as potent: Pan had brought syncopated, dangerous sounds into our world, was the ultimate progenitor of what some righteous people called the Devil's music, and was the god of fertility. As his psychic lover Romi had suggested, who was Brian really but a manifestation of Pan himself?

It was John 'Hoppy' Hopkins who commented that he never saw Brian smile except when he had a guitar in his hands. Yet Brian smiled often at Joujouka, a unique age-old spot where the earth was charged with a certain energy. Some ascribed this energy to the local saint, Sidi Ahmed Schiech, whose shrine dominated the village. Just like an early Christian basilica, the site, and the music connected with it, boasted special healing powers. In its early days, Islam incorporated older beliefs, as had early Christianity. The Bou Jeloud ceremony was the most potent example of this harnessing of ancient forces.

Brian and Suki flew in to Tangier around 30 July. Brian had called Olympic studios and requested an engineer the day before he left, so tape op and technical whizz George Chkiantz had just one afternoon to pack his bag, collect Brian's two Uher recorders (with dud batteries) from his new flat at the bottom of Hampstead Heath; then he returned to Olympic for a night session before getting a taxi to Heathrow. Suki and Brian were waiting for him when Chkiantz arrived at Tangier airport at 9 a.m. on 1 August.

Chkiantz had managed to stay out of the Stones' psychodrama; hence the Brian he encountered once he'd walked across the blazing hot tarmac was more like the Brian that Paul Jones remembered – 'my sort of bloke'. Brian encouraged the imposingly tall Chkiantz to step over the little rope separating the table and chairs from immigration, checking on his flight and the whereabouts of his luggage, and sharing the plan for his trip. 'He was totally together, and knew exactly what he was doing. He explained we were off to meet Hamri, and couldn't be late.'

Brian and Suki had a taxi waiting, a shiny new six-cylinder Chevrolet in which they travelled back to the El Minzah to have breakfast, and pick up Brion Gysin. Brian told Chkiantz they were going up to the mountains, where electricity was unheard of, so he used the one-hour break to stock up on batteries. Before long they'd picked up Hamri from the 1001 Nights and were making their way slowly, now with two cars, on a bumpy two-lane road. Chkiantz was in the Chevy with Brian, Suki and Gysin; the writer wove tales as they drove the ninety miles to their destination, of how the music they were about to see stretched back centuries, enthusing at the chance of capturing these old songs.

There was a brief stop-off, probably in the ancient town of Ksar el-Kebir, where Hamri, the local, picked up water and other supplies, then to the local Caid, who checked their passports. They were now in the old Spanish zone – a long-standing geographical link, for this area was ruled from the Spanish province as part of the Roman Empire. Then the Chevy struggled on a dirt road up the mountain, the final ten miles or so taking well over an hour.

When Brian, dressed in white, Suki, wearing trousers with her hair cut short, and the six-foot-tall Chkiantz finally pulled up in the village and walked into an olive grove, the villagers looked on, stunned, at these alien apparitions. The party settled down on rugs for a picnic with just a couple of villagers as the taxi driver con-templated his once shiny car, wrecked by the drive up the mountain, and mournfully handed his battery over to Chkiantz, who needed it to power the Uhers. Then the four outsiders sat down to watch the rituals.

Donkeys and chickens wandered around the fields as the music resounded around the mountain. The main performances took place in the middle of the village in an open space dominated by the saint's shrine, old gnarled olive trees and a communal well from which the villagers drew water. There were gentle, reflective moments: pastoral flutes, which recalled the courtly Elizabethan vibe Brian had brought to the Stones; small groups of women, singing in a modest courtyard, an obscure song Gysin had never heard before and whose lyrics he was keen to decipher. On the second day, they were told, they would hear the music of Bou Jeloud.

Brian, Suki and Chkiantz slept in a placid, spartan house of white stucco with blue doors, set around a courtyard with fig and palm trees. It was just up the hill from the main square, with views on to the Jebel mountain, an imposing, resonant presence which had in centuries gone by overlooked significant battles and had been settled since the Neolithic period; one stone cave was reputedly home to Bou Jeloud. Brian was happy, and had no problems drifting off to sleep in the clear, pure mountain air.

At some unknown time in the morning there was a scurrying noise outside the window of the bedroom the trio were sharing, and suddenly there came the deafening blaring of seven or eight rhaitas (primitive mountain oboes). Brian, Suki and Chkiantz emerged laughing and bleary-eyed but could see no trace of who'd given them their morning alarm call. Their little house was medieval in its simplicity: thick stone walls, pounded mud floors, water pulled up from a well splashed in your face for a morning shower, the toilet a simple drain, no electricity, no flunkies on call – and Brian had never seemed more content. 'He was so relieved for a moment from the pressure of being a Rolling Stone,' says Chkiantz. 'He didn't have to impress anyone. The villagers didn't give a toss – and he wasn't competing, he wasn't conscientiously being the bad boy. He'd come because he admired the musicianship and he was here, in a sense, to learn.'

Some people who knew Brian, like Stu's friend Keith Altham, saw his friendliness, the way he'd fuss over you, plying you with cups of tea, as designed to elicit sympathy or curry favour. That's not how George Chkiantz saw it in this remote, bare location, where Brian was 'considerate, together – concerned for people. I couldn't have been more comfortable.' Brian made sure Chkiantz could do his job, and was euphoric ('although', Chkiantz adds, 'his hand-clapping we could have done without').

The massed rhaitas and tbel drums, played by two banks of around twelve musicians, were probably recorded on the second day. Their set was abbreviated compared to their normal three-night-long ceremony, which was known to promote ecstatic states in the audience, but still, this was an experience beyond words: the rhaitas blared out a call and response, each theme modulating constantly, ancient melodies mapping out a cosmic meditation. Meanwhile, on the right, the drummers pounded out a juggernaut rhythm, powered by the zyeki and boomboo, small and big versions of the hand-hewn, military-looking tbel drum. Each drummer maintained a resounding heartbeat pulse on the bottom skin, and a fast machine-gun rat-a-tat on the top skin, the rhythms steady and hypnotic yet ever-changing via some deep telepathy. The volume was immense, echoing across the mountain, audible for miles around. Brian, Suki and Gysin sat back on cushions in the shade, calm, enraptured, their gaze steady, while Chkiantz scurried here and there, trying to work out how to capture the sound without overloading the Uher. In the end he decided to point the two microphones at the ground and record the sonic vibrations bouncing off the earth. The recordings therefore immortalized both this immense, profound music and the land that gave birth to it.

Bou Jeloud did not emerge that evening; the villagers explained he would come out only when the moon was full and the fruits of the earth were ready, for Pan's appearance was designed to enhance and celebrate the fertility of the land and its people. Brian would later write for the Joujouka album sleeve that this was something of a relief: 'I don't know if I possess the stamina to endure the incredible, constant strain of the [full] festival. Such psychic weaklings has Western Civilisation made of us.'

In the original ceremony, a goat would have been slaughtered, its skin stripped off, then laden with salt; a teenage boy would be sewn into the skin, the blood, salt, heat and the intensity of the music promoting visions, all the better to perform the dance, chasing young virgins and whipping them with olive branches. This was the role with which Brian identified. He discussed with Hamri whether he could return for the full festival to dance Bou Jeloud. Some young men were resistant to putting on the skins, knowing they would be forever changed – marked out, touched by Pan.

In their brief visit – one night and a full day, then departure the next lunchtime – they did partake in some of the ritual. Brion Gysin would remember, vividly, how he, Brian, Suki and Hamri were reclining on cushions when 'the most beautiful goat anyone had ever seen – pure white!' was led in front of them, and how Brian leapt up and shouted, 'That's me!' And then the goat was led off for slaughter. George Chkiantz remembers the goat being led in front of the group, although in his memory it was a less poetic grey. He is certain that Brian did not see the goat's sacrifice as a dark portent, 'But it was a powerful moment. By then, the music had become especially intense, and by then Brian had been smoking too much, too. And the goat knew what was happening. It's curious. It was quite resigned.'

A few hours later, the goat was brought to them, and they ate it in Roman style, holding the food in their right hand and wrapping it in bread. Gysin remembered Brian saying this moment was 'like communion'.

The next day, the exhausted group bumped their way back to Tangier in the two cars with hours of music on tape. Chkiantz had by now missed out on around two nights' sleep and crashed out the moment he reached his room at the El Minzah.

Brian shook him awake a few hours later. Grumbling at the intrusion and only dimly aware of his surroundings, Chkiantz staggered into the guitarist's room and plugged in a few cables as

Brian and a few friends waited. Later he'd wonder if he'd dreamt a pale, cadaverous figure in a raincoat, wearing a hat. Only now do we know, thanks to Burroughs' biographer Barry Miles, that the first person to hear the Joujouka tapes, along with Brian, Suki and Gysin, was William Burroughs, who also venerated the music of the Ahl Serif musicians, writing in *The Ticket That Exploded* about 'the Pan God of Panic piping blue notes through empty streets'.

The following morning, well rested, Brian and Suki took Chkiantz on a tour of the city Brian loved, to the site where Romans, and before them natives of long-lost Carthage, were buried. Then it was on to the beach. Again, Brian ministered to Chkiantz carefully, warning him not to swim far into the water, for the sea shelved rapidly at a certain point, beyond which there was a vicious undertow. 'If you do go in to cool off,' Brian told him, 'don't go any deeper than your ankles or they'll find your body fifteen miles down the coast.' Chkiantz snoozed in the August heat; when he awoke, he saw Brian swimming out into the Mediterranean. 'I remember the economy with which he swam, a fast crawl, very little splashing. He swam out a long way, and waved to us, then swam all the way back. And walked in his own footsteps back to the beach. With currents that strong, it gives you a good idea of what a good swimmer he was.'

After three days of being a good boy, maybe it was predictable that Brian should kick over the traces during Chkiantz's final night at the El Minzah. Brian had ventured down the Escalier Waller to Akhmed's little emporium and loaded up on hashish. As dawn broke the next morning, to the sound of Suki's furious complaints Chkiantz and Brian, his eyes half closed, were peering down from their balcony at passers-by making their way down the Rue de la Liberté and shouting out 'Salaam alaikum!' If any of the Tangerines failed to respond to this elegant, formal Arabic greeting ('Peace be upon you'), Brian would shout down a more Anglo-Saxon term: 'Fuck you!' Then suddenly, frighteningly, Brian simply passed out cold, keeling over on to the floor 'without even putting an arm out', says Chkiantz. 'I was thinking, Jesus, what's happening? Suki said, "Fuck him, this happens all the time." Then she put a blanket over him.'

Brian invited Chkiantz to stay on for more days in Tangier, but he had work to do, and he felt guilty about the £100 a day Olympic were billing Brian. Brian returned a week or so later, tanned and more healthy-looking, ready for an especially miserable September.

The month was laden with portent, for Brian's trial was due at the Inner London Sessions on 26 September. This month, Keith Richards would suffer his first real taste of Stones misery, as the sexually charged filming of *Performance* took place at Lowndes Square. Donald Cammell was the figure who'd tried to enmesh Linda Lawrence, Brian, Anita and countless others in his sex games from 1965 onwards; he doubtless took satisfaction from witnessing Mick's session with Anita. The pair's highly publicized fling would launch a feud that, as Keith revealed in *Life* with his observations about Mick's tiny todger, endures. Mick and Keith were now free to snap at each other, of course, because they'd effectively dispatched Brian.

Keith had temporarily left Redlands, where Brian had now holed up, to stay closer to the action at Robert Fraser's flat. He often sat, depressed, in his Bentley outside Lowndes Square, his grim mood eventually giving birth to Gimme Shelter, while Brian was some-times just a couple of doors down, with Mim Scala. In the first few days after his return from Joujouka, Brian was hugely enthusiastic. Although he'd initially intended to use the tapes as the basis for his own collages, like the Gnawa project, instead he started touting the release of the tapes as an album, to promote the music. But once back in the same old surroundings, his mood soon worsened.

One of the most poignant details of Brian's decline is that, even with close friends, he never bemoaned his lot. 'He never stated any resentment,' says Scala. 'You'd just get a morose face. You knew it was because he'd started this band called the Rolling Stones and was being blown out, but he never once slagged [them] off.' Instead, it was Suki who continued to share the pain. 'I think the secret had to be kept,' says Michael Rainey. 'So there was this kind of bravado, I'm all right, so he never complained. I actually didn't know how they were treating him until Suki gave me the lowdown. She told me how the emotional warfare went. "Oh come on, we're doing a session tonight, why don't you come round?" Brian would turn up with Suki at the studio, sitting on a sofa waiting to be called in . . . then at five in the morning, it was, "See ya, Brian!" It was that way that he simply got railroaded out of the picture.'

'Brian had become frightened to come in the office,' says Tony Calder. 'All those stories, the microphone not switched on, are absolutely true. He had no faith in himself, because it was all taken away.'

Some people, like Ian Stewart, had no sympathy at all. Glyn Johns, Stu's long-term friend, felt just the same: 'I wasn't sad, I was really frustrated – cos he was just a pain in the arse. He couldn't play – he was physically incapable of holding a chord down. It was pathetic. I didn't have a lot of sympathy for him, because he'd done it to himself.'

Though today Marianne Faithfull voices her sympathy for Brian, in 1968 she kept her own counsel. But now and again she'd share her concern with close friends. Like Mick, Marianne had her regular lovers on the side, one of whom, a young artist, stayed with her at Cheyne Walk during one of Mick's frequent absences that summer of 1968 ('It was a more sharing community then,' he laughs – respecting his discretion, we'll call him Jake). Marianne showed him a letter addressed to Mick, one of several Brian had sent to Cheyne Walk over recent weeks. She had opened this one in Mick's absence.

'Please let me come back in,' Brian had written. 'I'll play bongos, anything, but please let me come back in.'

Marianne, so witty and funny and unconcerned on the surface, was quite aware of the potency of this rift: it was beyond Brian being a fuck-up; this was a man being 'destroyed and humiliated' to his very core. And what Marianne witnessed in 1967 and 1968 was the concluding acts of a process that had started at the band's very beginning. Dawn Molloy, who'd given birth to Brian's son in March 1965, emerged profoundly damaged from her experience with the Stones, yet today she speaks as powerfully of the antagonism within the band as of her own treatment. 'Keith would be at Brian, all the time,' she says. 'It was often plain, bloody nasty.'

Fighting your bandmates is one thing, fighting the system quite another. As Stash observed, Brian's first drugs bust – almost certainly the result of Norman Pilcher's planted evidence – had been the most powerful factor in his subsequent decline, leaving him isolated and reliant on sleeping pills. There was no concealing his terror of his upcoming trial in London; yet this time he would be far more aggressive in his defence. This was a high-risk strategy which seemed all the more dangerous once Brian and his team realized that the judge who'd presided over his previous hearing, the nearly noble Reginald Seaton, was also overseeing his new trial.

Arriving at the Sessions in a dowdy suit on the 26th, Brian looked haunted, almost decayed; those once-clear blue eyes were hardly visible in his puffy face. When he took the stand, his plea of 'Not guilty' was hardly audible, but he seemed to pick up confidence once Detective Sergeant Robin Constable and two other policemen had presented their evidence. Brian's barrister, Michael Havers, then led him through his own version of the bust, focusing on the fact that he had no knowledge of the ball of wool which contained 144 grains of cannabis resin. Asked about the effect of the discovery, Brian replied, 'I just could not believe it. I was absolutely shattered.'

'Was the wool yours?' Havers continued.

'I have never had a ball of wool in my life. I don't darn socks, I don't have a girlfriend who darns socks.'

Asked if he had the slightest knowledge the wool contained cannabis, Brian insisted, forcefully, 'Absolutely not.'

Against all expectations, Judge Seaton's summing-up of the case was remarkably even-handed. He pointed out to the jury that there was only circumstantial evidence that the cannabis resin belonged to Brian Jones. Brian's defence team was feeling quietly confident when the jury withdrew. But when the foreman delivered their verdict just forty-five minutes later, it was devastating: guilty. Brian had his head in his hands and was rocking backwards and forwards as an official shouted for silence. A few minutes later he was asked to stand, to hear the sentence pronounced by his old adversary.

Remarkably, when the words came, they were ones of mercy – words that echoed William Rees-Mogg's insistence that for justice to be served, a celebrated rock star should receive no greater sentence than any other offender (doubtless, too, the prospect of losing another appeal aided Seaton's objectivity). 'I am going to treat you as I would any other young man before this court,' he told him. 'I am going to fine you, and I will fine you relative to your means: £50 with 100 guinea costs . . . but you really must watch your step and stay clear of this stuff. For goodness' sake do not get into trouble again.'

Mick and Keith had arrived in court just as the jury were

deliberating. The trio, and Suki, posed for photographs afterwards, Mick telling interviewers, 'We are very pleased Brian didn't have to go to jail – money doesn't matter.'

Brian's conviction had some disturbing implications, principally for his US immigration status, but the lenient sentence was a turn for the better. As was the country house he bought soon after his stay at Redlands, Cotchford Farm in Hartfield, East Sussex. A red-brick cottage set in a large sloping garden, the house was celebrated locally as the home of *Winnie the Pooh* author A. A. Milne. Romantic, with echoes of a childhood arcadia, it seemed to be the perfect location, far from the predations of the press and Norman Pilcher. For a while it seemed that with this second trial behind him, and his own rural refuge, somehow Brian would be able to rebuild his physical and psychological stamina.

That's what Al Kooper thought, anyway.

In November, the new songs were still flowing from Mick and Keith. The pair were calling in more musicians, including Ry Cooder, a friend of Jack Nitzsche, on slide guitar and mandolin; Cooder used Open G tuning, the same as Brian on some early Stones tracks, but played it in a more country-infused style. (Even today, Cooder finds the memory of those sessions painful. Maybe Mick and Keith did a number on him, like they did on Brian.) Al Kooper was another musician the band wanted to call in – the man who lit a fire under Bob Dylan's career when he came up with the unforgettable organ riff for Like A Rolling Stone.

Kooper was bushed, and had come to London to recuperate after working sessions for three months straight. Somehow, Denny Cordell, the producer and fixer, found out where he was staying and called him. Kooper told him he didn't want to play with any band in London. Not even the Rolling Stones. 'Forget it,' he told Cordell, 'I need a rest.'

It was later that day that he was walking down the King's Road on a fine autumn evening and he saw Brian Jones walking towards him. Brian was radiant, confident. 'Al, it's so exciting that you're playing at the session,' he told him, sweetly, irresistibly. They spoke for a few minutes, Brian telling him more details about the recording they had scheduled and how much he was looking forward to working with Kooper, whom he'd last seen at Monterey. It was impossible to turn him down. The session was the next day, the 17th.

When Kooper arrived, producer Jimmy Miller was presiding over the desk. Mick and Keith walked in and took control. Bizarrely, they handed acoustic guitars to each musician and asked them to play along. It was a weird device to break up the formality, and it worked: everyone was taken out of their comfort zone. Except Brian. As Mick and Keith walked around, Brian lay on his stomach on the studio floor, his eyes fixed on a book. 'It was a text-book on biology, I recall,' says Kooper. Brian was in his own world, unreachable. No one could work out what drug or combination of drugs he was on; the other musicians could cope only by ignoring him – 'not in a nasty way, it was simply that it was impossible to reach him', says Kooper.

The session was as loose as it was possible to be. Percussionist Rocky Dijon rolled up joints with one hand as the rhythm rolled without dropping a beat. Keith listened intently, hearing Kooper repeat a riff he'd lifted from Etta James's version of I Got You Babe which was incorporated into his own rhythm work. Out of the inchoate, thumping noises they crafted a magnificent, throbbing epic: You Can't Always Get What You Want. This was the birth of the Stones' gloriously shambling country-flavoured blues gumbo. And it was one of the last great Stones songs crafted in Brian Jones's presence. Except that he wasn't really there. Using the vestiges of that winning charm to persuade Kooper to attend and make the session a success was Brian's final contribution to the band he'd formed.

It is impossible to work out exactly what substances Brian was abusing in these last months of 1968; in the main, it seems it was Mandrax, other prescription medicines and alcohol, and that his depressed mental state was, as a psychiatrist would say, situational. He'd formed this band to escape his old life and now his band had escaped from him. Eddie Kramer, present at many of the later sessions, agrees that Brian's plight was 'very sad' but adds a crucial proviso: 'He was not a well person. I related to that as I suffered from asthma as a child. You could hear it, in his struggles with breath.' It's worth remembering the words of his neighbour, Roger Jessop, about Brian at the age of eleven, how he resented his asthma and 'he resented himself, because of it'.

Brian's final appearance with the Stones was a messy affair, all round. Mick and Keith had been bigging up the idea of a circus-style tour for a couple of months now, but when they finally embarked on filming a mini-movie, to be titled *Rock and Roll Circus*, the logistics proved beyond them. Guest act Taj Mahal had to be smuggled into the country without mentioning he was working. Jethro Tull had to rely on guest guitarist Tony Iommi, who pulled his hat down over his eyes hoping no one would notice him moonlighting with another band. John Lennon was the star guest, but his slot with Eric Clapton on guitar and Mitch Mitchell on drums was marred by Keith's horribly out-of-tune bass. Filming ran so late that the Stones didn't hit the stage until around two in the morning – at which point, says Tull's bassist Glen Cornick, a roadie had to lead Brian's hand to the fretboard before he could play.

Brian's sad state was a shocking revelation for those who cared about him. 'My favourite sound of the Stones was when Brian had his hand on the tiller,' says Taj Mahal. 'Something was off, and I was concerned, and shocked. There was some sort of disconnect – I should have said more, given more energy to him.'

Chris Welch, the *Melody Maker* writer, had got on well with Brian, and was the man with whom Brian had shared his vision of a post-Stones existence back in March 1965. They hadn't exchanged a word over the last three and a half years. Much later he realized that Brian had become upset because Welch had referred to him in print as a mere rhythm guitarist. The perceived insult still clearly meant something: 'He saw me in a corridor. Turned round. Then ran away.'

Pete Townshend had hung out with Brian at the Scotch for years, bonded with him over a love of pop music, and today remembers how Brian encouraged his writing. 'He was always very kind. He loved my first Who song, I Can't Explain.' He was 'very upset by Brian's condition. Brian was defeated. I took Mick and Keith aside and they were quite frank about it all; they said Brian had ceased to function, they were afraid he would slip away. They certainly were not hard-nosed about him. But they were determined not to let him drag them down – that was clear.'

11

Just Go Home

THEY SAY THAT pioneers get all the arrows. This would be the grim lesson as the 1960s shuddered to their end, and a succession of the decade's greater stars slipped away to form the infamous 27 Club. Today, even when we know more about depression, bipolar conditions and drug addiction, we still lose them. The story, says Pete Townshend, remains the same: 'We applaud, we wait, then we nod sagely when they burn out. It's despicable.'

By the beginning of 1969, it was obvious even to those who harboured no resentment of Brian that the show couldn't go on. Freed of Andrew Oldham and with Mick and Keith's drug bust comfortably consigned to the past, the band had a new artistic momentum – and Brian was holding them back.

There were odd moments when he pulled back into focus in early 1969: you can hear his booming drums (Moroccan tbel) after the breakdown in Midnight Rambler, and autoharp in You Got The Silver, all recorded in February or March. Overall, however, it was painfully clear that, as George Chkiantz puts it, 'He wasn't listening. If he was going to put anything on, it wasn't in the spirit of the track.' It's said he played on an early take of Honky Tonk Women, but his guitar part was wiped; still, it's been said for years that this happened to Ry Cooder too, who recorded one part, with a distinctive riff based around the top G string, which was wiped and replaced by Keith's version – a 'sponge job', just like Brian used to do to Keith's guitar parts all those years back, in 1964.

For one late-night session in March, Tom Keylock had driven Brian all the way from Cotchford to Barnes, and Brian decided he wanted to overdub a saxophone part on one of the tracks. No one present could imagine how it might work, but George Chkiantz set up a mic and screens around Brian, who was sitting on a plastic stacking chair all by himself in the cavernous main room at Olympic. After a couple of passes Brian stopped playing. Mick, Chkiantz and a couple of others listened in the control booth, until they heard Brian's voice over the monitors: 'Um . . . there's a problem with this reed. I need to change it.' Ten minutes passed, then another ten minutes. Chkiantz left the booth and walked over to Brian, who was staring foggily at the mouthpiece, struggling with the adjustment screws. He asked Brian if he could give him a hand changing the reed. 'No, no,' Brian told him, 'it's OK.'

And so it went on, for an hour, ninety minutes, Chkiantz, Mick, others walking over, and Brian, not aggressive, not stroppy, insisting he didn't need help. Of course, he did need help. 'You have no idea of how dreadful it was,' says Chkiantz today. 'But no one could reach him, no one could get close to him. It was clear, in that awful situation . . . [that] he was just a nuisance.'

And in that awful situation, did Mick and Keith seem considerate?

'Ha ha ha. Um . . . they were fed up with the whole bloody thing. No, I don't think they were very considerate.'

Other insiders share Chkiantz's perception of a hardness at the heart of the Stones, most notably Jack Nitzsche. Throughout 1965 and 1966 he'd noted rancour during the band's RCA sessions. When he resumed work with the band towards the end of 1968, he reckoned the atmosphere had changed – for the worse. His vignette of seeing Mick with Brian is chilling. 'Brian came up to me, looking pretty shaky, and asked me what I thought he should do – he didn't know where he fit[ted] in. I told him to just pick up a guitar and start playing. Then he walked over to Mick and asked, "What should I play?" Mick told him, "You're a member of the band, Brian, play whatever you want." So he played something, but Mick stopped him and said, "No, Brian, not that – that's no good." So Brian asked him again what to play and Mick told him again to play whatever he wanted. So Brian played something else, but Mick cut him off again – "No, that's no good either, Brian."'

The dysfunction at the heart of the band was all the more glaring in that Keith was looking at Mick, all the while trying to work out what had gone on between his primary school friend and the lover he'd taken from Brian. Nitzsche remembered that 'Keith and Mick weren't even speaking to each other during this period'. Mick, consequently, spent a lot of time with Ry Cooder. Today, Keith claims to have had his revenge by sleeping with Marianne. Such was the collateral damage in pursuing great music, and creating today's corporation. As Sam Cutler, road manager from that spring, points out, it was the dysfunction, the anger, that gave the music its power: 'That madness, that tension, is what makes bands. They use that negative energy, transmuting it into something else. It goes from lead to gold.'

Cutler has no love for Brian, but sees this period as one of utter, sickening coldness, as Bill Wyman was reduced to an irrelevance and Brian to a shell. 'No one realizes, to put it bluntly, what cold cunts Mick and Keith can be. They specialize in it. All I can remember from that time is Brian, sitting on the floor in the studio looking lost. It was too painful for him. A lot of people take drugs to mask their inner unhappiness and turmoil, don't they? And Brian was one of them. Yes, Mick and Keith did make it worse. They just treated him like he didn't exist. The Stones have a very cold way of dealing with people, man. OK, you're not on the radar any more. You don't exist. They treat you as if you're not there.'

At the end of the session for Sister Morphine, Mick walked up to the founder of his band and said, 'Just go home, Brian.'

Was Brian resigned to his fate, like the little grey goat he'd seen led in front of him as the tbels thundered? Undoubtedly he was. Even before his last spiral into despair began in late 1968, he knew how to escape. He simply chose not to.

Soon after his return from Joujouka, Brian had turned up to see Cleo Sylvestre, the woman who'd seen his very first Marquee show, to play records and chat. He mapped out an escape route that was just about as radical as the one that gave birth to the Rolling Stones. 'He'd been to Morocco, he was terribly excited, was talking to me about the rhythms, the drums, the instruments, how he wanted to have this group,' says Cleo. 'He wanted to bring over some of the musicians he'd met. Really, it was a vision of what we now call world music. In those days it was totally radical. It's amazing when you think of all the records you can get now; back then there was rock'n'roll, R&B, blues and jazz and everything was very well defined, and everything had a boundary. To have the vision, to break out and do something different, showed tremendous creativity and insight.' Brian had already planned the release of the

Joujouka album, which Elektra were interested in, but which was being stalled by Allen Klein. This conversation was very specific: Brian spoke about using the Moroccan polyrhythms, with guitars on the top, and Cleo singing. This, rather than the Robert Johnson blues which Brian had already explored, was the vision he wanted to follow.

Brian was articulate and coherent as he laid out his plans to Cleo over several phone calls. Cleo thought he had a good chance of realizing his vision, but she didn't react that positively to his suggestions. 'I was so insecure about my singing, I just said, "Oh Brian, you're sending me up." He said, "No, I'm serious." So I said let's meet, but I didn't pursue it.' Today, she dearly wishes she had been more responsive.

Others remember similar optimism at the prospect of starting over. During a shopping trip to Harrods over the winter of 1968/69, Brian had noticed a pair of paintings by the astronomical artist David A. Hardy, who had made his name via his artwork for Arthur C. Clarke novels and had recently been the subject of an exhibition at the London Planetarium. Brian was intrigued: around this time he'd built a telephone relationship with the science fiction author and even went to stay with him in his new home in Sri Lanka. The paintings were large, beautiful canvases, each around two by three feet: one was a view of Jupiter from Io, the other a depiction of Uranus from Titania, with a large methane lake. Brian asked about the works, only to be informed they were no longer available for sale, and were being returned to Hardy.

Some time later, the phone rang in Hardy's house. Hardy had a ten-minute-long conversation with the well-spoken caller, who asked whether he could buy the paintings. The pair chatted about space and astronomy for a while, and the caller soon agreed, without demur, to Hardy's asking price – a substantial amount, around

£50 each. As the conversation moved on to delivery and payment details, the caller gave his name: Brian Jones.

'That's easy to remember,' said Hardy. 'Like the Rolling Stone?'

'I am the Rolling Stone,' Brian replied.

Then the conversation took a different tack. Hardy was a bit of a music buff, and on his travels he'd bumped into other legendary guitarists such as Big Jim Sullivan and Hank Marvin. Soon they were chatting about Brian's plans. 'I want to get back to my roots,' Brian told Hardy. This wasn't a total surprise to Hardy, who'd heard the rumours of a falling-out, but he was surprised at how relaxed and open Brian sounded, coherent and full of energy. 'I can't wait to record a new album,' he told Hardy. The painter told him he was looking forward to hearing it, then the pair wished each other well. Of course, Hardy never got to hear this album, and the two large paintings seemed to vanish as completely as Brian's dreams. Over the decades since Brian's death Hardy has made investigations with specialist dealers and auction houses in an attempt to discover if either of the two canvases has passed through their hands. It seems they have both disappeared, without a trace.

Brian knew he needed to make the break, the leap he'd first contemplated back in 1965. Of course, he'd realized the significance of Ry Cooder being asked down for sessions – not that Cooder would have joined the band: he was too obviously, as Keith puts it, 'his own guy'. Of course, intimate as he was with the old blues scene, Brian knew very well that Mick had been chatting with John Mayall, who was forming a more acoustic line-up and therefore had a lead guitarist to spare – Mick Taylor, who rehearsed with the band from the middle of May 1969. Rather than confront the Stones, Brian probably took it out on Suki, who finally bailed around April. More isolated than ever, he was reduced to calling old friends like Zouzou. 'It was really sad. He said, "They think I don't know they are rehearsing." They never told him he wasn't a part of the Stones any more – but they'd taken on another musician! Mick had told him to fuck off – Mick didn't care at all about him.' Occasionally they'd talk about other subjects, and for an hour or so Brian would be lucid, talking quietly. Yet when it came to his old band 'he was talking crazy, telling stories that made no sense. It was then I thought, This is not Brian any more, this is somebody who's been destroyed.'

It was inevitable that rather than leave, as he should have done, Brian would wait for the blow to be delivered – by Mick, for he seemed to be the one he resented and feared, much more than Keith. The immediate imperative was money. Although there was always a possibility that with therapy, attention and an end to police harassment Brian would recover his powers, he would nevertheless have problems being admitted into the US, which would imperil future tours. Mick and Keith had just finished mixing Honky Tonk Women, with Mick Taylor on guitar, when they travelled down to see Brian late on the evening of Sunday, 8 June. Fearful there would be a fight, they took Charlie Watts along with them.

Keith Richards described the evening to *Rolling Stone* in 1971, telling Robert Greenfield that 'He left [the band]. We went down to see him and he said, "I can't do it again." And we said, "We understand."' According to Keith, the trio told Brian they 'didn't have Mick Taylor waiting in the wings to bring on' (Taylor had auditioned for the band three weeks earlier, on 14 May). But one element of Keith's version is true: Brian agreed readily to leave the band, almost relieved at the resolution. A press release was hurriedly assembled, with Brian stating, 'I no longer see eye to eye with the others over the discs we are cutting . . . we shall still remain friends. I love those fellows.'

Brian kept in fairly regular touch with the band over the next few weeks – Keith would later describe how Brian called every day, telling him how well the music was going. Brian had acquired a new girlfriend, Anna Wohlin, whom he'd met via Swedish photographer friend Jan Oloffson back in January during a party at the Revolution club. Anna moved in to Cotchford at the beginning of May, joining a small community including driver Tom Keylock, housekeeper Mary Hallett, gardener Mick Martin and a temporary guest, Frank Thorogood. Although in subsequent years many would speculate why Brian would hire this shadowy character, Thorogood had in fact been employed by the Rolling Stones office for around three years to repair and maintain the band's various properties, including Redlands. He had started work at Cotchford the previous November, and was currently sleeping over in a flat above the garage, returning home to Wood Green most Wednesday nights and weekends.

This small crew would soon be the subject of hundreds of newspaper articles, and many books over the coming years, starting in 1983 with Nicholas Fitzgerald's 'inside story'. The JFK-style industry of conspiracy theories continues to this day. Intriguing and contradictory as they are, they have perpetuated the image of Brian Jones as a corpse, which is a scandal, for it has overshadowed and obscured the legacy of Brian Jones as a musician.

What's beyond debate is that once out of the Stones, Brian was perilously low on friends. This wasn't, as some imply, unique to him, for as a huge number of people agreed, compared to the Beatles in particular the Stones had always been surrounded by hangers-on – gangster types and drug dealers – rather than friends. While there was a modest rebound in Brian's mental state, compounding his problems was the fact that he was reliant on Allen Klein for funds. Klein had always been tardy when it came to releasing money to the Stones, and Brian's position had worsened as he was sidelined. There have been many reports that Mick offered Brian a continuing salary, generally quoted as a one-off payment of £100,000 plus an annual wage of £20,000, but there seems to be no evidence that Brian ever received the money.

Brian did have one friend: the man who'd told him back in 1962 that blues was only niche music but who was happy to be proved wrong – and who believed, as his wife Bobbie points out, 'that Brian had been treated horribly by the Stones. Brian was a very special, curious young man.'

Alexis Korner had kept busy over the years, partly owing to his avuncular nature, beautiful radio voice and unrivalled connections. Although his record sales were modest, he remained busy as a radio and TV presenter, and a new avenue for live shows looked to be opening up in Europe where audiences appreciated his current, eclectic take on blues. Korner had assembled a reworked group, the New Church, just a few months before, with a younger line-up including his own daughter, Sappho, and bassist Nick South, a friend of Korner's son Nico. Korner and his wife drove over to see Brian around four or five times in June 1969; Korner also took his band over to play with Brian, and kept in constant touch with him on the phone.

Nick South had joined the veteran bandleader the previous year, and was just eighteen. He was thrilled to be in a bona fide rock star's house, all dark wood corridors which contrasted with the bright Moroccan blues on the paintwork. He arrived with Korner, and spent four or five days at the house. Korner had filled him in on the initial plan: to involve Brian in a short string of shows they had scheduled in Europe, something low-key to get Brian back on the horse.

The Korner family themselves stayed longer. Despite Brian's

troubles, Korner's twelve-year-old son Damian found the lost Stone a delight to be around: 'such a lovely man. He was kind, considerate and thoughtful. If you don't have children, you have to be a nice person to comfort them. Staying at the house was a problem for me, because it was haunted. But he had the capacity to make a young child who was feeling frightened feel OK.'

South, too, found Brian a pleasant host, but as a clear-eyed eighteen-year-old fixated on music he couldn't help noticing a few details: crates of wine by the front door, Brian's beer gut, and his bleary, distracted manner. Korner was 'a brilliant diplomat', South remembers, encouraging Brian, making him feel comfortable. Although he was also too much of a diplomat to say so at the time, Korner believed Brian's ejection from the Stones was a shabby affair, says his wife and confidante Bobbie. 'We really did think that, and that's why we went to see him.'

Korner's diplomacy continued posthumously, too: he'd later comment that he'd quietly dropped the idea of Brian playing with the New Church in Europe because Brian would overshadow them. The truth was that the rehearsals with Brian were a mess, and there seemed no chance of getting it together for July, when the New Church were scheduled to hit the road. Sadder still, Brian had abandoned the instrument that was his companion as he looked for gigs around Cheltenham at the age of fifteen; the instrument on which he'd first unlocked the secrets of the blues; the instrument he'd brought with him to London – his compass. Despite repeated urgings, Brian simply wouldn't play guitar. 'That was the strange thing. I was, "Put the guitar on, Brian." But he didn't play guitar – he left that to Alexis,' says South. 'And he would come in and play for a bit and wander off. He was playing soprano sax at one point, but it wasn't like a normal rehearsal where you'd sit down and play a song. It was more out there.'

Anna Wohlin described in her book *The Murder of Brian Jones* how his 'inspiration flowed unstemmed during the months I spent with him'. Another writer mentions how Brian was 'blind with enthusiasm for his [music] which had crystallised at last'. Sadly, there is no evidence to support such accounts. 'Brian didn't look too well,' says South. 'It would seem that he didn't have a support structure, from what I noticed. It looked like he had a habit of a few bottles of wine a day, and was looking a bit bleary. I don't want to be horrible . . . but I wouldn't say he was alert, not really. I think he was surviving. Trying to cope.' Korner and his band tried various songs in an attempt to get Brian to play along, 'but he'd be trying other instruments, then he'd go off and disappear, or say he had to make a phone call. There was no direction or energy coming from him.' Brian looked physically diminished. 'He was on those asthma inhalers all the time,' says Bobbie Korner. 'He wasn't in a good state.'

South's sadness at Brian's condition and his lack of ability to focus on his music was shared by the other musicians who went to see him. Korner asked his friend John Mayall to come down, saying that Brian was thinking about forming a new band and needed some encouragement. The pair sat down together, keeping it low-key. Mayall had only brought a harmonica with him, so this time Brian attempted to play guitar. 'It wasn't hanging,' says Mayall. 'His hands and his brain simply weren't matching up. It was a shame.' Mayall, like South, remembers that Brian was 'very wobbly. Not really in the condition to be putting something together.'

Brian's poor coordination and inability to focus weren't necessarily permanent obstacles to his forming his own band; upon a return to full health he could well have done so, as some people believed. But Nick South, John Mayall and Bobbie Korner's memories contradict practically every account of the run-up to

Brian's death, most of which culminate in a murder, which makes for a nice simple story, with cartoon villains. The reality is more complex, for Brian Jones was exploited by many people in his life and continued to be exploited in his death, even by those who profess to care for him.

The rehearsals weren't totally joyless: Brian was good company, occasionally joking around with the Korners, playing Proud Mary loud on a tape deck while banging a tambourine and shouting, 'We want Brian Jones!' over the chorus. But Bobbie thought he seemed very isolated: 'I didn't see any builders around, and there was no sign of any girlfriend at all in the time we were there.' She wondered how he could have founded a band like the Rolling Stones, whose career she had followed through the years, and be left so alone and vulnerable. Others agreed. Sam Cutler thought the Stones office bore some responsibility for his welfare and was horrified that this job was left to Tom Keylock. 'Keylock had been sacked by Keith – I was in the office when it happened. Keith had bought some furniture, and Keylock put his own furniture on the bill. He was a low-life.'

Brian rehearsed with Korner and Mayall throughout much of June; and according to Anna Wohlin, the couple were blissfully happy, Brian buying his new girlfriend three cocker spaniel puppies to add to their existing menagerie: Luther, an Afghan hound, and Emily, another cocker. Anna remembered one niggling irritant throughout that month, namely the building work being per-formed by Frank Thorogood, who was generally described as an old friend of Tom Keylock, despite the lack of any evidence. Anna's account, though hugely flawed, perhaps remains the best one there is, and she recalls ongoing disputes with Thorogood leading up to 2 July owing to problems with the shoddiness of his work. A few other people, notably Nicholas Fitzgerald, would later write that

Brian had called him to complain that he was being watched, of strange lights in the trees. Such allegations would form the basis of yet another book describing the murder of Brian Jones. But then Fitzgerald also wrote that Brian was planning a band 'with Jimi Hendrix. In the same outfit [with John Lennon]', suggesting that dark forces wanted to prevent this supergroup overshadowing the Stones. Those who actually worked with Hendrix in June 1969, like Eddie Kramer, describe such stories as 'silly nonsense'.

Alexis Korner was the one outsider who spoke frequently with Brian. Again, some books suggest that Korner, too, thought there were dark forces at work. His wife Bobbie rejects this: 'There were a lot of phone calls – Brian did feel underrated, got at, but I wouldn't interpret that as anybody out to kill him. If there were plots, it was that he felt excluded.'

Wednesday, 2 July was a muggy, oppressive day, bad weather for someone who suffered from asthma. Frank Thorogood had been staying in the garage flat since the beginning of the week, and the previous night had been joined by a friend, Janet Lawson. Each evening, Thorogood joined Brian and Anna for dinner; they drank wine every night, usually the then obligatory Blue Nun, and then Brian would drink brandy and Thorogood would have vodka. Most evenings running up to the Wednesday night, two or three of them would go for a swim after their meal. The previous night, Anna had cried off, telling Brian the pool was too cold, so for the Wednesday evening he raised the thermostat to ninety degrees.

That day, Anna later stated, she and Brian got up around eleven and watched the tennis from Wimbledon on TV for most of the afternoon (Bill Wyman, in contrast, would later write that Brian had been in London in the morning and travelled back to Cotchford in a limo hired by the Stones office). They had a salad for lunch, another snack later, and watched TV that evening –

probably *Rowan and Martin's Laugh-In* – sending Frank into the village to fetch more drinks. Around 10.15 Brian decided to go for a swim. Again Anna wasn't keen, so Brian walked over to the flat to invite Janet and Frank to join him, loaded up a tray with drinks, then went back to change into his multicoloured swimming trunks.

Anna (who had been persuaded), Frank and Brian spent some time in the pool, the trio recounted later, although Janet stayed away as 'I considered that Frank and Brian were in no fit condition to swim. I felt sufficiently strongly about this that I mentioned it to both the men.' Later Janet went to the music room 'and played a guitar' while Anna continued swimming before eventually return-ing to the house and getting changed. Frank stayed in the pool with Brian for a while, then returned to the house himself, for a cigarette or to get a towel. A few minutes later, Janet looked out at the pool and 'saw Brian. He was face down in the deep end. He was motion-less and I sensed the worst straight away.' Janet called to Anna and Frank, and eventually the trio managed to get Brian out of the water. Janet attempted mouth-to-mouth resuscitation, then left that task to Anna while she performed cardiac massage, for around fifteen minutes.

Brian died before midnight, yet his death is still widely reported as having occurred on 3 July. The reports surrounding the end of his life would be just as contradictory. The police investigation was cursory, and the industry that grew up around his death exploit-ative, with a remarkable reliance on deathbed confessions. In the years that followed, several witnesses, notably Anna Wohlin and Janet Lawson, reappeared to accuse Frank Thorogood of pushing Brian under the water, although neither had actually witnessed the deed. Tom Keylock, ludicrously, claimed that Thorogood had made a deathbed confession to him. Everybody blamed somebody else –

except for Brian's real friends, who mostly blamed themselves. As Pete Townshend puts it, 'I've become angry about a business in which people, especially the press, sneer if someone tries to save their skin by going into rehab after raising hell. Brian should have been sectioned into a mental hospital, not allowed to flounder around in a heated swimming pool taking downers. If I'm honest, I suppose, I was one of the friends who should have called the ambulance.'

Keith Altham was at Olympic, where Brian's old band were working on *Let It Bleed*, when the Stones heard the news. There was shock, tears, and curiously contrasting reactions. Most of the tears came from Marianne, who was overwhelmed with grief. The strangest but most telling reaction was Mick's. '[He] got quite angry about it,' says Altham, 'almost as if Brian had committed hara-kiri on purpose, cos the Stones were planning their Hyde Park concert later that week.' Some of Mick's anger was doubtless directed at the tragedy of the death, the waste of it all. Yet the chilling fact remains that the man who has often accused Brian Jones – the founder of the Rolling Stones, who gave Mick a job that would last for half a century – of being a self-centred, jealous type was upset because Brian's death threatened to overshadow his big media event.

Many people suggest, quite rightly, that Brian deserved better from the authorities who investigated his death. It's undeniable that he deserved much better from those authorities who harassed him until he was a broken man, particularly as that group included Detective Norman Pilcher, who colluded with the media, planted evidence and was finally convicted of perjury in November 1973. Most undeniable of all is that Brian deserved better from his friends.

Chris Barber brought blues to English coffee clubs before Brian brought blues to the world. His appearance at Cheltenham was the first step in Brian forming the Stones. 'I was glad we were useful to Brian,' he says. 'But given what happened, maybe we weren't useful at all.'

The hurried aftermath of Brian's death had a dark momentum to it, just as the run-up had, as if there was an inevitability about it all. When Hartfield beat officer Albert V. Evans arrived at the scene shortly after midnight, he had a 'policeman's instinct' that he wasn't being given the full story but had no evidence to support his feelings. The investigation of Brian's death was assigned to a senior officer, Detective Chief Inspector R. Marshall, assisted by Detective Sergeant P. Hunter, who concluded fairly early that the case seemed to be a 'normal drowning'.

The autopsy, by Dr Albert Sachs, a consultant pathologist at Queen Victoria Hospital in East Grinstead, was extraordinarily brief. There were some elementary errors, too: Brian was described as being 5ft 11in tall when he was in fact around 5ft 8in. Sachs ruled out an asthmatic attack, although this was not necessarily implausible according to other pathologists. Still, there was no evidence of manipulation, and the top line of the verdict, 'Death By Misadventure', was simplistic but has never been proved wrong. In delivering the verdict, coroner Dr Angus Sommerville could not resist adding his own moral censure: 'He would not listen. So he drowned under the influence of alcohol and drugs.'

In the years that followed there was a concerted attempt by Brian's minder, Tom Keylock, to shift blame on to Frank Thorogood, in the main with his unverified account of a last-words confession by the builder. More recently reports have emerged that an investigation by Allen Klein pinpointed Keylock as the guilty man. Yet once again these accounts (detailed in the coda) have never been verified. In 2003, a story in the *Toronto Sun* reported how club owner and Stones aficionado Jerry Stone had bought two gold records, one for Paint It, Black and one for Little Red Rooster, which commemorated Brian's proudest moments. He described in the story how these were Brian's copies, mentioning as their provenance that he had bought them from 'former Stones chauffeur Tom Keylock'. Thus we have convincing evidence of Keylock's theft of Brian's property – although thieves are not necessarily murderers.

The focus on Brian's death seems over the decades to have transformed a visionary into a victim. 'I don't think of him like that,' says Bobbie Korner. 'I don't know why people have all these theories. It's a reflective thing. They don't want to let go.' Today, Bobbie still remembers the sadness of seeing the charismatic young boy she and her husband had given a home so reduced. 'One knew it wasn't good, so it didn't come as any shock. Only a great sadness.'

At least some of those who speak for Brian seem to have bizarre agendas of their own. The murder scenario was kicked off by Nicholas Fitzgerald, whose book contains the obligatory hallmarks: implausibly detailed reconstructed dialogue, vague reports of assaults and threats, and reliance on the deceased for corroboration. Fitzgerald claimed to have been a close friend and lover of Brian, yet he sold his story to the *News of the World*, the one publication that had done the most to destroy him.

Brian's funeral took place on 10 July in Cheltenham, the city of secrets and lies. Some townsfolk considered that the vicar, Hugh Evan Hopkins, was too forgiving in presiding over the rite, at the request of Lewis and Louisa Jones. Suki Potier walked alongside Barbara and her parents. Keith and Anita stayed away, while Mick was contractually obliged to remain in Australia to film *Ned Kelly*, so Charlie and Bill were the only Stones in attendance. Nico and Pete Townshend wrote songs for him, but perhaps the most incisive tribute came from George Harrison, the man who first recommended his band to Decca:

> When I met him I liked him quite a lot. He was a good fellow, you know. I got to know him very well and I felt very close to him; you know how it is with some people, you feel for them, feel near to them. He was born on February 28, 1942, and I was born on February 25, 1943, and he was with Mick and Keith and I was with John and Paul in the groups, so there was a sort of understanding between the two of us. The positions were similar, and I often seemed to meet him in his times of trouble. There was nothing the matter with him that a little extra love wouldn't have cured. I don't think he had enough love or understanding. He was very nice and sincere and sensitive, and we must remember that's what he was.

It's unlikely that Lewis and Louisa, who had now suffered the terrible fate of losing two of their children, ever quite came to terms with their son's death – or his life. When Alexis Korner, Brian's greatest mentor, wrote a note to them after Brian's death, Lewis wrote back, saying that the Korners' attendance at the funeral would be 'inappropriate'.

The Stones made great music without Brian, with *Sticky Fingers* (1971) an unqualified masterpiece, and *Exile on Main Street* (1972) a magnificent, sprawling epic. But they were working on a kind of residual mojo, and a massive quality drop-off soon followed. When the band assembled in 2012 to celebrate their half century, they barely mentioned Brian's name. But then, in most performances Mick and Keith avoided eye contact, while the spectacle of Bill Wyman, asked back in order to be stuck on the side of the stage and studiously ignored, was a reminder that inter-band feuds add a dark energy for the first few years, and then they become deadly dull. 'It is tedious,' says Andrew Oldham. 'It's Mick with instrumental accompaniment.'

Yet if in 2014 the Stones seem banal, everyday, that's because they did change the world in their image: a world where in London in 1962, black culture was an oxymoron; a world where in 1965, when Brian Jones presented Howlin' Wolf to the American public, the venerable bluesman believed he would never cross to mainstream TV in his lifetime. Brian's pioneering status as a musician has become steadily less obvious thanks to the very success of his mission. The blues and world music that he championed and dragged into the mainstream have become so ubiquitous that we all suffer a hindsight bias – we find it impossible to imagine what the world was like *without* this music. As counter-intuitive as it might seem, this is proof of Brian's accomplishment.

Set alongside his powerful musical legacy is a less welcome distinction. After his death came the untimely ends of Jimi Hendrix, Janis Joplin, Jim Morrison, Kurt Cobain and Amy Winehouse, who together make up the 27 Club – stars who crashed, burned and then died at that fateful age. Being the inaugural member of such a club seems a gloomy achievement – though Brian would have been the first to point out that this distinction should really be credited to Robert Johnson, the visionary bluesman who also died aged twenty-seven. Johnson had lived a life on the edge of established society, where you could get thrown in jail for being a musician and no one much cared if you died. It's worth repeating, of course, that Brian was as much a victim of the establishment as Johnson: it was sustained harassment by an officer since proven to have planted evidence that isolated him and engineered, as Stash puts it, 'the breaking of

Brian'. An establishment which carried out a minimum of seven raids on a vulnerable rock star surely bears a bigger, more demonstrable share of the guilt than any of the shady characters around Brian's beloved Cotchford Farm.

Beyond the establishment's contemptuous treatment of Brian Jones, the dysfunction and repression around his family add to the air of tragedy and loss. One can only imagine the feelings of Lewis and Louisa Jones when they buried their second child. However, imagine was all most people could do, for Lewis avoided the advances of people such as Alexis and Bobbie Korner, and other acquaintances. Fans and friends noticed Lewis and Louisa chose not to use the word 'love' on Brian's tombstone, which was marked merely 'in affectionate memory'. Brian's parents also showed little interest in his children: letters from Pat Andrews and others went unanswered, and their contact with Julian Leitch, Brian's son by Linda Lawrence, was fitful. Unsurprisingly, Julian has found the burden of being Brian's son heavy to bear, despite being brought up with obvious love and sensitivity by his adopted father, Donovan Leitch. Yet the passing of time has brought some healing.

For several of Brian's girlfriends who bore his children, the misogyny of society in the sixties was a bigger source of pain than their relationship with the Stones founder. Dawn Molloy was 'one of thousands of women who were forced to give a baby up for adoption'. Finally, thanks to new regulations, she was contacted by her and Brian's son; it was a joyful moment, which brought some closure, as her son John learned about his dad. Simon, Brian's son by Valerie Corbett, went through a similar emotional journey, and has become friends with Graham Ride, Brian's old flatmate. Mark, Pat Andrews' son, is still close to his mother, but is generally resistant to talking about his absentee father; Belinda, Brian's daughter, has over the years spent more time finding out about her father and herself seems reconciled with her past.

Most poignantly, Joolz Leitch, Brian's first grandson, born in 1997, has, like many kids his age, become fascinated with the music of the sixties, which still permeates our cultural landscape. Tall (unlike his grandad), with close-cropped hair and a laid-back charm, he's emerged from the wreckage of the Jones family with a deep, enduring pride in his grandfather's legacy and a mature acceptance that what will be, will be, for he remembers Brian Jones not as a man who had his life cut short but rather as a man who had completed his mission. 'It's odd, it's weird – but it couldn't have happened any other way.'

In the closing stages of writing this book, I spent an evening with Joolz in Donovan and Linda Leitch's peaceful, sprawling Georgian rectory in County Cork, chatting for a while before we picked up guitars and played them late into the evening. Joolz is already a fluid guitarist, hinting at some of his grandfather's musical insights. It was a moving, warm experience, one of family pride, with only one strand of disappointment: while Brian's legacy, the way he opened up black music to a huge young audience across the world, has deepened with time, the memory of his impact has arguably diminished thanks to the sustained sniping of his brother Stones, and an unending obsession not with his life but with his death. 'I do think all the focus on his death has taken the music away from him,' says Joolz. 'The death doesn't matter; it's what he did in his life, while he had time, that matters. He definitely did change the world.'

Just as vexing is the recent history of the Stones, whose Hyde Park show contained no reference to Brian. Incredibly, over the course of several interviews to mark the anniversary of the band's formation, Mick Jagger managed to explain how the Stones got together and his discovery of the blues without any significant mention of Brian Jones. In contrast, Keith Richards, whose *Life* did so much to minimize Brian's role (as it did Bill Wyman's), mentioned Brian's loss as his biggest regret around the fiftieth anniversary of the band's Marquee debut.

Those who knew the band in the early days have become puzzled by the lottery of life, the way Mick seems to have succeeded in a Stalinesque revision of history, airbrushing Brian out of the story. 'Brian Jones was the main man in the Stones, Jagger got everything from him,' says Ginger Baker, who helped out the pair on some of their first shows back in 1962. 'Brian was much more of a musician than Jagger will ever be – although Jagger's a great economist. Yet sometimes Brian seems to have been forgotten, which is very sad.'

Just as sad is the way the value of Brian's estate seems to have dwindled. His mum and dad, and after their death his sister Barbara, inherited some money, but the Stones' early catalogue generates fewer royalties than their later work because the band was compelled to hand over their pre-1971 catalogue to Allen Klein in order to retain control of their later material. In the meantime, several songs credited to Nanker Phelge – the name Brian came up with for early band compositions – have now been reassigned by BMI to Mick Jagger and Keith Richards.

Still, Brian wouldn't have carped, believes his grandson Joolz. Brian's mission was to champion his beloved R&B, and he succeeded. Nothing can erase that. 'He changed the face of rock'n'roll. There was nothing more to do. Nothing more needed in this world.'

The commercial behemoth that is the Stones today should not overshadow the force of nature that was the Stones in 1963. The Beatles launched a revolution, the Stones electrified it; they interposed a blue note in the Beatles' white notes, added the dark danger of Pan to the Beatles' Apollonian optimism. It's understandable why the survivors resent Brian Jones beyond the grave: he formed the band, he named the band, he taught Keith Richards Open G tuning, and he taught Mick Jagger how to bring a girl to orgasm. Like his inspiration, Pan, Brian Jones may be demonized but his music plays on. Not in his old band, but in the sounds, the magnificent panic, which he unleashed on the world. For the battle between Pan and Apollo, ecstasy and elegance, the magnificently flawed and the imposingly perfect, goes on for ever. We bow our heads to Apollo, but we should all have sympathy for the devil.

Coda

Unreliable Evidence: the Death of Brian Jones

IN THE YEARS since the death of Brian Jones late in the evening on Wednesday, 2 July 1969, the focus has changed from the impact of his life to the drama of his death. The circumstances of his leaving this earth are undoubtedly disturbing, messy and contradictory. Yet in my view this focus on conspiracy theories, along with some revisionism by Mick Jagger, Keith Richards, Andrew Oldham and others, has diminished the importance of one of the most visionary musicians of the twentieth century.

Without doubt the official coroner's verdict on Brian's death was perfunctory and lazy. The initial view of the police was that this was a simple drowning and most of the anomalies in witness accounts were not investigated. The police had, in the main, exhibited contempt for Brian Jones during his life and there's good evidence that they continued to do so after his death. Furthermore, the motives of many people around Brian in his final days were dubious, and their accounts are suspect. However, from my

324

interviews with objective witnesses of Brian's last weeks, including musicians who played with him and old friends like Bobbie Korner, I've come to share their belief that Brian's death was most likely a tragic accident. I've also come to believe that many of the existing theories that his death was in fact murder rely on unreliable witnesses, most of whose accounts are markedly more contradictory than the official witness statements.

Police version: Brian drowned

As flawed and cursory as the original verdict is, compared to the complexity of most conspiracy theories, this remains the most likely scenario, partly because it is supported by most disinterested witnesses and people who knew Brian. Brian had blacked out in the past, under the influence of alcohol and prescription drugs, for instance with George Chkiantz at the Minzah hotel, and according to Suki Potier, this was a frequent occurrence.

There are, of course, crucial discrepancies in the witnesses' descriptions of Brian's death, all of which were shared with police in the early hours of 3 July. Anna Wohlin stated that she heard Lawson shout, 'Something has happened to Brian' and she rushed out to the pool at the same time as Thorogood; Thorogood stated he had left Brian in the pool to get a towel when Wohlin shouted, 'He is lying on the bottom'; meanwhile, Lawson states that she was in the house, returned to the pool and found Brian motionless. There are also discrepancies about what each party did that day, whether they watched TV and in particular about the timeline.

There are several other disturbing elements in the official chain of events, principally the rush to convene a coroner's court and the reliance on medical information communicated via telephone rather than in writing. In addition, there are anomalous elements in the autopsy which have never been explained: there is the mention of 'punctuate haemorrhages' in Brian's brain, for instance – a term familiar from shaken baby syndrome.

However, anyone involved in criminal trials will know that witness statements usually differ, and witnesses often recall the timeline of simple events in a different order. If there had been collusion between witnesses, concealing a murder, it's likely there would have been fewer discrepancies. Likewise, if the authorities had colluded in covering up a murder they would in all likelihood have made more of an effort.

For all these reasons I believe that Brian's death was most likely a sad accident.

Nicholas Fitzgerald's account

Nicholas Fitzgerald's book, *Brian Jones: The Inside Story of the Original Rolling Stone*, combined with an earlier *News of the World* story on 27 February 1983, contained the first allegations that Brian was murdered. Fitzgerald, a cousin of Tara Browne, claimed that he, like Browne, was a close friend of Brian's. He related how he and a nineteen-year-old friend and gofer, Richard Cadbury – who had died by the time the story appeared – had visited Brian at Cotchford on the day of his death. Brian had shared with Fitzgerald his stories of an imminent supergroup with John Lennon and Jimi Hendrix, and warned him, 'Don't say anything ... it could be dangerous!' Fitzgerald and Cadbury had visited a pub, then returned to Cotchford at 11.15, leaving their car some distance from the house; when they walked into the grounds they saw three men near the pool, one of them pushing someone under the water, while two bystanders – a man and a woman – looked on. Suddenly, a 'burly man' (probably Keylock) leapt out of the bushes and snarled, 'Get out of here, Fitzgerald, or you'll be next.'

Fitzgerald refused to make a formal statement to the police, and a detailed investigation by Detective Chief Superintendent J. F. Reece in August 1983 concluded Fitzgerald was a 'Walter Mitty type person', and that the allegations had been made primarily to help promote his book. Reece's interviews with Fitzgerald were hostile; he informed him several times that he might well be committing offences by withholding information, and become an accessory after the fact. Yet Fitzgerald's evidence was bizarre, full of un-verifiable claims that he, too, had escaped murder attempts, that Cadbury might have been involved with the murderers, and that Cadbury, too, had died 'in mysterious circumstances'.

In the event, the stories heard by Reece were quite possibly less ludicrous than many of those contained in Fitzgerald's book, which revealed none of the insider information its title promised. The book mostly seemed a sad fantasy, especially the assertion that Brian was possibly bumped off because of the planned supergroup (the implication was that it was Tom Keylock who oversaw the murder). Hendrix's producer Eddie Kramer describes the story as 'silly', and John Lennon, in later interviews, commented that he thought Brian was another victim of the drugs scene, and how his sad state in the latter days meant 'You'd dread he'd come on the phone' – hardly the comment you'd expect from someone whose supergroup with Brian was sabotaged by a contract hit.

Fitzgerald's account is remarkable for how few encounters there are with others who knew Brian who were still alive and could therefore verify or disprove his presence. Fitzgerald implied that Suki Potier, who died in 1981, was aware of dark dealings, but Suki never mentioned this in the wake of Brian's death to friends, like Michael Rainey. Stash was with Brian at the Hilton after his bust, when Fitzgerald describes Brian calling him. Stash doesn't remem-ber the call, nor did he ever hear Fitzgerald's name mentioned. One of the few named friends is James Phelge. Today, Phelge says, 'Nick

Fitzgerald? Who the fuck is he? I never met him that I recall, and do not recognize him from the photo. His story of meeting me does not sound real.' The same, sadly, can be said of many of the events in Fitzgerald's book. But that hasn't stopped his story being the basis of many subsequent murder theories.

Fitzgerald went to live near his mother after the publication of the book, did not surface to refute any of the accusations of inaccuracy, and died in 2009.

A. E. Hotchner

Hotchner's 1990 book *Blown Away: The Rolling Stones and the Death of the Sixties* concluded that Brian had been murdered on the basis of two witnesses, Dick Hattrell and an anonymous cockney with long sideburns called 'Marty'. In this account, Hattrell claimed to have visited Brian at Cotchford shortly before his death, became worried about him, then later bumped into a party-goer who had witnessed Brian's murder. 'Marty' also claimed to have witnessed the incident, which was watched by (among others) two women. Hotchner incorporated Fitzgerald's story, as well as the hearsay of other bystanders, such as the story that Linda Lawrence was another witness of the cover-up and was spirited out of the country (Linda last saw Brian in 1968). Today, Hattrell says the story is nonsense, that he never visited Cotchford and '*never* told the story about Brian being murdered . . . this information is *not* correct'. Meanwhile, 'Marty' has since kept his counsel. This version of events is also incompatible with Anna Wohlin's two books. Unless Linda Lawrence and Dick Hattrell are part of the conspiracy, Hotchner's thesis doesn't stack up.

David Gibson

David Gibson was employed to fit carpets at Cotchford Farm; he later surfaced to make allegations in the *Brighton Evening Argus*. He reckoned Brian had been absent from Cotchford most of the day, as had Anna Wohlin; but Brian had reappeared later in the evening, and begged Gibson not to leave. Gibson believed that Brian had been murdered, and that Tom Keylock was responsible. There have been second-hand reports, says Stones road manager Sam Cutler, that Gibson saw Princess Margaret at Cotchford – hence rumours of a cover-up to protect the controversial princess's reputation. It is thought that Gibson never contacted the police and, like Fitzgerald, believed he had been the victim of threats and murder attempts.

Gibson's story is incompatible with most of the rival conspiracy theories bar the air of paranoia and Brian's conviction that someone was out to get him. However, Brian didn't share this with witnesses, like Bobbie Korner, who were known to be his confidants. Gibson's story is detailed at the Brian Jones fan club site, www.brianjonesfanclub.com.

Janet Lawson

In a *Daily Mail* interview with Scott Jones published on 29 November 2008, Janet Lawson claimed that much of her original statement was suggested to her by the questioning officer, Detective Sergeant Peter Hunter. This interview provided new evidence: that Lawson was in fact Keylock's girlfriend, and that Keylock had suggested she go down to keep an eye on Brian. In this interview, Lawson suggested that Frank Thorogood had been acting strangely and that she believed he had killed Brian, most likely by accident.

Lawson's account is consistent with the facts as we know them although her memories do, of course, provide only the most tenuous evidence of Thorogood's guilt, and equally prove that Keylock was economical with the truth. In the various police reviews of the case, some officers have concluded, 'It is possible that

Thorogood was larking about . . . [but] this is of course pure speculation.' It remains the second most likely scenario, that if Frank Thorogood was responsible, it was an accident – a possibility which Lawson and Wohlin's accounts could well support.

Tom Keylock

Most of the murder conspiracy theories around Brian's death emanate from Tom Keylock, Brian's driver and minder, who around 21 February 1994 claimed to have heard the deathbed confession of builder Frank Thorogood. In a sworn statement, Keylock said, 'I visited [Thorogood] at the North Middlesex Hospital on Sunday 7th November 1993. Mr Thorogood was terminally ill and close to death . . . Mr Thorogood stated he would finally like to set the record straight in relation to the death of Brian Jones. Mr Thorogood stated he physically held Brian Jones under the water and that this resulted in the death of Brian Jones.'

Any cynic would point out that a deathbed confession is value-less; if anything, the 'confession' attaches more guilt to Keylock than to Thorogood, especially as Thorogood's daughter Jan Bell later surfaced to deny that Keylock had spent any time alone with their father, who had been admitted to hospital with a respiratory problem and therefore, not being aware he was on his deathbed, could not have made a 'deathbed confession'.

Keylock's reminiscences were a key source for Terry Rawlings' book *Who Killed Christopher Robin?* (Boxtree, 1994), an updated version of which is promised soon. Keylock was likewise an adviser for Stephen Woolley's 2005 film *Stoned* (based on Janet Lawson and Anna Wohlin's recollections), which again accused Thorogood. Perhaps there is truth to some of Keylock's stories, but I feel they should all come with a health warning.

Keylock himself died on 2 July 2009. Sam Cutler reported that he, too, made a deathbed confession which was videoed and offered for sale. Several years later the video remains just a rumour.

Jan Bell

In 1994, Jan Bell, the daughter of Frank Thorogood, denied that her father had made any confession to Tom Keylock. Jan also related a story which she recalled her father sharing with her, of Mick Jagger and Keith Richards driving down to Cotchford on the day of Brian's death and arguing with Brian over ownership of the name Rolling Stones; during the argument, Keith pulled a knife on Brian. But the Stones were at Olympic on the day in question, observed by several witnesses. It's possible that Thorogood had indeed witnessed an argument between Mick, Keith and Brian, but if it did happen it probably took place at Redlands earlier in the year.

'Joe'

Early theories, inspired by Keylock, that Thorogood murdered Brian were given additional weight by Geoffrey Giuliano's *Paint It Black*, published in 1994. Giuliano's book relied heavily on interviews from Mandy Aftel's and Laura Jackson's earlier books; recycled the allegations of the pseudonymous Marty from Hotchner's book as well as Dick Hattrell (who denies speculating that Brian was murdered); added another anonymous industry insider, 'Sean'; and for good measure one more mysterious bystander, 'Joe', who claimed to have held Brian underwater 'for the fucking crack. For a joke, like.' On the tape, 'Joe' claimed that Thorogood had subsequently fled the scene: 'Frank had got this old Ford Anglia . . . we jumped out of the pool . . . We went to London.' However, Thorogood was present at Cotchford when police officer Albert Evans arrived around 12.10 a.m. Subsequently, the police concluded the tape was a fake, 'prepared in America for a number of radio programmes in New York'.

Anna Wohlin

Anna's book, with the emphatic title *The Murder of Brian Jones*, was published in 1999. Her story was broadly consistent with her original witness statement, except she detailed more tension between Thorogood and Brian who, she said, had argued over bills for work on Cotchford Farm with the result that Brian had sacked the builder. There was little explanation of why, if Brian had fallen out with Thorogood, he went over to his flat to invite him for a swimming session. Although Anna didn't witness it, she wrote that she believes Thorogood killed Brian because of his reaction after the death: 'Frank was as cold as ice. He didn't show any sympathy.'

Anna Wohlin made the accusation when Thorogood was dead and therefore not able to defend himself; she also suggested that Stones PR Les Perrin, who died in 1978, was involved in a cover-up. Unless one believes other ludicrous theories that Anna was involved in a (different) cover-up, one must feel sympathy for the trauma she underwent. None the less, most of her recollections of Brian being focused, in control of his music, and planning a new life with her are contradicted by objective witnesses like Bobbie Korner and Korner's bassist, Nick South.

Some people believe that Anna's story validates Keylock's assertion that Thorogood was responsible. But Anna's conviction that Thorogood murdered Brian seems to have arrived only once Thorogood's name was already in the frame, according to Jan Oloffson, the Swedish writer and photographer who introduced Anna to Brian. 'Anna came over [from Sweden] and I met her through a friend of mine, a Swedish girl called Inga Rose,' he says. 'I wrote and took pictures for Swedish Images, she was impressed by this, and I took her down to the clubs.' Jan introduced Anna to Brian at the Revolution and the three remained good friends; Anna and Brian spoke to Jan several times on the phone from Cotchford, and were planning to come to his wedding on 12 July. Of course, they never made it. After Brian's death, Jan was one of the few who stayed in contact with Anna. 'She came to see me . . . we spoke, and it was definitely a drowning thing. Whether Brian might have drunk or smoked too much was another matter. But as far as she was concerned, there was no one involved in drowning him.' Anna's latter-day belief that Brian was murdered is, says Jan, a recent development: 'Early on she didn't [believe that]. Definitely not.'

The 'Allen Klein report'

In 2009, one-time Stones road manager Sam Cutler mentioned the 'Allen Klein report' on his blog. He detailed how Klein had employed private detectives to investigate Brian's death; they concluded that Keylock was the guilty man. As detailed elsewhere, there is some evidence to suggest Keylock's guilt, principally his attempt to blame Frank Thorogood, his apparent theft of some of Brian's belongings, and Janet Lawson's revelation that she was actually Keylock's girlfriend, and Keylock had persuaded her to conceal this fact. Yet in October 2013, Cutler told me that there was now confusion as to whether the Klein report does in fact exist.

The *Toronto Sun* and Tom Keylock

In 2003, the *Toronto Sun* ran a story on Jerry Stone, proprietor of a Stones-themed bar in the city, that described his acquisition of two exciting items of memorabilia, gold records for Paint It, Black and Little Red Rooster, both of them (according to Stone) once owned by Brian Jones. The bar owner remarked on the pedigree of the two items, for he had acquired them from 'former Stones chauffeur Tom Keylock'.

This was a fascinating development for some Brian Jones diehards, for it was well known that many of Brian's possessions had disappeared after his death. Some items, including master tapes and clothing, had been returned to the family; others, such as David A. Hardy's paintings and quite possibly some of Brian's guitars, have never been traced. Keylock's possession of the gold discs apparently verified that he had stolen items from Brian, thus confirming his dishonesty. This also seemed like supporting evidence for the theory that Keylock was the mastermind behind Brian's death (as borne out by Fitzgerald's alleged sighting), and made Keylock's dubious claims of Frank Thorogood's deathbed confession appear to be an obvious attempt to put sleuths off his trail.

Many people who met Keylock disliked or distrusted him, Stones confidant Keith Altham for instance: 'I didn't like him. And no, I didn't trust him. There was something about him that was unpleasant, a little bit like Jimmy Savile, where you sensed there was something malevolent.' This view was shared by many in the Stones circle, and even by outsiders like Brion Gysin. For this reason, over recent years Keylock's name has increasingly been suggested as Brian's murderer, perhaps the mastermind in a bigger conspiracy.

Keylock as a villain makes much more sense than Thorogood. There's only one flaw in this version, which is that Keylock was in London on the evening in question, namely at Olympic studios in Barnes, where he was seen by, among others, Altham. 'I had got to Olympic around eleven on my way home; he came in about midnight, or one o'clock.' Keylock had received a call from Cotchford with the news of Brian's death, and broke the story to the band.

Witness accounts of Brian's death put it after eleven o'clock; Fitzgerald reckoned he had turned up at the house at 11.15, and would have been 'threatened' by Keylock some minutes later. The notion that Keylock could have chased off Fitzgerald or other bystanders, threatened and instructed the various witnesses, hit the road for an eighty-minute drive and arrived in the studio by one o'clock stretches credulity to the limit. 'It's ludicrous,' says Altham. 'Keylock was unpleasant, but why would he have murdered Brian when Brian was the goose that kept laying the golden egg?' Of course, it's possible that Keylock could have been involved if he'd organized a murder with split-second timing – but as with so many conspiracy theories, this makes more assumptions, and generates more inconsistencies, than the official version.

Who was responsible?

Keylock's presence at Olympic undermines the most plausible conspiracy theory about Brian's murder. Yet it doesn't eliminate many of the deep and justified misgivings around Brian's death.

Brian was ill served by the establishment, and by his own band. The former had a statutory duty to investigate his death but did so in a casual manner; the latter had a duty of care to the man responsible for forming the Rolling Stones, however maddening, irritating and unreliable he was.

Although the police did assign experienced detectives to the scene, their investigation jumped to a conclusion early on, and failed to adequately consider other alternatives. The police failed to control the site, too, allowing Keylock and others access to the area, which allowed evidence to be destroyed and Brian's property to be removed. Similarly, the Rolling Stones seemed content to leave Keylock, a man who Keith Richards and others believed was a thief, in charge at Cotchford.

In the years since Brian's death the band has shown little interest in protecting his legacy, and it appears from the limited amount of evidence available that the current value of Brian's estate is only modest. It's quite possible that Lewis Jones, who died in 2009, was not aggressive in protecting the value of his son's estate. After the death of Louisa, in 2011, the estate passed to Brian's sister Barbara, who has one son. Today, by most estimates, Brian Jones's estate receives less than £20,000 a year in income, which seems exceptionally low considering the band's back catalogue has been extensively reissued, along with DVDs. It is undeniable that Mick Jagger, Keith Richards and Charlie Watts have no legal duty to look after Brian's financial or other interests; perhaps it's naive to suggest they have a moral duty.

Only Bill Wyman has stood up for the band's founder: 'As the years go by, I become ever more convinced he's entitled to [a] free pardon.'

Notes

Chapter 1: Secrets and Lies

Main interviewees: Robert Almond, Trudy Baldwin, June Biggar, Roger Dagley, Colin Dellar, Graham Keen, John Keen, Anna Livia, Roger Limb, Roger Jessop, Dave Jones, David Mercer, Linda Partridge, Tony Partridge, Tony Pickering, Robin Pike, Pip Price, Alvin Smith, Ian Standing, Carole Woodcroft. Architectural information from Nikolaus Pevsner's *Gloucestershire* (Penguin, 1974); 'so gay it was unbelievable' quote is Barry Miles. Many thanks to Robin, John and Pip for their guided tours of the area. Most accounts of Lewis and Louisa's role in the Welsh and musical community come from John and Graham Keen, and Roger Jessop. Recollections of Lewis primarily draw on interviews with Robert Almond and Linda Partridge; information on the local church was from Trudy Baldwin. Thanks to Shirley Park of Pate's Grammar School, formerly Cheltenham Grammar School, for her invaluable help. (Initially, Pate's, the girls' grammar school, and Cheltenham, the boys' school on the high street, were separate institutions; they have now merged, based in the bigger building on the girls' site.) 'Beatnik horror' refers to the 7 August 1960 *Sunday People* story on Jack Kerouac, Jack Corso, William Burroughs and 'hate merchant'

Allen Ginsberg, 'men who have nothing to offer but despair'. 'Essentially a sensitive and vulnerable boy' comes from Brian's obituary, by Dr Arthur Bell, in *The Patesian* (1969); Brian's O level and A level results likewise come from *The Patesian*. I have not managed to trace Hope's current whereabouts, and have changed her name to protect her privacy.

Chapter 2: Crossroads
Main sources: Ken Ames, Pat Andrews, Chris Barber, Harry Brampton, Jane Filby, Dick Hattrell, Tony Holbrook, Buck Jones, Paul Jones, Graham and John Keen, Richard Pond, Graham Ride, Graham Stodart, Pete Sumner, David Widdows. Previous accounts have Val realizing she was pregnant after leaving school. Anna Livia suggests she was still at school when Brian was in London. In addition, while other accounts suggest different timelines for Brian's dates with the Ramrods, I believe most of his dates with them were in 1960, as Tony Holbrook and Graham Stodart remember he still lived at Hatherley Road. This chapter revolves around the accounts of Pat Andrew, Dick Hattrell, Graham Ride and John Keen, to all of whom I'm indebted, especially John, with whom I'd often debate interpretations of events. I couldn't have asked for a better observer than John, who came from a similar background to Brian – and, given his subsequent career as an educational psychologist, he is well versed in the psychology of groups. Re Chris Barber in Cheltenham: Graham Ride believes Alexis Korner and Cyril Davies visited Cheltenham early in September; my own belief, based on the research of Todd Allen, is that Cyril didn't play with Alexis until December of that year, which means Graham's recollections are of a later show, and that Barber's performance on 10 October was the date of their first, crucial meeting. There is also confusion about the Sonny and Brownie show – Graham Ride

believes it was 10 October, and that Alexis was there. More defini-
tively, although many writers have rendered accounts of Brian
watching Sonny Boy Williamson in Cheltenham, this is fantasy.
Williamson's first visit to the UK is well documented, and was in
1963. I think Dick Hattrell has confused his memories of Sonny
Terry with Sonny Boy Williamson. There are other incompatibili-
ties in various accounts. Dick Hattrell thinks Brian finally moved to
London after his third trip to Ealing; Graham Ride is certain he'd
already decided to move before his first show, so I've followed his
account. Dick Taylor believes he, Mick and Keith attended the second week of the club, 24 March, although other versions differ. Many
accounts, like Philip Norman's, suggest Brian played with Paul Jones
after Brian moved to London, rather than before, partly because this
was Paul's initial memory. However, that chronology is impossible,
and Paul now agrees he'd met Brian in Oxford, late 1961. For further
reading, I'd recommend Graham Ride's *Foundation Stone*.

Chapter 3: A Bunch of Nankers

Main interviews: Pat Andrews, Geoff Bradford, Rick Brown, Norrie
Burnette, Janet Couzens, Billie Davis, Andy Hoogenboom, Glyn
Johns, Bobbie Korner, Jeffrey Kruger, Harold and Barbara
Pendleton, Mike Peters, James Phelge, Keith Richards, Keith Scott,
Cleo Sylvestre, Dick Taylor. Early Little Boy Blue and the Blue Boys
background based on Dick Taylor's account, as is much of the
information on early Stones rehearsals. Main Ian Stewart background comes from Hamish Maxwell, while Ben Waters provided
insight into his style. Description of Bill Wyman being drawn into
the band is based around his account in *Stone Alone*. Main
reference for 1963 gigs is Karnbach and Benson, *It's Only
Rock'n'Roll*. For further reading, I'd recommend *Phelge's Stones*, a
hilarious, witty account of the atmosphere around the Stones in

1963. I did trace 'Sal', mentioned in the final paragraphs, through another interviewee, but she declined to be interviewed. For that reason I've changed her name.

Chapter 4: I Can't Be Satisfied

Main interviewees include those listed for Chapter 3, plus Keith Altham, Tony Bramwell, Eric Burdon, Tony Calder, George Chkiantz, Jeff Dexter, John 'Hoppy' Hopkins, John Keen, Linda Leitch, Andrew Oldham, Nicky Wright, Patrick Wright. Information on the life and background of Andrew Oldham from my interviews with him, plus Oldham's three volumes of memoirs. Dick Rowe section: I have relied heavily on Johnny Rogan's excellent story on Brian Epstein, *Starmakers and Svengalis* (p109). 'Blotches all over his face' quote is from *Stone Alone*. I Wanna Be Your Man account draws on Paul McCartney's *Many Years From Now*. Further reading: Andrew Oldham's *Stoned* and *2Stoned* are a great reference for this era. Although his own recollections are sometimes unreliable, they are always entertaining, and counterpointed by the other insiders' accounts.

Chapter 5: How Many More Years

Main interviewees: as for Chapter 4, plus Toni Basil, Tosh Berman, Peter Guralnick, Chris Hutchins, Stash Klossowski, Ken Kubernik, Harvey Kubernik, Gered Mankowitz, Phil May, Scott Ross, Guy Webster. Account of Mick and Keith's meeting on Dartford train platform based on my interview with Keith. Charlie Watts quote is from an interview by Sylvie Simmons in *MOJO* (2003). 'Brian was Welsh' quote is from Hotchner, *Blown Away: The Rolling Stones and the Death of the Sixties* (Simon & Schuster, 1990, p206). Astrid Lundstrom quote is from *Stone Alone*. Dave Thomson references throughout the book from his interview with John McGillivray.

'They had done the whole thing, and left him to overdub': some accounts conflict with this one, in particular Dave Thomson's, Brian's friend, who thought the band recorded the track together. But Ian Stewart's account in *Blown Away* corroborates that of Phil May. If the pair are mistaken, it's in attribution, i.e. it was during the recording of another song that the event occurred.

Chapter 6: Paranoia Meter

Main interviews: Toni Basil, Ken Boss, Denny Bruce, Eric Burdon, Tony Calder, Jeff Dexter, Marianne Faithfull, Christopher Gibbs, Chris Hutchins, Stash Klossowski, Ken Kubernik, Linda Leitch née Lawrence, Gered Mankowitz, Michael Rainey, Scott Ross, Pete Townshend, Hilton Valentine, Chris Welch, Peter Whitehead, Zouzou. 'Jumped along the pavement' quote comes from Wyman's *Rolling With the Stones* (Dorling Kindersley, 2002). Description of Allen Klein draws on Johnny Rogan's *Starmakers and Svengalis*, and Johnny Black's feature in *MOJO*'s *The Beatles: 10 Years That Shook the World*. Nico quotes come from Witts's *Nico: The Life and Lies of an Icon*. As Witts points out, Nico is an exceptionally unreliable witness – Stash, Zouzou and others suggest Nico's relationship with Brian was briefer than her notes for Witts indicate. Meeting Klein: in *Stone Alone*, Wyman says it's in Miami, mid July 1965. Jack Nitzsche mentioned Keith and Mick's abuse of Brian in context with the later 1968 session, in his November 1974 *Crawdaddy* interview; however, it seems certain that this incident took place in the *Aftermath* sessions, during the period Denny Bruce stayed with Nitzsche.

Chapter 7: Paint It Black

Main interviews: Tosh Berman, Tony Bramwell, Denny Bruce, Eric Burdon, Jeff Dexter, Marianne Faithfull, Christopher Gibbs, Dana Gillespie, Stash Klossowski, Eddie Kramer, Donovan Leitch,

Michael Rainey, Harriet Vyner, Nigel Waymouth, Peter Whitehead, Bill Wyman. Gene Clark quote is from a 1983 TV interview. Wyman 'funnily enough' quote is from *Rolling With the Stones*. The analysis of how many Stones gigs Brian really missed comes from Karnbach and Benson's *It's Only Rock'n'Roll*. The total of missing shows comes to either 11 or 12 (depending on references) from around 934. Some Hamri background comes from John Geiger and Michelle Green (see Further Reading). 'Witches coven' quote is from *Faithfull*. Stan Blackbourne interview courtesy of Simon Spence. References for the Beatles' parallel developments are Mark Lewisohn's *Complete Beatles Chronicle* and Neil Spencer's 'Eastern Rising' from *The Beatles*.

Chapter 8: Butterflies and Wheels

Main interviews: Tony Bramwell, Tony Calder, Glyn Johns, Kenney Jones, Stash Klossowski, Sonja Kristina, Linda Leitch, Michael Rainey, Mim Scala, Volker Schlöndorff. Tom Keylock interview is courtesy of Pat Gilbert, Stan Blackbourne interview courtesy of Simon Spence. Robert Warren quote is from the BBC Radio 2 documentary *Who Breaks a Butterfly on a Wheel?* Although all other Christopher Gibbs quotes come from my interview with him of 18.6.13, the 'obnoxious behaviour' quote is taken from Harriet Vyner's wonderful *Groovy Bob*. The Morocco trip: main sources are Tom Keylock, Marianne Faithfull (including her book *Faithfull*), Keith Richards' *Life*, Christopher Gibbs, Brion Gysin's 'Moroccan Mishaps with the Strolling Ruins', Cecil Beaton's diaries, John Geiger's *Nothing is True Everything is Permitted*, and the newspaper *La Dépêche* (January 2011). Beaton's diaries are courtesy Hugo Vickers, © The Literary Executors of the late Sir Cecil Beaton. Several quotes by Gysin are taken from the book by John Geiger entitled *Chapel of Extreme Experience* (Soft Skull Press): © 2003 by

Brion Gysin, used by permission of the Wylie Agency LLC. Each of their accounts contradicts the other to some extent. Keylock suggests Anita returned to London from Marbella rather than Tangier, and arrived in Marrakesh directly with Brian and Anita. However, Gysin's diaries maintain the party assembled in Tangier, and as they were written more or less contemporaneously I've gone with his timeline – even though Gysin, like the others, contradicts himself over various accounts. For good measure, Marianne's book seems to splice in the story of Brian breaking his wrist – an incident that took place eight months earlier. Keith's 'he never stopped whining' quote is from *Life*. Through this and Chapter 9, one key source on the character and background of Norman Pilcher is Simon Wells' *The Great Rolling Stones Drugs Bust*. Although it contains odd factual errors derived from secondary sources, it's a fantastic overview and analysis of the bust, and is especially good on the character of Judge Leslie Block and the identities of the police squads that raided Redlands.

Chapter 9: The Kindness of Strangers
Interviews: Keith Altham, Stan Blackbourne, Tony Bramwell, Caroline Coon, Jeff Dexter, Stash Klossowski, Eddie Kramer, Gered Mankowitz, Mim Scala, Murray Zucker. In this and the following chapters, I reveal several new attempted police busts on Brian, which clearly demonstrate he was the Rolling Stone pursued most consistently by the police. When I've written Brian was 'reportedly' busted, for instance, this comes from Simon Wells: I've used 'reportedly' because he doesn't mention the source of the information. Beatles recording info comes from Mark Lewisohn's *Complete Beatles Chronicle*. Nico 'spotty' quote is from Richard Witts. The story of the Monkees' Royal Garden attempted bust comes from Blackbourne. Dr Green's quote about Brian calling at

three in the morning comes from Mandy Aftel's *Death of a Rolling Stone* (I normally wouldn't quote from another biography, but this is the only direct evidence I've seen of what a difficult patient Brian was) – the name Dr Green is apparently a pseudonym. Wyman's 'their idea of a joke' is from *Rolling With the Stones*. The details of Brian's loan from Major Dawson, and Keith's £20,000 wall, also come from Wyman.

Chapter 10: Bou Jeloud

Interviews: Tony Bramwell, Sam Cutler, George Chkiantz, Christopher Gibbs, Blanca Hamri, Boualem Hamri, Glyn Johns, Adam Kinn, Al Kooper, Eddie Kramer, Linda Leitch, Taj Mahal, Roger Mayer, Michael Rainey, Keith Richards, Mim Scala and Ron Schneider, plus Simon Spence's Stan Blackbourne interview. Chronologies of Brian's interactions and recordings with Jimi Hendrix courtesy of Caesar Glebbeek. Timeline and background of Brian's drug bust use information from Simon Wells (notably the 2001 reference) and the British Library Newspaper Collection. Timeline of the Stones recording session based on Felix Aeppli's *Rolling Stones: The Ultimate Guide* plus Karnbach and Benson's *It's Only Rock'n'Roll*. Thanks to Andrew Lott at the London Metropolitan Archives, which holds details of the Inner London Sessions. Description of Mick's approach to *Performance* and Brian's encounter with Mick at Redlands based on *Faithfull*. Nitzsche 'aloof' quote is from his interview with *Crawdaddy*. Timing for Brian's visit to Marrakesh is from Glyn Johns' records – this trip has often been confused with Brian's visit to Tangier, this time with Suki, which Bill Wyman dates as 4 July. It's been written that Brian visited Joujouka in July to make an early attempt at recording: I'm certain this is incorrect, as neither Boualem Hamri, Christopher Gibbs nor others on the scene remember it. Ron

Schneider is certain that his night with Brian at the Hilton took place after the second bust, and that he was not present for the first. This conflicts with Wells and others who suggest Brian went straight to the Priory, but given that Ron was there, I've gone with his version. Likewise, Al Kooper's account of the You Can't Always Get What You Want recording in November might be confused with a further session on 15 March 1969. Brian's condition suggests the latter, but Al is adamant that the 'biology textbook' moment came during the first session, when Jimmy Miller was playing drums, while Glyn Johns, who engineered the later session, didn't witness the incident. It's possible James Karnbach's personnel list for the later session is incorrect, as Glyn does not remember Al being present at the later session. Joujouka, Bowles and Gysin background: Michelle Green, John Geiger. If anyone thinks I'm being hard on Bowles, they should have been present at Dean's Bar on 17 June 2013 when I met a Moroccan psychiatrist who informed me he is still dealing with the psychological damage inflicted by Bowles on the young men of Tangier.

Chapter 11: Just Go Home

Interviews: Keith Altham, George Chkiantz, Sam Cutler, David A. Hardy, Bobbie Korner, John Mayall, Nick South, Cleo Sylvestre, Zouzou. Keith Richards' 'He left [the band]' quote is from his *Rolling Stone* interview with Robert Greenfield in 1971. Jack Nitzsche quotes from his interview with *Crawdaddy*. Damian Korner quotes from Harry Shapiro's *Alexis Korner*. Quotes from Janet Lawson, and timings, are all taken from their witness statements.

Coda

Sources for the various conspiracy theories around Brian's death are all cited in the text (the Laura Jackson book mentioned is *Golden Stone*, Smith Gryphon, 1992). My own quotes come from Bobbie Korner, Nick South, John Mayall, Dick Hattrell, James Phelge and Stash, all interviewed in 2013 and 2014.

Acknowledgements

As ever, I owe endless thanks to my agent Julian Alexander, a vital, inexhaustible source of wisdom and insight, as is my American agent, Sarah Lazin. Michelle Signore, my editor at Transworld, and Julie Miesionczek of Viking were likewise crucial in helping me see the wood for the trees. Any errors or shortcomings in this book are mine.

The many breakthroughs and new information in this story are due to the help and assistance of countless people. Music writers are sometimes thought of as a competitive bunch, yet Sean Egan, Richie Unterberger, Mark Paytress and Simon Spence in particular were invariably helpful in assisting me to delve into areas they've investigated already, and sharing their knowledge and contacts. I owe a debt to all of my interviewees, many of whom went to huge trouble to help me with further contacts, and submitted gracefully to request after request. I should particularly single out Robin Pike, who helped me when this idea was in germination; John Keen, who has been a good friend and a (much-needed) voice of sanity throughout; and Stash Klossowski, whose cordless phone often gave up the ghost in the face of relentless interviews. Thanks also to Linda and Donovan Leitch for their wonderful hospitality. A brief list of others who provided vital assistance: Todd Allen, Mark Blake, Joep Bremmers, Julian Carr, Jeff Dexter, Ben Edmonds, Caesar Glebbeek, Carl Glover, Marcus Gray, Giorgio Guernier, David Holzer, Ken Hunt, Nicola Joss, Harvey Kubernik, Tony Leppard, Pen Lister, Barry Miles, Kris Needs, Shirley Park, Pip Price, Robert Rimell, Frank Rynne, Harry Shapiro, Mat Snow, Phil Sutcliffe, Barbara Temsamani, Harriet Vyner, Val Wilmer, John Wurr, Alistair Young. Thanks also to Rob Chapman, always one of our favourite writers in my time at *MOJO*, who wrote a cover story on Brian – the Nicky Wright quotes used in this book are mainly from an interview I added to Rob's story. And thanks to Nicola Joss for permission to use Pete Townshend's appreciation of Brian, written for the same issue.

My thanks once again to my interviewees: Robert Almond, Keith Altham, Ken Ames, Pat Andrews, Fery Asgari, Mick Avory, Ginger Baker, Trudy Baldwin, Chris Barber, Toni Basil, Tosh Berman, Dave Berry, June Biggar, Ken Boss, Geoff Bradford, Harry Brampton, Tony Bramwell, Rick Brown, Dennis Bruce, Eric Burdon, Norrie Burnette, Tony Calder, George Chkiantz, Caroline Coon, Janet Couzens, Sam Cutler, Roger Dagley, Billie Davis, Colin Dellar, Jeff Dexter, Jess Down, Marianne Faithfull, Penny Farmer, Jane Filby, Kim Fowley, Christopher Gibbs, Dana Gillespie, Peter Guralnick, Buddy Guy, Blanca Hamri, Bouallem Hamri, David A. Hardy, Dick Hattrell, Tony Holbrook, Andy Hoogenboom, John 'Hoppy' Hopkins, Chris Hutchins, Roger Jessop, Glyn Johns, Buck Jones, Dave Jones, Kenney Jones, Paul Jones, Graham Keen, John Keen, Adam Kinn, Stash Klossowski, Al Kooper, Bobbie Korner, Eddie Kramer, Sonja Kristina, Jeffrey Kruger, Harvey Kubernik, Ken Kubernik, Linda Leitch, Donovan Leitch, Joolz Leitch, Roger Limb, Anna Livia, Taj Mahal, Gered Mankowitz, Hamish Maxwell, Phil May, John Mayall, Roger Mayer, Barry Miles, Dawn Molloy, Rod

Morris, Roy Moseley, Dave Myers, Laurence Myers, Andrew Oldham, Carl Palmer, Colin Partridge, Linda Partridge, Barbara Pendleton, Harold Pendleton, Mike Peters, James Phelge, Tony Pickering, Robin Pike, Ken Pitt, Richard Pond, Pip Price, Michael Rainey, Keith Richards, Graham Ride, Scott Ross, Mim Scala, Keith Scott, Volker Schlöndorff, Ron Schneider, Nick South, Ian Standing, Graham Stodart, Pete Sumner, Cleo Sylvestre, Nedra Talley, Dick Taylor, Hilton Valentine, Harriet Vyner, Dick Waterman, Ben Waters, Nigel Waymouth, Guy Webster, Chris Welch, Peter Whitehead, David Widdows, Val Wilmer, Carole Woodcroft, Nicky Wright, Patrick Wright, Bill Wyman, Zouzou. Stan Blackbourne interview transcript courtesy of Simon Spence. Tom Keylock interview transcript courtesy of Pat Gilbert. This book also draws on the transcript of an interview with Brion Gysin, conducted by Genesis P. Orridge.

Further Reading

All written sources used in the book are cited in the notes. The following books made for invaluable background reading on Brian Jones.

Aeppli, Felix, *Rolling Stones: The Ultimate Guide* (Record Information Services, 1996)

Aftel, Mandy, *Death of a Rolling Stone* (Sidgwick and Jackson, 1982)

Bockris, Victor, *Keith Richards* (Hutchinson, 1992)

——— *The Life and Death of Andy Warhol* (Bantam, 1989)

Booth, Stanley, *The True Adventures of the Rolling Stones* (Abacus, 1985)

Cutler, Sam, *You Can't Always Get What You Want* (ECW, 2010)

Dawson, Julian, *And on Piano . . . Nicky Hopkins* (Backstage, 2011)

Donovan, *Hurdy Gurdy Man* (Arrow, 2005)

Dylan, Bob, *Chronicles* (Simon & Schuster, 2004)

Faithfull, Marianne & David Dalton, *Faithfull* (Cooper Square, 1994)

Geiger, John, *Nothing is True Everything is Permitted* (Disinformation, 2005)

Green, Michelle, *The Dream at the End of the World* (Bloomsbury, 1992)

Herbst, Peter (ed.), *Rolling Stone Interviews 1967–80* (Arthur Barker, 1981)

Karnbach, James & Carol Benson, *It's Only Rock'n'Roll* (Facts on File, 1997)

Lachman, Gary, *Turn Off Your Mind* (Dedalus, 2010)

Lewisohn, Mark, *The Complete Beatles Chronicle* (Pyramid, 1992)

Mahal, Taj, *Autobiography of a Bluesman* (Sanctuary, 2001)

Melly, George, *Revolt into Style* (Penguin, 1972)

Miles, Barry, *Paul McCartney: Many Years From Now* (Vintage, 1998)

MOJO magazine, *The Beatles: 10 Years That Shook the World* (Dorling Kindersley, 2004)

Norman, Philip, *The Stones* (Penguin, 1993)

Oldham, Andrew, *Stoned* (Vintage, 2000)

—— *2Stoned* (Vintage, 2002)

—— *Stone Free* (Escargot, 2012)

Phelge, James, *Phelge's Stones* (Buncha Asshole Books, 1999)

The Q Encyclopedia of Rock Stars (Dorling Kindersley, 1996)

Richards, Keith, *Life* (Weidenfeld & Nicolson, 2010)

Ride, Graham, *Foundation Stone* (Broad Brush, 2005)

Rogan, Johnny, *Starmakers and Svengalis* (Macdonald, 1988)

Ross, Scott, *Scott Free* (Chosen, 1976)

Rous, Henrietta (ed.), *The Ossie Clark Diaries* (Bloomsbury, 1998)

Scala, Mim, *Diary of a Teddy Boy* (Review, 2001)

Shapiro, Harry, *Alexis Korner: The Biography* (Bloomsbury, 1997)

Spence, Simon, *Immediate Records* (Black Dog, 2008)

Vickers, Hugo (ed.), *Beaton in the Sixties* (Phoenix, 2003)

Vyner, Harriet, *Groovy Bob* (Faber, 1999)

Wells, Simon, *The Great Rolling Stones Drug Bust* (Omnibus, 2011)

Witts, Richard, *Nico: The Life and Lies of an Icon* (Virgin, 1993)

Wyman, Bill, *Stone Alone* (Penguin, 1991)

All magazines and periodicals quoted within the text are detailed in the notes. The principal magazines used for background reading include *Billboard, Circus, Creem, Disc, DownBeat, East Village Other, Entertainment World, Evo, Fifth Estate, Fusion, Goldmine, GQ, The Guitar Magazine, Guitarist, International Musician, Jazz Chronicle,* Jazz *News, Jazz & Pop, Melody Maker, MOJO, Motorbooty, NME, The*

Patesian, Pavilion, Phonograph Record Magazine, Q, Record Mirror, Record World, Rolling Stone, Sounds, Stereo Review, Strange Things, Trouser Press, Variety, Village Voice, Wire, ZigZag. Copies of the *Gloucestershire Echo* and other local information courtesy of Cheltenham Public Library. Copies of the *News of the World, Times, Sunday People, Sunday Times, Sun* and *Daily Mirror* were all accessed courtesy of the British Library reading rooms. Thanks to *Q, MOJO,* Johnny Black, Fred Dellar and Richard Morton Jack for use of their archives.

Picture Acknowledgements

Every effort has been made to trace copyright holders, but any who have been overlooked are invited to get in touch with the publishers.

Images are listed clockwise from top left:

Section 1
Brian aged twelve in Cheltenham: David Mercer.

Brian as a baby, 1943: Popperfoto/Getty; Barbara Jones and friends in Cheltenham: Trudy Baldwin; Brian and Valerie Corbett, 1961: Graham Ride; John Keen band, Cheltenham: John Keen; Alexis Korner: Keith Scott; Brian and Valerie, Symonds Yat: Graham Ride; Brian at Crich tramway museum: National Tramway Museum; Brian aged seventeen in Filby's basement: John Keen.

Rolling Stones, Marquee, 12 July 1962: © Pictorial Press Ltd/Alamy; Brian with Pat Andrews: Pat Andrews; Brian with Linda Lawrence: courtesy Linda Leitch; Dawn Young: Dawn Molloy Young; Zouzou, Castel nightclub, 1967: Mary Evans Picture Library/Epic; Andrew Oldham and the band, *c.* 1963: Getty Images.

Stones in the street before recording I Wanna Be Your Man and (below) in the studio, 1963: both Gus Coral; Brian, Hollywood, 4 June 1964: Mirrorpix.

Brian with Howlin' Wolf on TV show *Shindig*, Hollywood, May 1965: Michael Ochs Archives/Getty Images; Brian, Clearwater, May 1965: Redferns via Getty Images.

Section 2
Brian and Anita Pallenberg photographed for *Men in Vogue*, November 1966: Michael Cooper.

Brian playing the sitar, *Ready, Steady, Go!*, May 1966: Jan Olofsson; Brian and Mick Jagger, Escalier Waller, Tangier, March 1967; Brian, Keith Richards and Anita, Es Saadi hotel, Marrakech, March 1967; Brian, Café Phoenix, Morocco, March 1967: all Michael Cooper; Robert Fraser's birthday party, Hotel Minzah, Tangier, 20 September 1965: White of Reading/Mirrorpix.

Brian with Andrew Oldham, Monterey, June 1967: Fred Arellano vintagerockphotography.com; Brian leaving for the High Court, 12 December 1967: © Bettmann/Corbis; Brian in Sri Lanka, 1968: both Record Mecca; Brian and Suki Potier, Marbella, 3 August 1967: Getty Images; Brian and Anita arriving at the screening of *Mord und Totschlag*, Cannes, 5 May 1967: Getty Images; Brian with Stanislas Klossowski de Rowla, West London Magistrate's Court, 5 May 1967: © UPPA/Photoshot.

Brian and Keith, Redlands: Michael Cooper; Brian and Mick on the set of *The Rolling Stones Rock and Roll Circus*, December, 1968: Rex/Globe Photos Inc.; Brian's funeral, Barbara Jones, Suki Potier,

Louisa and Lewis Jones and Tom Keylock, 10 July 1969: Mirrorpix; Tom Keylock, Cotchford Farm, 10 July 1969: Mirrorpix; Cleo Sylvestre, 16 October 1969: Rex/Philip Jackson/Associated Newspapers; Joujouka: Archives of the Master Musicians of Joujouka; Brian leaving Marlborough Magistrates Court, 21 May 1968: AP/Press Association Images.

Brian, Sri Lanka, 1968: Record Mecca.

Index

ABOUT THE AUTHOR

Paul Trynka is a respected music writer, known both for his groundbreaking role as editor of *MOJO* magazine and as author of *Starman* and *Open Up and Bleed*, biographies of David Bowie and Iggy Pop which attracted laudatory reviews worldwide. *Portrait of the Blues*, his collection of oral histories with over sixty blues musicians (a collaboration with photographer Val Wilmer), is regarded as a landmark work. Paul was also editor of the widely respected *International Musician* magazine, and founding editor of *The Guitar Magazine*, for which he first interviewed Keith Richards over twenty years ago. Paul lives with his wife, Lucy, and son, Curtis, in Greenwich, London, just down the road from Mick and Keith's old stomping ground of Dartford.

For more information on Paul Trynka and his books, visit his website at www.trynka.net